DATE DUE

12-21-95			

DEMCO 38-297

Studies in Modern Literature, No. 34

A. Walton Litz, General Series Editor

Professor of English
Princeton University

Linda Wagner

Consulting Editor for Titles on Ernest Hemingway
Professor of English
Michigan State University

Thomas C. Moser

Consulting Editor for Titles on Joseph Conrad
Professor of English
Stanford University

Other Titles in This Series

William Faulkner's Short Stories

by
James B. Carothers

UMI RESEARCH PRESS
Ann Arbor, Michigan

Produced and distributed by
UMI Research Press
an imprint of
University Microfilms International
A Xerox Information Resources Company
Ann Arbor, Michigan 48106

Library of Congress Cataloging in Publication Data

Carothers, James B.
  William Faulkner's short stories.

  (Studies in modern literature ; no. 34)
  Bibliography: p.
  Includes index.
  1. Faulkner, William, 1897-1962—Criticism and
interepretation.   I. Faulkner, William, 1897-1962.
II. Title.   III. Series.
PS3511.A86Z7543   1958   813'.52   85-8523
ISBN 0-8357-1500-0 (alk. paper)

For Beverly

William Faulkner lecture in the McGregor Room, University of Virginia
Library, May 26, 1961
(Photograph: Rip Payne. William Faulkner Collection (N495-593),
University of Virginia Library)

Contents

List of Abbreviations

References to Faulkner's texts, noted parenthetically, are to the following editions:

AA   *Absalom, Absalom!* N.Y., Random House, 1936.

AILD   *As I Lay Dying.* N.Y., Random House, 1964.

BW   *Big Woods.* N.Y., Random House, 1955.

CS   *Collected Stories of William Faulkner.* N.Y., Random House, 1950.

DM   *Doctor Martino and Other Stories.* N.Y., Random House, 1934.

EPP   *Early Prose and Poetry,* ed. Carvel Collins. Boston, Little, Brown, 1962.

ESPL   *Essays, Speeches & Public Letters,* ed. James B. Meriwether. N.Y., Random House, 1966.

FA   *Father Abraham.* N.Y., Random House, 1984.

FAB   *A Fable.* N.Y., Random House, 1954.

FIU   *Faulkner in the University,* eds. Frederick L. Gwynn and Joseph L. Blotner. N.Y., Vintage, 1965.

GDM   *Go Down, Moses and Other Stories.* N.Y., Random House, 1942.

HAM   *The Hamlet.* N.Y., Random House, 1964 (third edition).

KG   *Knight's Gambit.* N.Y., Random House, 1949.

LIA   *Light in August.* N.Y., Harrison Smith & Robert Haas, 1932.

LIG   *Lion in the Garden: Interviews with William Faulkner, 1926-1962,* eds. James B. Meriwether and Michael Millgate. N.Y., Random House, 1968.

MAN   *The Mansion.* N.Y., Random House, 1959.

NOS   *New Orleans Sketches,* ed. Carvel Collins. N.Y., Random House, 1968.

NOTES   *Notes on a Horsethief.* Greenville, Miss., Levee Press, 1950.

REQ   *Requiem for a Nun.* N.Y., Random House, 1951.

REV   *The Reivers.* N.Y., Random House, 1962.

S&F   *The Sound and the Fury.* N.Y., Jonathan Cape and Harrison Smith, 1929.

SAN   *Sanctuary.* N.Y., Jonathan Cape and Harrison Smith, 1931.

SAR   *Sartoris.* N.Y., Harcourt, Brace, 1929.

SLWF   *Selected Letters of William Faulkner,* ed. Joseph Blotner. N.Y., Random House, 1977.

SP   *Soldiers' Pay.* N.Y., Boni & Liveright, 1926.

TWN   *The Town.* N.Y., Random House, 1957.

UNV   *The Unvanquished.* N.Y., Random House, 1938.

USWF   *Uncollected Stories of William Faulkner,* ed. Joseph Blotner. N.Y., Random House, 1979.

WP   *The Wild Palms.* N.Y., Random House, 1939.

Preface

When I completed the first version of this study in 1970, relatively little scholarly or critical attention had been given to Faulkner's short fiction, many of the texts of his uncollected and unpublished stories were difficult to locate, important materials related to a developmental study were restricted or unavailable, and nobody seemed to be doing developmental studies of Faulkner anyway. With the publication of James B. Meriwether's checklist of Faulkner's short fiction in 1971, responsible description and classification began. Joseph Blotner's *Faulkner: A Biography* (1973, 1984), his edition of the *Selected Letters of William Faulkner* (1977), and his edition of the *Uncollected Stories of William Faulkner* (1979) each provided invaluable texts for continuing study. Hans H. Skei's *William Faulkner: The Short Story Career* (1981) offers explicit aid in sorting out the chronology of the many variants of particular stories and describes Faulkner's labors in the genre. Doreen Fowler, Gary L. Stonum, and Karl F. Zender, among others, have shown that developmental readings of Faulkner are illuminating. If we don't always see eye to eye, as Faulkner put it to Saxe Commins, we are, nevertheless, all looking at the same thing. None of us is, of William Faulkner, "Sole Owner and Proprietor."

In revising the original text of this study I have sought to eliminate unfounded speculations and downright errors, to cite appropriate editions of short story texts, and to note what seem to me to be the better recent readings of some stories and subjects.

Acknowledgments

Portions of this study were supported by a grant from the University of Kansas General Research Fund. Readings of all or part of the original text by B.M. Carothers, Douglas T. Day, Edward F. Grier, Kelley Hayden, John H. Langley, J.C. Levenson, George Y. Trail, and James Gray Watson helped eliminate errors and refine arguments. I, of course, remain responsible for whatever errors persist. Jane Garrett and Barbara Paris typed the manuscript and provided valuable editorial assistance. Special thanks go to my colleagues at the "Faulkner and Yoknapatawpha" Conferences for their encouragement and to Joseph Blotner.

Introduction

Most discussions of Faulkner's fiction deal primarily or exclusively with his novels, treating the short stories as though they did not exist, or, at most, allowing them cursory treatment. For the student of the short stories, it is tempting to reverse this procedure, though hardly convenient. Faulkner's short stories are considerably more than rough drafts or minor footnotes to his novels; they deserve serious study in their own right and are of sufficient merit to assure Faulkner's place in the first rank of twentieth-century writers, even had he never written novels.

Since he did write the novels, however, it is impossible to ignore them. Though my thesis is that the short stories are essentially independent of the novels, I have chosen to present that argument in large part by comparing the stories with the novels to which they are related, to show the differences which indicate that individual texts in the Faulkner canon, though demonstrably reflexive, are not as mutually dependent as they have sometimes been made out to be.

The first chapter includes a brief survey of past estimates of Faulkner's stories and of Faulkner's contributions to modern fiction. His development of the Yoknapatawpha chronicle has suggested to many that all of his fiction is part of one grand design, and the usual assumption is that the short stories are only incidental to that design. Faulkner's design, however, was a dynamic one, and in view of the many significant differences between the short stories and novels which supposedly treat the "same" characters and incidents, it is best first to read each of his texts as self-contained.

In the second chapter six different relations between single stories and novels are described, in an effort to support the contention that each text is essentially independent. Though there are many reflexive connections between Faulkner's texts, no single connection is binding, and no one short story or novel is absolutely dependent for its understanding on any of the others. The latter portion of this chapter is concerned with a description of Faulkner's gradual development from pessimism to optimism, a development which has often been ignored or misunderstood, and which the short stories help to define.

The third chapter considers individual stories in themselves, and in relation to the collections or "cycles" in which they appeared. The text of any individual Faulkner story has an integrity and coherence quite apart from the volume in which it is included, but the context of such collections as *Collected Stories, Knight's Gambit,* and *Big Woods* often affects our response to the stories. A comparison of the magazine versions of the short stories with the corresponding episodes in *The Unvanquished* and *Go Down, Moses* leads to the conclusion that those two books are best read as unified novels rather than as collections of autonomous stories or as story-cycles. Removing separate chapters of these two books, such as "The Bear" and "An Odor of Verbena," from the context of the novel may present grave difficulties for the reader. Some stories which Faulkner did not collect or publish are discussed here, and some tentative explanations of their exclusion are offered.

The fourth chapter deals with the short stories about the Snopes family, from the first treatment in *Father Abraham* through the stories incorporated into the Snopes trilogy. The Snopes stories illustrate the related themes of this study: that Faulkner's short stories are autonomous texts, and that his outlook on the human condition altered considerably over the years.

The brief concluding chapter summarizes points made elsewhere in the study, and examines assumptions on which the current downgrading of Faulkner's short story work is based.

Faulkner's short stories, in addition to being entertaining in themselves, are important because they reflect his constant and developing themes and techniques. They can add measurably to our understanding of his novels, and they are of vital importance in assessing two of his distinctive contributions to twentieth-century literature: his creation of a related series of narratives, and his eventual development of an affirmative, comic view of man in his struggle. The lasting value of Faulkner's stories is that they are moving, often amusing, occasionally tragic. They are the products of the same passionate and deliberate craftsmanship which characterizes Faulkner's novels. They are a major part of the major work of a gifted artist.

Faulkner has suffered both early and late from the fraternal twins of criticism, reduction and amplification. His mythologizing, his technical innovations, his extension of the Gothic tradition, his humanism, and his style have all been singled out at one time or another as his primary virtue or primary defect. That each of these readings is now usually developed to Faulkner's credit does not mean that they are correct in their assessment. Faulkner's superiority as a writer of fiction comes not from any one attribute, but from his repeated demonstration of their natural combination. If it is possible to isolate, for the purposes of discussion, one area of his achievement, it is more desirable to consider them in their mutual relations. The short stories are of signal importance in understanding and appreciating the rich and complex unity of Faulkner's fiction.

1

"With A Kindred Art": Reading Faulkner's Short Stories

A skilful literary artist has constructed a tale. If wise, he has not fashioned his thoughts to accommodate his incidents; but having conceived, with deliberate care, a certain unique or single *effect* to be wrought out, he then invents such incidents — he then combines such events as may best aid him in establishing this preconceived effect. If his very initial sentence tend not to the outbringing of this effect, then he has failed in his first step. In the whole composition there should be no word written, of which the tendency, direct or indirect, is not to the one preestablished design. And by such means, with such care and skill, a picture is at length painted which leaves in the mind of him who contemplates it with a kindred art, a sense of the fullest satisfaction.   — Edgar Allan Poe

To read Faulkner's short stories "with a kindred art" requires us to accept the paradox that each of Faulkner's texts is at once autonomous and interdependent. Faulkner's short stories, though more multiple in their effects and less mechanically calculated than Poe's formula prescribes, are to be first approached as self-contained, unified works of prose fiction, possessing coherent structure and discoverable significance in themselves. At the same time, the short stories are indispensable segments of the continuum of Faulkner's *oeuvre,* considered as a whole, "the same story over and over," as Faulkner once described it, "which is myself and the world."[1] In reading Faulkner's short stories, as in reading his novels, we recreate Faulkner's changing conception of himself, of the world, and of the dynamic relations between them.

Faulkner often said that the short story was, after poetry, the most difficult of literary forms, and his comments on his own short stories were frequently self-deprecating, but his work in the short story was long and intense, beginning in his student days at the University of Mississippi, continuing through his period of literary apprenticeship in New Orleans, paralleling and counterpointing his greatest years of achievement as a novelist, diminishing after the early 1940s, and apparently ending in the mid-1950s. Faulkner wrote well over one hundred short stories, collected them in a number of carefully structured volumes, and drew frequently and extensively on them in constructing his novels. Within and among his short stories are to be found all the elements of his peculiar narrative genius.

Whereas all of Faulkner's novels can now be assembled with no particular difficulty, it is considerably more difficult to bring together all his short stories. Faulkner's early work in short fiction is available through Carvel Collins' editions of the *Early Prose and Poetry* and of the *New Orleans Sketches,* usefully supplemented by Leland H. Cox's edition of *Sinbad in New Orleans.* Other early shorter works in prose — one would not want to call them short stories — are available in the editions of *Mayday* and *The Wishing Tree.* Of the volumes of short stories Faulkner published himself, *These 13, Doctor Martino and Other Stories, Knight's Gambit, Collected Stories,* and *Big Woods* are essential, and *The Faulkner Reader* is of interest. Since it includes all thirteen stories of *These 13,* and twelve of the fourteen stories of *Doctor Martino,* as well as twenty-seven other stories published between 1930 and 1948, and since he gave extended careful attention to its arrangement, *Collected Stories* is the single most important volume in all of Faulkner's work in short fiction. Joseph Blotner's 1979 edition of the *Uncollected Stories* gathers forty-five more stories, including most of those Faulkner apparently chose not to collect because he had revised them for later books, a number that had been published under a variety of circumstances but never collected, and a number previously unpublished. While a few stories remain unpublished or uncollected, and while several pieces published in *Uncollected Stories* are not, strictly speaking, short stories, it is nevertheless true that a reader in possession of the volumes listed above has available the vast preponderance of Faulkner's work in short fiction.[2]

It is now relatively clear just when Faulkner wrote each novel, although some of the chronology of composition remains problematic. But we know, for example, that he wrote the original version of *Sanctuary* before beginning *As I Lay Dying,* even though the latter precedes the former in publication; we know that he wrote *Pylon* after he had begun work on the novel that became *Absalom, Absalom!;* we know that both *Intruder in the Dust* and *Requiem for a Nun* were written during the period in which he was also working on *A Fable.* Just when he wrote each of his short stories, however, is considerably less clear, for Faulkner did not often date his short story manuscripts as he dated the manuscripts and typescripts of his novels, and also because so many of the short stories exist in more than one manuscript or typescript version. Faulkner's correspondence with his agents and editors is often useful in determining the approximate completion date of a story, though it tells us little about when stories may have been conceived and drafted. Hans H. Skei has made an ambitious attempt to gather facts, inferences, and speculations regarding the chronology of composition of Faulkner's short stories,[3] but the exact dates and stages of composition for many must remain conjectural.

We assume that a writer of Faulkner's stature is essentially self-consistent, that his writings are all of a piece, and we assume that the reader's art is to discover the principles of this self-consistency in the repeated subjects, themes, rhetorical strategies, or styles of the successive texts. In thus reading Faulkner it is common to select a passage from a public or private statement, or a characteristic rhetorical device, or a philosophical position and to employ it as the "key" to all of his texts. In such readings Faulkner's early work in poetry, prose, and criticism is seen to manifest his struggle toward realization of the "key" principles and techniques, which are then seen to be embodied in his great novels of 1929-1942, though his subsequent "lesser" texts are seen to compromise or misapply these principles and techniques, as though Faulkner had, in his last twenty years of writing, lost his key, or, like Leopold Bloom, left it in his other pants.[4]

Faulkner's most important achievement, according to the readings that have dominated Faulkner studies since the time of George Marion O'Donnell and Malcolm Cowley, is his creation of a body of fiction in which each individual text is less significant than the whole, and is dependent on its place in the design of the whole. This whole — whether called a legend, a saga, a series, a chronicle, a history, or a myth — centers in Faulkner's novels and stories set in Yoknapatawpha County, Mississippi, and in individual characters, entire fictional families, and corresponding incidents and events which figure in more than one text. This whole, so goes the argument, is of primary importance for the Faulkner reader, for only within the larger design can particular texts be fully understood and appreciated. It is within this larger context, often denominated by the approbative term "myth," that Faulkner's contributions to twentieth-century fiction are now understood.

His short stories, however, are not often numbered among his major contributions, and they have received, as a group, substantially less attention than other aspects of his work. Recent studies have gone some distance toward describing how Faulkner reworked short stories into novels, close attention has been given to Faulkner's organization of his short story volumes, and the predictable few of his stories have found their way into the anthologies and have been studied with care.[5] But Faulkner is considered primarily as a novelist, a mythmaker, an innovator in fictional technique, or a moralist, before he is considered as a short story writer. His short stories, when they are treated at all, are considered incidental to his larger design. The short stories, read as individual texts, and read in relation to each other and to the texts of the novels, not only substantiate but also significantly modify some of the continuing assessments of Faulkner's development and overall achievement, and they help to identify and resolve some of the apparent paradoxes and contradictions in those readings.

The argument from design has a sound basis in Faulkner's own description of his work, most memorably expressed in his 1956 interview with Jean

Stein: "With *Soldiers' Pay* I found out writing was fun. But I found out after that not only each book had to have a design but the whole output or sum of an artist's work had to have a design."[6] His invention of Yoknapatawpha County was crucial in this development: "Beginning with *Sartoris* I discovered that my own little postage stamp of native soil was worth writing about and that I would never live long enough to exhaust it, and by sublimating the actual into apocryphal I would have complete liberty to use whatever talent I might have to its absolute top." This discovery, Faulkner continues, "opened up a gold mine of other peoples, so I created a cosmos of my own." As though anticipating or responding to those who would call attention to the apparent discrepancies and contradictions among his texts, Faulkner asserts: "I can move these people around like God, not only in space but in time too. The fact that I have moved my characters around in time successfully, at least in my own estimation, proves to me my own theory that time is a fluid condition which has no existence except in the momentary avatars of individual people." Faulkner then rings changes on a theme that sounds at intervals throughout his novels, from *The Sound and the Fury* and *As I Lay Dying* through *The Wild Palms* to *The Reivers:* "There is no such thing as *was* — only *is*. If *was* existed there would be no grief or sorrow." "I like to think," he concludes, "of the world I created as being a kind of keystone in the universe, that, as small as that keystone is, if it were ever taken away, the universe itself would collapse. My last book will be the Doomsday Book, the Golden Book, of Yoknapatawpha County. Then I shall break the pencil and I'll have to stop" (*LIG*, 255).

If individual phrases and sentences are isolated from this famous statement, there is some justification for the inference that Faulkner had in mind a hard core of narrative "fact" upon which his Yoknapatawpha cosmos rests, and many readers have sought to trace an outline of Faulknerian history. But Faulkner repeatedly declined to be bound by the "facts" he had posited in one text when he was creating another. The problem for the reader is to determine how far, if at all, to allow the knowledge of one Faulkner text to shape the reading of another. Even the notion of "autonomy" can be a misleading and debilitating preconception, as Mark Spilka pointed out early on, and as a host of present-day "intertextual" readers would insist.[7] If it is wrong to ignore the many reflexive connections among Faulkner's works, and if it is equally wrong to deny that there is, in several senses, a "design" within the Faulkner canon, it must nevertheless be argued that the connections among Faulkner's texts are problematical rather than absolute, that there are several different kinds of connections, that it is useful to discriminate among them, and that, above all, Faulkner's "design" was dynamic. Reading *a* Faulkner short story, then, is one thing, reading "Faulkner's short stories" is another, and "reading Faulkner" is still another. The art of reading Faulkner's short stories requires the reader to focus, as Faulkner did, on the immediate text, and to read among and between the texts for a sense of the developing design.

Faulkner's attitude toward the variety of his texts appears to have changed, for he originally mentioned the possibility of a collected edition of his works, in which factual discrepancies and contradictions would be eliminated.[8] When Malcolm Cowley pointed out the differences between the Compson Appendix to *The Sound and the Fury* and the 1929 text of the novel, however, Faulkner defended his changes:

> The inconsistencies in the appendix prove that to me the book is still alive after 15 years, and being still alive is growing, changing; the appendix was done at the same heat as the book, even though 15 years later, and so it is the book itself which is inconsistent not the appendix. That is, at the age of 30 I did not know these people as at the age of 45 I now do: that I was even wrong now and then in the very conclusions I drew from watching them, and the information in which I once believed.[9]

Much the same note is sounded in the headnote to *The Mansion,* in which Faulkner informs the reader that the discrepancies and contradictions in the thirty-four-year progress of the Snopes chronicle are an indication of his own vitality, "contradictions and discrepancies due to the fact that the author has learned, he believes, more about the human heart and its dilemma than he knew thirty-four years ago, and is sure that, having lived with them that long time, he knows the characters in this chronicle better than he did then " (*MAN,* unnumbered page). Both observations, it may be noted, are based on the same theory of "life as motion" which is central to Faulkner's concept of his own design. The problem with much Faulkner criticism, the desire to bring a semblance of order from apparent chaos, is a too-narrow, too-rigid conception of Faulkner's design. It is consistent with my argument for the autonomy of individual stories, then, that I will here be as much concerned with the uniqueness of single stories, and with significant differences between stories and novels, as with Faulkner's supposedly constant themes and techniques. Approaching the design through the short stories rather than approaching the short stories through some extrinsic conception of the design implies a radically inductive method, based on the assumption that useful generalizations about Faulkner's work must derive from responses to particular stories and novels.

The materials relevant to this study are extensive and various. Faulkner's stories are extant in several forms, including manuscript, typescript, magazine, and collected versions. The most important single volume is *Collected Stories* (1950), which contains verbatim reprintings or slightly altered versions of all the stories which appeared in *These 13* (1931), all but two of the stories which appeared in *Dr. Martino and Other Stories* (1934), and seventeen stories which had been previously published but not collected. Those forty-two stories in *Collected Stories* represent less than half of Faulkner's production. Other collections were *Knight's Gambit* (1949) and *Big Woods* (1955). *The Unvanquished* (1938) and *Go Down, Moses* (1942) have been treated as story-cycles.[10]

The magazine versions of the stories in these five volumes are worthy of more attention than they have thus far received, for changes between magazine and collected versions often suggest shifts in Faulkner's attitudes and intentions, both in single stories and in whole volumes. Magazine versions of stories such as "Thrift," which Faulkner did not choose to collect, are instructive, as are the separately published stories *Idyll in the Desert* and *Miss Zilphia Gant.* Joseph Blotner's edition of *The Uncollected Stories of William Faulkner* (1979) provides convenient texts and groupings of such stories. Many of the stories, published or unpublished, collected or uncollected, were subsequently worked into novels, so each of Faulkner's novels, from *Soldiers' Pay* to *The Reivers,* is germane to a reading of the short stories.

A second body of useful materials consists of Faulkner's comments on his own work. Especially important collections of these observations are found in the interviews Faulkner granted at the University of Virginia, at West Point, in Japan and elsewhere. *Faulkner in the University, Faulkner at West Point,* and *Lion in the Garden* each present difficulties resulting from Faulkner's sometimes perverse attitude towards interviewers, and from the circumstances of transcription.[11] Malcolm Cowley's *The Faulkner-Cowley File* and James B. Meriwether's edition of Faulkner's *Essays, Speeches, and Public Letters* are important sources, as is Joseph Blotner's edition of Faulkner's *Selected Letters.*[12]

The third body of relevant material consists of the published scholarship, criticism, and journalism directly concerned with Faulkner. Since he has been the subject of several dozen books and hundreds of articles, a comprehensive review of scholarship and criticism is beyond the scope of the present study. Nor do I propose to treat the history of critical reaction to Faulkner's works, assuming that the main outlines of this aspect of his career are well-known or readily available elsewhere. On the other hand, I will refer to a number and variety of scholarly and critical works sufficient, I hope, to indicate the kinds of treatment the short stories have so far received.[13] Though a few of Faulkner's short stories have been singled out for explication and praise, and though few anthologists of the modern short story fail to include a sample of Faulkner's work in the genre, Faulkner's stories have most often been treated as mere adjuncts to the novels. The reasons behind this relative lack of attention are not hard to find. Faulkner is, after all, a novelist of the first rank, and the earliest critical priority was given to a discussion of his achievement in that form. His habit of retelling his stories in the novels and his stated preference for some of the novel versions have suggested to some that the stories are less important than the novels.[14] Similarly, Faulkner's neglect of the short story during the last years of his life might be interpreted as a rejection of the form.

Faulkner's habit of referring to himself as a "failed poet" provides a convenient introduction to his notion of the short story, for he often compared the two forms and contrasted them with the novel. "I think that every novelist is a failed poet," he told an interviewer. "He tries to write poetry first, then finds he can't. Then he tries the short story, which is the most demanding form after poetry. And failing at that, only then does he take up novel-writing" (*LIG*, 217). Faulkner repeated this formula on several occasions,[15] and it obviously describes his own experience. The short story is more demanding than the novel, Faulkner explained, because a novelist "can be more careless ... can put more trash in and be excused for it. In a short story that's next to the poem, almost every word has got to be almost exactly right. In the novel you can be careless but in the short story you can't" (*FIU*, 207). The aim of the poet, which the short story writer can only approximate, is to create "some moving passionate moment of the human condition distilled to its absolute essence" (*FIU*, 202).

The implications of this notion for Faulkner's novels have been explored by a number of critics, but comparatively few have applied it to the short stories. Walter J. Slatoff, for example, describes Faulkner's characteristic use of the oxymoron, and concludes that oxymoronic structures are dominant in Faulkner's art, "to place motion and immobility or differing velocities in tense antithesis."[16] Richard P. Adams examines in detail the relation between Faulkner's poems and early novels, showing that both contain many such attempts to arrest motion, which is, Adams argues, Faulkner's constant artistic aim. Both Slatoff and Adams, however, are interested in the novels; to explore the process of arresting motion in the later short stories, Adams says, would be redundant.[17]

Olga Vickery, developing a similar view, says that Faulkner's short stories are "adjunctive, projective, and parodic," the proper labelling of each story being determined by the story's relation to the rest of the Yoknapatawpha cycle.[18] In *The Achievement of William Faulkner,* Michael Millgate makes a number of illuminating comments on the contrapuntal structuring of individual volumes of stories, but has only relatively brief comments on the stories themselves.[19] Guides such as those provided by Dorothy Y. Tuck, Harry Runyan, and Walter K. Everett contain short discussions of single stories.[20] Though some of Faulkner's stories, says Lawrance Thompson in his study of Faulkner's novels, "are so excellent that they leave an indelible and searing hurt ... any reader who learns to handle Faulkner's difficult idiom, as it operates in the novels here considered, can transfer from that exerience the wherewithal for handling the short stories."[21] Irving Howe attends briefly to a few stories, but prefaces his remarks with the observation that *Collected Stories* "contains a half-dozen brilliant pieces of writing and another dozen reasonably good ones; but it does not persuade one that Faulkner, the story writer, is nearly as important or original as Faulkner, the novelist."[22] Cleanth Brooks has studied Faulkner's early stories and sketches and the stories that went into *Go Down, Moses,* and has offered readings of several other well-known stories.[23]

Most good readings of individual short stories are found in such journals as *The Mississippi Quarterly* and *Studies in Short Fiction*. The bulk of the criticism of Faulkner's short stories consists of close readings of single stories in such journals, though the bibliographical work of James B. Meriwether and the chronological investigations of Hans Skei may provide the basis for more extended textual and intertextual studies. To sum up the current state of scholarship, then, it seems clear that Faulkner's short stories as a group have received comparatively little serious attention from the critics, although there have been numerous *obiter dicta* in consideration of his development as a novelist, and many stories have been mined for particular themes, while a relative few have been studied with care.

In view of the high esteem in which Faulkner held the short story, and in view of the energy and skill which he devoted to individual stories and collections, an attempt to redress the critical balance would seem to be in order. A more important consideration, however, is simply that Faulkner wrote good stories, and those stories are often deliberately neglected or misread. In order to show how the stories are good, to show why they are worth reading, to show how they are best appreciated, it is necessary to show what they are; similarly, it is necessary to answer some of the objections which have been raised against them, to explain what the short stories are *not*.

Each of Faulkner's short stories, then, ought to be read first as a self-contained, unified work of prose fiction, dealing with significant change in the life of the story's central character or characters. In reading each story we should concern ourselves with the specific nature of this change, with the ways in which it is brought about, with the characters' response to it, and with the implications this change has for the characters, for their world, and for the storyteller. This definition is consonant, I think, with Faulkner's assertion that "the aim of every artist is to arrest motion, which is life, by artificial means and hold it fixed so that 100 years later when a stranger looks at it, it moves again since it is life" (*LIG*, 253). Something always happens in a Faulkner short story, and what happens has meaning and value. Faulkner's stories are not derivative, dependent *addenda* to a rigidly ordered and clearly conceived Yoknapatawpha scheme. They are not conscious mechanical explorations of a single abstract idea or system of ideas. They are not repetitive exercises in a rigidly conventional prose form. Nor, finally, are they self-indulgent experiments in monstrosity, sentimentality, or reflexivity, though Faulkner's stories have often been explained or dismissed according to one or more of these misconceptions.

It is convenient, too, to put the stories in their generic place by critical *fiat*, to decree, for example, that "Dry September" is a short story, while the *Go Down, Moses* version of "The Bear" is not. Faulkner's own definition of the short story, as the form demanding the highest degree of perfection after the poem, is suggestive but inconclusive, for the aesthetic criteria of "unity and coherence and emphasis" which he mentioned on several occasions are never clearly defined.[24] We do, of course, have Faulkner's authority for calling some texts novels and some texts collections of short stories, and we have similar authority for calling some separately published texts short stories and some excerpts from novels.[25] The arbitrary criterion of length is not a useful tool of definition, though Faulkner once remarked that a short story was 3000 words or less and anything longer was "a piece of writing" (*LIG,* 58). Only the *Go Down, Moses* text of "The Bear," the title story of *Knight's Gambit,* the two counterpointed stories in *The Wild Palms,* and longer excerpts from novels, such as the "Spotted Horses" section of *The Hamlet,* tend toward the "short novel" or novella classifications.

Faulkner's stated concern with unity, and my description of his short stories as autonomous and unified, for example, might suggest the appropriation of Poe's famous description of the tale of single effect. But Faulkner apparently did not conceive of his stories in terms of their effects, single or otherwise.

A story begins, according to Faulkner:

> Sometimes with a person, sometimes with an anecdote, but the short story is conceived in the same terms that the book is. The first job that the craftsman faces is to tell this as quickly and as simply as I can, and if he's good, if he's of the first water, like Chekhov, he can do it every time in two or three thousand words, but if he's not that good, sometimes it takes him eighty thousand words. But they are similar, and he is simply trying to tell something which was true and moving in the shortest time he can, and then if he has sense enough stop. That is, I don't believe the man or the woman says, Now I'm going to write a short story, or Now I'm going to write a novel. It's an idea that begins with the thought, the image of a character, or with an anecdote, and even in the same breath, almost like lightning, it begins to take a shape that he can see whether it's going to be a short story or a novel. Sometimes, not always. Sometimes he thinks it'll be a short story and finds that he can't. Sometimes it looks like it's to be a novel and then after he works on it, he sees that it's not, that he can tell it in two thousand or five thousand words. No rule to it. (*FIU,* 48-49)

"A Rose for Emily," Faulkner said, began with the picture of "a strand of hair on the pillow in the abandoned house" (*FIU,* 26). Had he been writing according to Poe's formula, he would have begun with the intention to horrify. Or, more didactically, he might have set out to convey the terrible nature of the conflict between the North and the South, or to describe the conflict between the individual and the community, between the past and the present, between men and women. These are, of course, popular readings of "A Rose for Emily," but no one of them ought to be argued to the exclusion of all the others. The effect of "A Rose for Emily" is perhaps single, but it is profound and complex as well, and it is clear that Faulkner did not begin the story with the intention to affect the reader or impress on him a simplistic theme. On the

contrary, Faulkner seems to have written many of his works without considering the emotional or intellectual effects they might have on the audience.

"I think I have written a lot and sent it off to print before I actually
realized strangers might read it," Faulkner wrote Cowley.[26] Yet he later maintained that every artist must sooner or later come to realize the existence of his
audience, "and probably a writer, whether he intends to or not, or knows it or
not, is going to shape what he writes in the terms of who will read it" (*FIU*, 41-
42). Joseph Gold has argued that Faulkner's growing awareness of his audience
accounts for many of the changes in style in the later novels, that Faulkner
became progressively more rhetorical, more discursive, and less metaphorical
as he grew older.[27] Such a notion of change and development is essential, I
think, to an understanding of the Faulkner canon, and of the place of individual texts within it. But if he gradually approached Poe's view, the fact should
remind us that he started elsewhere. Though Poe's theory has been extremely
influential, it has only limited application to Faulkner, and thus warns us
against selecting a single notion of the short story and forcing Faulkner's works
to conform to it. Too, though it is tempting to see Poe as one of Faulkner's
major influences — for, like Poe, Faulkner wrote tales of terror and tales of
ratiocination — Faulkner specifically denied that there was any special inter-
play between him and Poe, whom he called "a transplanted European" (*LIG*,
95).

The definitions of the short story form supplied by critics and scholars are
also of limited usefulness in their application to Faulkner. One critical definition of the short story offered by Ray B. West, though originally intended to
apply to Hawthorne, Melville, Mark Twain, and James, seems made to order
for Faulkner: "the American story was a story of initiation, a recognition of
the significance of evil, a pessimistic rather than an optimistic view of man."[28]
The pattern or theme of initiation is a standby of Faulkner criticism, but Faulkner's variations on the pattern are many, and many of his stories seem rather to
imply an optimistic view of man. A discovery of evil is basic to many of
Faulkner's best stories — "That Evening Sun," "Wash," and "Barn Burning," to name only a few. Faulkner's protagonists, however, are not always as
perceptive as Quentin Compson, Wash Jones, and Sarty Snopes. Many live in
the presence of evil — their own or others' — without recognizing it. The old
man in "Pennsylvania Station" fails to realize the perfidy of his nephew;
Georgie in "That Will Be Fine," is oblivious to the true character of his Uncle
Rodney; and the title character of "Elly" refuses to understand her own will-
fulness. In such stories the discovery of evil is made by the reader, rather than
by the character, and the relation of these two kinds of initiation stories to each
other may recall the two different notions of Joyce's epiphany: one in which
the character reveals his true nature to others, one in which the character
reveals his true nature to himself. In Faulkner's stories the two types of initia-

tion are often simultaneous, but it is only in rare instances — "Wash," for one — that they fuse. The modern critical preference for complexity, for the kind of story such as "The Dead" in which both reader and character make the same discovery at the same moment, may go far to explain why much of Faulkner's fiction has been ignored or dismissed. Another factor is the assumption, implicit in West's definition, that initiation necessarily entails a discovery of evil. When a reader or character is led to the discovery of goodness in men, the modern equation of truth and evil suggests that the story is invalid. Thus, stories like "The Tall Men," "Race at Morning," "Shingles for the Lord," and "Mule in the Yard" are sometimes dismissed as sentimental, untrue to life. But surely it is as much a mistake to reject as invalid the virtue and humor of Faulkner's characters and situations as to reject the evil and horror.

The definition of a Faulkner short story which I have advanced is broad enough to overcome the objections mentioned. It is consistent with Faulkner's own comments, and with my understanding of what he accomplished in individual stories. The most radical aspect of this definition, I think, is in the assertion that the short stories are self-contained. By this I mean that their texts are complete in themselves and are not dependent on any extrinsic work or idea of Faulkner's. The problem is that Faulkner uses so many characters in more than one text that it is difficult not to assume that the reading of one text must absolutely shape the reading of another. "Most of Faulkner's fiction projects," says Hugh Kenner, "a leisurely saga, Gothic in its violences and its genealogical intricacy, of characters who need not be 'presented' because from story to story everyone has come to know them."[29] The danger of such "knowledge" may be seen in comparing the three works about the Compson family: *The Sound and the Fury,* "That Evening Sun," and *Absalom, Absalom!* The two novels are almost universally held to be among Faulkner's very greatest, while the short story is occasionally glanced at by readers in search of help in dealing with the two novels. To what extent are the three works about the "same" people?

The Sound and the Fury describes a Quentin Compson who commits suicide at the age of nineteen. The narrator of "That Evening Sun," also named Quentin Compson, is twenty-four when he tells the story of Nancy and Jesus. Quentin's suicide in *The Sound and the Fury* is in part a result of his failure to accept his sister Caddy's dishonorable marriage. No sister is mentioned in *Absalom, Absalom!* There are many similarities between the Compson family in *The Sound and the Fury* and the Compson family in "That Evening Sun." Mr. Compson is ineffectual, Mrs. Compson complains, Caddy is inquisitive about sexual matters, Jason is mean, Dilsey is calm, and Quentin is sensitive, but the novel simply does not count in a reading of the story; they are two different texts, operating according to two different histories. Only in a limited sense can the Quentin who narrates "That Evening Sun" be instructively compared with either the guilt-ridden suicide of *The Sound and the Fury* or the past-haunted student of *Absalom, Absalom!*, and, in any event, he cannot be *equated* with either. The narrator of the story projects a calm, dispassionate, mature voice, a voice very different from that of the two Harvard Quentins.

"That Evening Sun" may, as Cleanth Brooks argues, show that "the Compson children have already assumed the personality patterns we shall find later."[30] But it is a questionable assumption that this revelation is the most important function of the story, or even an operative one. The only "later" the story treats is implied in the adult voice of Quentin. The disparity between the mature voice of the narrator of the opening paragraphs, and the child-like voice which the narrator gradually adopts gives us a clue to what the story is "about." "That Evening Sun" concerns Quentin's childhood, a particular experience in that childhood which has implications for his adult life. The experience of the child Quentin involved Nancy and Jesus, but it is not the outcome of their terrible conflict that is important — the narrator Quentin deliberately makes the reality of Nancy's danger ambiguous — the chief concern is the boy Quentin's realization that something has changed. Like so many first-person stories, "That Evening Sun" may be understood as a kind of *Bildungsroman* or *Kunstlerroman,* though neither education nor art is discussed explicitly in it. This happened to me, Quentin seems to be telling us; it is part of why I am what I am, and I am telling it to you so that you can feel what I felt and learn what I learned. In the process of telling his story, the mature Quentin involves himself again in the experience of the incident, and his narrative prose resembles that of a bright child.

Because this process is implied, rather than expressed directly, it is easy to overlook, and in an effort to understand the story, readers have looked to *The Sound and the Fury, Absalom, Absalom!, Requiem for a Nun,* or "A Justice," in which one or more of the characters of "That Evening Sun" also appear. When this happens, they create difficulties such as the belief that the Compson children have "already" assumed personality patterns in the story, though the story was, in all likelihood, written after *The Sound and the Fury.* A well-known example of the confusions of the "mythological" approach is provided by Dorothy Y. Tuck:

> Nancy's fate is not disclosed in this story, but there is a strong suggestion that she will actually be killed. She is resurrected to become a central character as Nancy Mannigoe in *Requiem for a Nun* (1951). It is ironic that in the short story the white family she loyally serves refuses to take her fears seriously and thus is partially responsible for her death, while in *Requiem* she sacrifices her own life so that her white employer, Temple Drake, might find some kind of moral salvation.
>
> 'That Evening Sun' ... displays some of the best elements of his fictional technique, particularly in the contrast between Nancy's calm horror of the death she knows awaits her and the children's total failure to see that horror; they comment on her strange actions, but are untouched by the fear behind them. This is particularly brought out in the last sentences with Quentin's question, 'Who will do our washing now, Father?' With the impersonal curiosity of childhood he placidly accepts Nancy's expected death.[31]

What "That Evening Sun" says is that Nancy expects to be killed and that Mr. Compson does not expect her to be killed. If there are strong suggestions that Nancy is going to die, there are also suggestions that her fears are groundless. In any event, the story does not tell us that Nancy did die. *Requiem for a Nun* is another text with another Nancy, neither a continuation of the story nor a resurrection of a character. Similarly, Nancy's death cannot be inferred, as one early critic assumed, from *The Sound and the Fury.*[32] The supposed "irony" of the contrast between "That Evening Sun" and *Requiem* presumes both a death which is not established and a direct continuity between a story and a novel which are separate texts and ought to be treated as such. Nor is it accurate to say that the Compson children are untouched by Nancy's fears. The nervous quarrelling of Caddy and Jason, their instinctive wish to stay away from Nancy's cabin, and Quentin's final acceptance of Nancy's statement of her plight all indicate that they are indeed affected. It is significant, moreover, that the mature Quentin who narrates the story selects this incident, these characters, and this method of telling a story. The contrast between time past and time present which he evokes in the opening sentence of the story is consistent with the implied constrast between the child and the man. We may interpret the latter as the difference between innocence and knowledge of sex, violence, or death, but these are themes which the child could not be expected to articulate. Quentin's question, "Who will do our washing now, Father?" shows that he, unlike Caddy and Jason, is aware that things are irrevocably different, and if his question is childlike, its ironic inadequacy is not lost on the mature Quentin who tells the story.

In emphasizing the autonomy of "That Evening Sun" and other Faulkner stories, I do not mean to imply that Faulkner's reuse of his characters and stories can or ought to be ignored. But an understanding of Faulkner's so-called mythology must take account of the many significant discrepancies and contradictions between separate stories and novels. What we find in Faulkner's best fiction is the forceful expression of a comprehensive and generally coherent intelligence, but each story or novel constitutes a different expression and implies a different intelligence. The genesis and development of Faulkner's continuing stories, through both shorter and longer texts, help illustrate and define the extensive modal shift which took place in Faulkner's writing between 1919 and 1962. Despite his occasional public utterances to the contrary, Faulkner's conception of himself, of the world, and of their mutual relations was always changing. Faulkner's fiction develops an evolving world view, moving from the desultory irony and pathos of *Soldiers' Pay, Mosquitoes,* and the *New Orleans Sketches* to the romance of *The Reivers*. This shift is gradual rather than radical, and can be discerned in an examination of Faulkner's consecutive treatments of individual characters such as Flem Snopes, Temple Drake, Surratt-Ratliff, or Benbow-Stevens. The shift is clear, too, in Faulkner's reworking of individual themes: Snopesism, social and racial justice, sexuality, and time. Faulkner and his characters proceed from an initial expression of resentment toward a universe which is either indifferent to the prosperity of evil or antagonistic to the virtuous. In time they gain a qualified acceptance of things as they are, and they develop a capacity for the appreciation and celebration of the occasional benevolence of Providence, nature, and humanity. This development is not to be understood as a progression (or regression, as some would have it) from one thematic pole to its opposite. I do not wish to be understood as arguing for a Faulknerian version of the pattern of Manifest Destiny. Faulkner is neither totally ironic in his early fiction nor totally romantic in the end. There are elements of comedy and endurance in *Soldiers' Pay* just as there are elements of evil and transience in *The Reivers*. Nor can the watershed be located precisely. For some critics, *Go Down, Moses* is the crucial text, but there are elements of the later mode in *Light in August*, published ten years earlier. At that time Faulkner told an interviewer that he had passed through three stages in his attitude toward people and, therefore, toward his characters: "There is the first stage when you believe everything and everybody is good. Then there is the second, cynical stage when you believe that no one is good. Then at last you come to realize that everyone is capable of almost anything — heroism or cowardice, tenderness or cruelty" (*LIG*, 32).

A work of art establishes a world for us, a comprehensive and coherent universe in which relations among elements are ordered according to some discoverable rationale. Such worlds, naturally, invite comparison with our own — though this is not necessarily the artist's primary or conscious purpose — and they may differ radically from our own conception of the real world, encompassing anomalies, contradictions, or absurdities. Fictional worlds, however, are best understood as linguistic approximations of parts of the "real" world, imposing their own realities in the form of literary traditions, conventions, and innovations. Faulkner's fictional world is sometimes judged to lack verisimilitude, but when this judgment is proclaimed, it is important to stipulate whether it means that his characters and their world do not sufficiently resemble real people acting in real situations, or that his characters and their world are not rendered in accepted mimetic conventions. It is further necessary to stipulate whether Faulkner's alleged lack of verisimilitude or his infidelity to convention is to be construed as a fault. The ways in which a Faulkner story projects a comprehensive and coherent universe, then, require explanation, for Faulkner's stories and novels have been praised and condemned for their lack of realism or of historical or sociological accuracy, and they have been praised and condemned for their realism and their historical and sociological authenticity.

The most simple proof of Faulkner's lack of verisimilitude is advanced by those who have pointed out the disparity between Faulkner's characters and "real" people, concluding that this disparity constitutes a weakness. A useful example of such reasoning was provided long ago by Winthrop Tilley, who attempts to show that the behavior of Benjy in *The Sound and the Fury* does not conform to textbook descriptions of idiot behavior.[33] The argument concentrates on Benjy's attack on the Burgess girl and on his subsequent castration, for it is contended that idiots are normally sexually apathetic, and it is demonstrated that castration was illegal in Mississippi in 1913. Inasmuch as Faulkner clearly intends for Benjy's section of the novel to approximate an idiot's experience and behavior, such a reading would seem to have merit. But it is not altogether clear that Benjy's attack on the little girls is sexual in nature, though it is interpreted as such by Jason Compson and Mr. Burgess. Here is Benjy's account of the incident:

> I could hear them talking. I went out the door and I couldn't hear them, and I went down to the gate, where the girls passed with their booksatchels. They looked at me, walking fast, with their heads turned. I tried to say, but they went on, and I went along the fence, trying to say, and they went faster. Then they were running and I came to the corner of the fence and I couldn't go any further, and I held to the fence, looking after them and trying to say. (*S&F*, 63)

> They came on. I opened the gate and they stopped, turning. I was trying to say, and I caught her, trying to say, and she screamed and I was trying to say and trying and the bright shapes began to stop and I tried to get out. I tried to get if off of my face, but the bright shapes were going again. They were going up the hill to where it fell away and I tried to cry. But when I breathed in, I couldn't breathe out again to cry, and I tried to keep from falling off the hill into the bright whirling shapes. (*S&F*, 64)

"I don't reckon he even knew what he had been trying to do," Jason remarks later, "or why Mr. Burgess knocked him out with the fence picket" (*S&F*, 328). But the text does not make clear that Benjy is trying to do what Jason and Mr. Burgess think. Rather, it is at least as likely that he is "trying to say." Nowhere in this incident or in any other part of *The Sound and the Fury* does Benjy clearly manifest or articulate sexual lust, though the family is obviously concerned that he will, and so they refuse to allow Caddy to continue to sleep in the same bed with him. Extrinsic support for Jason and Mr. Burgess' reaction is available in a letter Faulkner wrote to Ben Wasson. "He tries to rape a young girl," Faulkner explained, "and is castrated."[34] The novel does not fully document this incident, however, and the later Compson Appendix does not help to resolve the ambiguity. It is clear that Benjy associates the incident with the girls with his subsequent castration, but that is all. Critics have similarly argued that Benjy's violent reaction to Luster's driving around the left side of the monument is a result of his memory of the trip he was forced to make to Jackson, but on this point, as with Benjy's attack, Faulkner seems to have been deliberately ambiguous. Tilley may be correct in designating some of Benjy's other characteristic actions, such as crying, as atypical of idiotic behavior, but in the most important part of his case against Faulkner's "stuffed literary idiot" he depends heavily on a questionable reading of the text. The question of the legality of the castration is more aptly put, though Tilley proves only that the incident would have been illegal, rather than impossible.

If Tilley's brand of argument and evidence were admissible in the literary court, one would be forced to reject a good many of Faulkner's stories and novels out of hand. General Nathan Bedford Forrest did not write the battle-field citation transforming Lt. Backhouse into Lt. Backus in "My Grand-mother Millard." The behavior of the Indians in stories like "Red Leaves," "A Justice," and "A Courtship" is sociologically and historically suspect, as is the Jefferson officials' countenancing of Miss Emily's refusal to pay her taxes. Considerable efforts have been expended in attempts to determine the historical and geographic accuracy or inaccuracy of Faulkner's characters and settings,[35] but a common reaction to arguments such as Tilley's is to admit their truth while denying their relevance to literary appreciation and judgment. Cleanth Brooks, for example, labels Tilley's activity "sociologizing," and contends that Tilley has merely gathered "sufficiently devastating evidence of how little Faulkner's story ... is to be taken as a sound medical and legal account of what can happen to idiots in Mississippi." One must distinguish, Brooks says, be-tween "truth of reference" and "truth of coherence."

> Faulkner's novels and stories, properly read, can doubtless tell us a great deal about the South, but Faulkner is primarily an artist. His reader will have to respect the mode of fic-tion and not transgress its limitations if he is to understand from it the facts about the South — that is, he must be able to sense what is typical and what is exceptional, what is normal and what is aberration.[36]

Similarly, Robert Scholes and Robert Kellogg refer to Tilley's contention as irrelevant: "Some psychologist has proved that Benjy is not a true psychotic but a literary construct. This being so, it is fortunate that Benjy is in a book, where he belongs." Actually, they argue, Faulkner uses Benjy's supposed mental limitations "as a means of getting away from routine rhetoric and intro-ducing a more poetic verbal pattern into the monologue."[37]

Although I am not convinced that Tilley has conclusively proved his case against Faulkner's characterization of Benjy, it is significant that we are willing to accept such arguments to the extent that Brooks, Scholes, and Kellogg accept Tilley's rejection of Benjy's realism. Faulkner is only occasionally described as a "realist," and those who do not consider realism the single or essential valid mode of fiction are usually willing to grant many of the objections of those who do. But Faulkner is more concerned with verisimilitude than has been supposed. "Truth of reference" and "truth of coherence" are hardly separate, and proper discrimination between the two truths must be based on something more than an intuitive sense of the rightness of the literary "facts." In Benjy's case, for example, it is instructive to note that the character resembles an Oxford neighbor of Faulkner's, whose behavior has been recalled by two men close to Faulkner. Faulkner's brother John maintains that the Oxford proto-types of the fictional Snopes family tormented "Benjy" to such an extent that his family had to keep him away from the street. Faulkner's friend John Cullen says that the idiot "chased little girls and frightened them." Cullen says that there is "more brutality in fiction than there was in fact," but John Faulkner's account suggests that "Benjy" was mercilessly provoked. The point is that in creating Benjy, Faulkner was drawing on an experience of a real-life idiot, an idiot who was not "sexually apathetic."[38] In this case, as with the famous sensationalism of Temple Drake's story in *Sanctuary,* Faulkner's grotesque characters and outrageous incidents are hardly more grotesque than the real people and events that may have suggested them.[39] The world which can be inferred from Faulkner's stories and novels, of course, does not depend for its success or failure on the existence or nonexistence of real-life prototypes for characters, or of historical and sociological parallels for incidents and condi-tions. The discovery of such prototypes and parallels may help us understand what Faulkner is doing in a given text, but the world of a Faulkner story ought not to be understood as Oxford transmuted.

Nor should the Faulkner world be understood as a composite of all the worlds of all the separate stories and novels, with discrete "facts" of the fictional world, composite or otherwise, inferred from one text to another. The stories are autonomous. When a particular piece of information is required for the proper understanding of a narrative, Faulkner supplies it, and when it is not required, he omits it, and attempts to obtain fictional "facts" from other texts will produce confusion and contradiction as often as enlightenment. It is both possible and desirable to discriminate a different world in each of Faulkner's stories and novels — possible because Faulkner offered the stories to the world as complete in themselves, and desirable because such an approach helps avoid drastic or questionable misreadings of Faulkner's particular texts and overall achievement. Again, this is not to say that the reuse of characters and incidents is without significance for Faulkner and his readers, but rather that a prema-ture recourse to the variants of Faulkner's mythology creates problems which cannot be satisfactorily resolved and which, in many instances, should never have been raised in the first place. However, a consideration of the Faulkner canon as a series of independent stories and novels, each having its place in Faulkner's personal chronology, reveals the abundance, the variety, and the changes in his fiction.

The protean volume in this connection is *Collected Stories.* Although several texts have been nominated for the honor, it is better not to think of Faulkner in terms of a single masterwork, a *Moby Dick,* a *Huckleberry Finn,* a *Gatsby.* There is, to use Faulkner's own metaphor, no Golden Book of Yoknapatawpha County which embodies the sum and substance of the artist's vision. *The Sound and the Fury, Light in August, Absalom, Absalom!,* the Snopes trilogy, the Nobel Prize address, and "The Bear" have been declared touchstones by various critics, but *Collected Stories* reveals, better than any other single volume or excerpt, the range and — to use what must be Faulkner's favorite word — the *myriad* scope of his fiction. All of the important Yoknapatawpha families appear in the volume. Sartorises, Snopeses, Compsons, McCaslins, de Spains. Stories include single characters such as Dilsey, Gavin Stevens, V.K. Ratliff, Boon Hogganbeck, and Thomas Sutpen, who figure prominently in the major novels. In addition, *Collected Stories* contains some of Faulkner's best-known and most-admired short stories, including "Barn Burning," "A Rose for Emily," "That Evening Sun," and "Red Leaves;" some excellent but lesser-known stories, such as "Mule in the Yard," "Turnabout," and "Carcassonne"; as well as such lesser efforts as "Victory," "Shall Not Perish," and "That Will be Fine." Most of the stories are set in the familiar territory of Yoknapatawpha, but there is a sufficient number of good stories set elsewhere to raise questions about the traditional view that Faulkner is a literary Antaeus who loses his strength when his feet are not planted in Mississippi soil. *Collected Stories* contains material demonstrating Faulkner's characteristic themes and forms, from both the earlier and later phases of his career.

The characters who appear in *Collected Stories* link the stories with most of Faulkner's novels. Some of the connections are obvious: "Wash" describes a crucial episode in *Absalom, Absalom!* and both "Centaur in Brass" and "Mule in the Yard" are retold in *The Town.* "There Was A Queen" develops the characters of *Sartoris,* bringing a conclusion to one incident in the novel and death to Miss Jenny. "My Grandmother Millard" deals in a comic vein with the Sartorises of *The Unvanquished.* The reappearance of less important figures such as Uncle Willy Christian of "Uncle Willy" in *The Town, The Mansion,* and *The Reivers* constitutes another kind of linkage. Monaghan of "Ad Astra" and "Honor" appears in both *Sartoris* and *A Fable.* Res Grier of "Shingles for the Lord" is mentioned in *The Mansion.* Captain McLendon of "Dry September" appears also in *Light in August, The Town,* and *The Mansion.* Gerald Bland of "Ad Astra" is Quentin Compson's adversary in *The Sound and the Fury.* Such linkages, of course, are not confined to the various *Collected Stories,* but also obtain among uncollected stories and *The Unvanquished, Go Down, Moses, Knight's Gambit,* and *Big Woods.* If, as many have held, Faulkner's chief literary distinction is as a mythologist, *Collected Stories* is an essential text.

The short stories can be useful, too, to those primarily interested in Faulkner's technical experiments. Though many of his stories were thoroughly revised between their original manuscript and typescript versions and their eventual magazine texts, there are even more significant differences between many of the magazine texts of stories and the versions found in story collections, story-cycles, and novels. Two conclusions may be drawn from this. First, a short story is likely to provide a fairly clear indication of Faulkner's attitude toward the world at a given point in time, though it must be noted that there was often a lapse of several years between the time Faulkner wrote a story and the time it was finally published. Second, both major and minor differences between story texts provide evidence of the nature and extent of his changing attitudes. But since there were delays between the writing and publication, generalizations based only on chronological order of publication are suspect and often misleading. The revisions Faulkner made between manuscript, magazine, and novel texts also indicate his developing notions of literary craft, and his work in the short stories generally shows the same concern for experimentation and innovation manifested in his novels.

Faulkner's virtuosity in the manipulation of point-of-view, for example, is probably his best-known technical innovation and represents a notable point of departure from realistic literary conventions. To whom is Benjy's section of *The Sound and the Fury* addressed, and how was it recorded, for example? Is Quentin's section of the same novel articulated from beyond the grave, as Addie Bundren seems to speak in *As I Lay Dying?* To whom does Jason Compson tell his version of the story, and why does he include so many details and incidents which would generate antipathy towards him? Ishmael, Huckleberry Finn, and Holden Caulfield are writing stories which are meant to be read; they are self-conscious craftsmen. The speakers in Ring Lardner's "Haircut" and the Cyclops episode of *Ulysses* are talking in a familiar style to a congenial audience; these texts are a record of what such men might say. Similarly, when Robert Browning's dramatic monologists speak, their utterances are located precisely in place and time, and Browning is careful to provide each speaker with an initial motive for discourse. Guido addresses the court in defense of his life. Ferrara desires to impress the envoy of his prospective father-in-law. Mr. Sludge wishes to avoid exposure as a fraud. Clearly a different set of conditions obtains in Faulkner's stories and novels.

In the short stories we find Faulkner experimenting with many possible variations of point-of-view, exploring the rhetorical techniques which distinguish novels like *The Sound and the Fury, As I Lay Dying,* and *Absalom, Absalom!* One might suppose that opportunities for experimentation with point-of-view are more limited in short stories than in novels, but within the short story form Faulkner constantly varied the point-of-view and the assumptions of what Wayne Booth calls "the implied author."[40] Roughly equal numbers of Faulkner's stories depend upon first-person and third-person narrators. Among his first-person narrators are central characters, such as Quentin Compson in "That Evening Sun"; participants, such as the Grier boy in

"Shingles for the Lord"; observers such as the unnamed narrator of "Divorce in Naples"; and those who repeat stories they have heard, as Quentin Compson does in "A Justice." They may be innocently naive, like the Grier boy in "Two Soldiers," or damnably naive, like Georgie in "That Will Be Fine." They may be humorous, sophisticated, disillusioned, or misanthropic, sympathetic, neutral, or antipathetic. Eloquence and poetry may be the natural qualities of their narrative voice, or they may be terse and reportorial.

In the stories told from the third-person, the omniscient narrator or implied author may employ any of a number of voices. He may speak as the interested but uninvolved member of the community, as in "A Rose for Emily," or he may be a more or less objective reporter, as in "Turnabout." The narrative voice in "Artist at Home" is mock-bardic, while that of "Red Leaves" is often lyrical. Some of Faulkner's stories, like his novels, feature several narrative voices: fluctuating first-person in "A Justice," different applications of omniscience in "Dry September," a hybrid first- and third-person in "A Bear Hunt." Point-of-view is as important in Faulkner's short stories as it is in his novels, for the location and range of the narrative voice go far toward determining the effects of particular stories. To employ the visual metaphor: where the narrator chooses to stand and what he is able and willing to see from there have significant consequences for the story he tells.[41]

Just as they demonstrate different stages of Faulkner's mythology and technical experiments, the short stories are also valuable in assessing Faulkner's development of particular themes. A story like "Dry September" personalizes the excessive and irrational qualities of a racist mob in ways that *Light in August* and *Intruder in the Dust* do not. "Lo!" and "Tomorrow" explore the sense of right relations to the land in a different manner than does *Go Down, Moses*. The hill people who are treated with irony and perhaps with contempt in *As I Lay Dying* and *The Hamlet* fare differently in the Grier stories and in the *Knight's Gambit* stories. The chicanery of the Snopeses is viewed with considerably more tolerance in "Mule in the Yard" and "Centaur in Brass" than in the corresponding sections of *The Town*. Frustrated women in "A Rose for Emily," "Elly," "The Brooch," and "Miss Zilphia Gant" are related to Mrs. Compson in *The Sound and the Fury* and Ike McCaslin's wife in *Go Down, Moses,* but the individual treatment of these women suggests that they are considerably more than the mere types that some critics have persisted in describing.[42] Black slavery and emancipation are explored humorously, sentimentally, and ironically in the stories which went into *The Unvanquished* and *Go Down, Moses,* and other aspects of contemporary racial attitudes come under scrutiny in "Dry September," "That Evening Sun," "Elly," and "There Was a Queen." No one theme receives exactly the same treatment in every story and novel in which it figures. In fact, Faulkner is capable of diametrically opposite renderings of a single theme. Violence issuing in murder, for example, is developed in very different ways for Ernest Cotton in "The Hound," Wash Jones in "Wash," Miss Emily in "A Rose for Emily," McLendon in "Dry September," Vatch in "Mountain Victory," Bayard Sartoris and Grumby in *The Unvanquished* stories, and Gavin Stevens' clients and opponents in *Knight's Gambit*.

The ways in which the short stories contribute to our understanding of Faulkner's achievement as the creator of Southern Gothic romances are somewhat less easy to identify. Faulkner's stories are often and in many ways peculiarly Southern in setting, subject, and characters, and some of them may be considered Gothic in their blend of sentiment and grotesquerie.[43] Remembering Brooks' warning against sociologizing, however, we might well be warned against the early and late critics who chided Faulkner for supposedly exploiting violence for its own sake. Violence is a tool that naturally and inevitably comes to Faulkner's hand in specific fictional situations, but never is it the result of motiveless malignancy. The so-called Gothic trappings, ruined mansions and "ghosts" in particular, are indigenous to the country about which Faulkner wrote, but it is doubtful that Faulkner ever deliberately exploited a cult of cruelty, Gothic or otherwise.[44]

More can be said about the ways in which the short stories disclose Faulkner's virtues and limitations as a prose stylist. In both his dialogue and his descriptive prose certain identifiable habits are readily apparent. Several of these can be observed in a short passage from "Shingles for the Lord," in which the Grier boy describes his father's disastrous attempt to remove shingles from the roof of the old church:

> He laid back on the bar and this time it got a holt. It wasn't jest a patch of shingles, it was a whole section of decking, so that when he lunged back he snatched that whole section of roof from around the lantern like you would shuck a corn nubbin. The lantern was hanging on a nail. He never even moved the nail, he jest pulled the board off of it, so that it looked like for a whole minute I watched the lantern, and the crowbar, too, setting there in the empty air in a little mess of floating shingles, with the empty nail still sticking through the bail of the lantern, before the whole thing started down into the church. It hit the floor and bounced once. Then it hit the floor again, and this time the whole church jest blowed up into a pit of yellow jumping fire, with me and pap hanging over the edge of it on two ropes. (*CS*, 39)

The boy speaks in the colloquial idiom, using approximations of dialect ("jest," "a holt") and grammar ("never even," "blowed up," "me and pap"). The longer idiomatic sentences contrast with the short functional narrative lines ("The lantern was hanging on a nail." "It hit the floor and bounced once."). The negative qualification ("He never even moved the nail") followed by the positive assertion ("he jest pulled the board off of it") is a typical Faulkner device, and the whole passage is concerned with establishing a single image, a frozen moment. The boy employs metaphor appropriate to his background and experience ("like you would shuck a corn nubbin") and the details he selects in describing the structure of the church indicate his familiarity with the particulars of carpentry and construction. Faulkner's use of dialect, colloquial idiom, metaphor and simile, negative qualification and definition, and oxymoronic devices is basic to his style, and the style varies much more widely than is often assumed. But in many stories, as in "Shingles for the Lord," artistic success depends directly on the consistency and propriety of the narrative voice in relation to the events being described.[45]

It is in his disputed capacity as a moralist, however, that Faulkner is best served by careful readings of his short stories. Because of his use of violent situations and grotesque characters, as well as his preoccupation with experimental techniques, Faulkner was condemned for years. The most startling assertion for George Marion O'Donnell's readers in 1939 was not that Faulkner's works are "a series of related myths" but rather that Faulkner "is really a traditional moralist, in the best sense."[46] In light of the later fiction, and especially in light of the Nobel Prize address, it has become common to discuss the positive implications of Faulkner's earlier works. His name and his fame were established, however, on the sensational success of *Sanctuary,* and it was only after that that he found lucrative work in Hollywood and more receptive editors in the national magazines.[47] Few of Faulkner's readers then considered that his stories and novels might have moral implications. "A Rose for Emily," the first story which Faulkner published in a national magazine, could be read as a sensational and violent story without moral implications, a typical performance "by the author of *Sanctuary.*" But there are, of course, moral implications to Miss Emily's story, though they are neither directly expressed nor obvious from an exclusively structural and technical examination of the story. The "pure event" is primary in the reader's consciousness. "A Rose for Emily" is, in a sense, one of Faulkner's greatest mystery stories, but the only mystery which it even partially solves is "what happened?" The further mystery, "why was it done?" is implied in the "pure event," as is the final mystery, "what is the meaning of it all?" Far from being a mere Gothic exercise or a facile combination of the horrible and the commonplace, "A Rose for Emily" is, among other things, an expression of moral outrage, an indictment of those conventions and customs which drive Miss Emily to murder Homer Barron. Because this indictment is expressed ironically, indirectly, many have failed to read it.

To the original definition of a Faulkner story must be added the assertion that the significance of change is moral in nature. If Faulkner does not merely exploit the violent and sentimental aspects of human behavior, neither does he merely record them. In the wide range of his short stories, there is always evaluation, a moral assessment of the fictional people who represent "the problems of the human heart in conflict with itself." Not every story makes the same evaluation or assessment. Only the most general moral classifications are broad enough to apply to all of Faulkner's stories and novels, and none is an adequate substitute for the direct apprehension of Faulkner's complex texts. The short stories, individually and collectively, are no more the "key" to Faulkner's morality than they are the "key" to his mythology, his technique, his Gothicism, or his style. Faulkner's short stories are not a way in, a means to an end; they are a part of the rich domain to which the various keys give access.

2

Stories and Novels

"You don't know about me," Huck tells us, "without you have read a book by the name of *The Adventures of Tom Sawyer,* but that ain't no matter." Though Faulkner seldom chose to provide such explicit links between his texts, there are obvious connections among his short stories and his nineteen novels as strong as those between *Tom Sawyer* and *Huckleberry Finn;* and, as with Mark Twain's works, there is a sense in which such connections do not matter, and a sense in which they matter a good deal. They do not matter insofar as each story or novel is an autonomous text, having a discoverable existence independent of all other stories or novels, succeeding or failing on its own terms. Thus, as I have suggested, a knowledge of *The Sound and the Fury* may be a hindrance to a proper reading of "That Evening Sun," and "Shall Not Perish" is a weak story even though it is set in Yoknapatawpha County and is related, through the de Spains, to superior works. But, since all the stories and novels are the creation of a single author, each may be at least partially understood in relation to the others, through similarities of technique, theme, character, setting, and style. Each text, moreover, takes on intertextual significance according to its place on the continuum of Faulkner's personal development. "That Evening Sun," for example, invites comparison with Faulkner's other first-person stories, with his other treatments of the relations between whites and blacks in Yoknapatawpha, and with his other renderings of Nancy, Dilsey, and the Compsons. "Shall Not Perish," in addition to its kinship with other texts involving the de Spains and the Griers, reflects something of Faulkner's attitude toward the Second World War, and also provides evidence for Faulkner's adoption, after 1940, of a rhetoric of advocacy. The point is that each of Faulkner's stories can and ought to be understood without recourse to his other texts, though the intertextual relations may lead to genuine insights concerning the individual text and the whole canon. This apparent paradox of simultaneous autonomy and interdependence is especially prominent in works such as *The Unvanquished, Go Down, Moses,* and the Snopes trilogy, and it obtains in all the stories and novels which involve the Yoknapatawpha setting and characters. It may be observed, in addition, in a few of the works set outside Yoknapatawpha, such as *A Fable,* and "Honor." In this chapter I will describe the several ways in which Faulkner's short stories and novels are related, in an attempt to establish some criteria by which both the autonomy and interdependence of his works may be appreciated.

Faulkner's stories and novels are related in two general ways. First, particular stories and novels are related as sources, sequels, and analogues. Second, they provide evidence for an understanding of Faulkner's technical and thematic development. Accordingly, I will first discuss the different kinds of relations between particular stories and novels, and then I will examine several pairs of novels, and short stories related to them, in order to specify the nature and characteristics of the profound evolution in outlook and method which Faulkner experienced over the years. This transformation, at once the most significant pattern in Faulkner's development and the most difficult to describe exactly and evaluate properly, may be observed in its most obvious form in a comparison of an early novel such as *Soldiers' Pay* or *Sartoris* and a later novel such as *The Mansion* or *The Reivers,* or in a comparison of an early story such as "Landing in Luck" or *Father Abraham* with a later story such as "Mr. Acarius" or "By the People." The stages in this development, which may generally be described as a movement from ironic pessimism to romantic optimism, can be inferred from an analysis of the stories and novels written in the thirties, particularly those connected to earlier and later texts through common characters, incidents, and settings in place and time.

There are six distinct ways in which particular Faulkner stories and novels are related. First, several novels are largely structures of material originally conceived in short story form. *The Unvanquished* and *Go Down, Moses* are in this group, as is, to a lesser extent, *The Hamlet* and, more doubtfully, *The Wild Palms.* Second, a number of novels incorporate single stories with relatively few changes, though the novelistic context always alters the significance and emphasis of the elements of the original story. The Jackson stories which were written into *Mosquitoes,* the story "Wash" which was worked into *Absalom, Absalom!,* and the stories "Centaur in Brass" and "Mule in the Yard" which were incorporated into *The Town* all provide instances of this practice. Third, a number of stories were extracted and published from novels-in-progress and from novels completed but unpublished. In this group are stories clearly labeled as excerpts, such as the opening section of *Absalom, Absalom!* which appeared under that title in *The American Mercury,* the *Perspectives USA* and *Vogue* versions of "Notes on a Horsethief," and the episodes from *The Mansion* and *The Reivers* published in *Esquire.* Other extracts, such as the Levee Press *Notes on a Horsethief,* were published without allusion to the novels from which they were taken.[1]

The fourth relationship involves stories which appear to be sequels to novels. "There Was a Queen," for example, continues the story of Miss Jenny and Narcissa from *Sartoris,* and "Honor" follows Monaghan from the same novel. "All the Dead Pilots" and "Ad Astra," too, develop characters and incidents treated in *Sartoris,* but since these stories are not chronologically later than the incidents of the novel, a term such as Lawrence Durrell's "sibling" may be more proper than "sequel."[2] In this manner "My Grandmother Millard" takes up the characters of *The Unvanquished,* and "That Evening Sun," "A Justice," and "Lion" reconsider the youth of Quentin Compson first described in *The Sound and the Fury.* The fifth relationship involves stories which contain analogues to characters, situations, incidents, and techniques which figure in the novels. Miss Zilphia Gant and the grandmother in "Elly" are clearly related to Miss Rosa Coldfield in *Absalom, Absalom!,* and McLendon (or Plunkett, as he is named in the *Scribner's* version) of "Dry September" is similar in many respects to Percy Grimm of *Light in August.* Hawkshaw's situation in "Dry September" is analogous to that of Chick Mallison in *Intruder in the Dust,* and of Horace Benbow in *Sanctuary.* Mister Ernest's refusal to kill the deer in "Race at Morning" recalls similar choices by Ike McCaslin and Sam Fathers in *Go Down, Moses* as well as Quentin's request in *The Sound and the Fury* that the boys leave the old trout alone. The sixth connection between particular stories and novels consists of Faulkner's countless allusions to previously developed characters and incidents. Such reflexive allusions are apparently superficial, and are of two types. An instance of *functional* allusion occurs in the story "Uncle Willy":

> And Uncle Willy was sitting by Reverend Schultz looking littler than ever, and I thought about one day last summer when they took a country man named Bundren to the asylum at Jackson but he wasn't too crazy not to know where he was going, sitting there in the coach window handcuffed to a fat deputy sheriff that was smoking a cigar. (*CS*, 228)

The narrator here develops from his own experience an analogy which serves to dramatize the pathetic situation of Uncle Willy, but is not employed primarily to refer the reader back to *As I Lay Dying,* though, for some readers, that reference is inevitable. Many allusions, by contrast, seem to be *decorative,* rather than functional, as when Flem Snopes is mentioned in *The Reivers,* and when a variety of characters in the Yoknapatawpha saga return for a last bow in *The Mansion.* These decorative allusions, which appear with increasing frequency in the later fiction, are at once the least important and most troublesome of Faulkner's self-reflexive practices, insofar as they incorporate earlier texts by reference into later ones and at the same time invite reconsideration of the earlier texts. Thus, such allusions place a double burden upon the reader. Some apparent allusions, too, are mere repetitions, such as the appearance of distinct characters named Everbe Corinthia in "The Leg" and *The Reivers.*

There are few stories or novels in which one or more of these six connections is not operative, and the way we respond to the individual text often depends on the relative importance we attach to the different connections involved. But from the beginning of his career as a novelist, when he incorporated elements of the story "Moonlight" into *Soldiers' Pay,* to the end of *The Reivers,* Faulkner drew on his short stories in the making of his novels, and he drew on his novels in the making of his short stories.[3]

Four apparent variations of Faulkner's practice of transforming short stories into novels can be observed in *The Unvanquished, The Wild Palms, The Hamlet,* and *Go Down, Moses,* published consecutively between 1938 and 1942. It is not always accepted that *The Unvanquished* and *Go Down, Moses* are actually novels, and it is highly questionable whether *The Wild Palms* was originally conceived as two distinct stories. *The Unvanquished,* the story of young Bayard Sartoris, consists of seven chapters, the first six deriving from short stories previously published in magazines. Since *The Unvanquished* appeared only a short time after the last of the six stories was published, since many of the changes between the stories and the novel are slight, and since Faulkner did not choose to collect any of the magazine versions of the stories, the relations between the stories and the novel have received relatively little attention.[4] But *The Unvanquished* is often considered a unified collection or cycle of short stories, and individual chapters, particularly "An Odor of Verbena," are regularly included in short story anthologies.

Go Down, Moses, published in 1942 with the crucial attention to the title *and Other Stories,* appears to have been composed in a manner similar to that of *The Unvanquished,* since Faulkner first published versions of several chapters as stories in magazines and then rewrote the stories, often with substantial revisions, to achieve novelistic unity. The *Go Down, Moses* volume, however, follows the apparent order of composition and the known order of publication of the separate stories much less closely than does *The Unvanquished.* There are also substantial differences between the several stories and the corresponding matter in the novel. Many of the characters' names are changed, for example. The *Harper's* version of "Lion" is narrated by Quentin, rather than by Ike McCaslin. In "Lion," Ike is "Uncle Ike" to the narrator, and is not among the important characters. The narrator of the *Post* version of "The Bear" and *Harper's* version of "The Old People" are nameless; these two stories, and "Lion," feature conversations between the narrator and his father, while the analogous portions of *Go Down, Moses* are ascribed to Ike McCaslin and his cousin, McCaslin Edmonds. Similarly, the *Story* version of "Delta Autumn" names Don Boyd the white miscegenist whose conduct creates a dilemma for the aging Ike McCaslin, while in the novel this role is given to Roth Edmonds, significantly, a McCaslin descendant. Two stories, "Gold Is Not Always" and "A Point of Law," were combined in the section of *Go Down, Moses* entitled "The Fire and the Hearth," and "Lion" and the *Post* version of "The Bear" were reworked for the most famous section of the novel. Although there can be little doubt that Faulkner's final intention was that *The Unvanquished* and *Go Down, Moses* should be read as novels, his public statements about both texts were often vague or contradictory. The current practice of anthologizing excerpts from the two books is questionable, for such excerpts do not clearly stand alone, and are in many particulars incomprehensible without heavy annotation. The evidence for these arguments, however, is both various and complex, and the two volumes will be examined together in the following chapter.

The Hamlet, the first volume of the Snopes trilogy, published in 1940, combines material from published and unpublished stories written as early as 1926 and as late as 1938. Whereas the stories revised for *The Unvanquished* were not altered in their basic structure but were subjected to several extensive additions and minor substitutions and deletions, the stories revised for *The Hamlet* were often radically altered with respect to emphasis, character, and structure. "Barn Burning," for example, is primarily concerned with the filial dilemma of young Colonel Sartoris Snopes, who is alluded to but briefly and obscurely when Ratliff tells the story of Ab and de Spain in *The Hamlet*:

> — there was another one, too, a little one; I remember seeing him once somewhere. He wasn't with them. Leastways he aint now. Maybe they forgot to tell him when to get outen the barn. (*HAM*, 13)

The story of Mink Snopes and Jack Houston in "The Long Summer" section of *The Hamlet* was appropriated from the short story "The Hound," first published in *Harper's* and collected in *Doctor Martino*. In "The Hound," the central character is not a Snopes, but a kinless bachelor named Ernest Cotton. The lyric passages describing the idiot Ike Snopes' pursuit of the cow may have originated in Faulkner's self-parodic *fabliau,* "Afternoon of a Cow." The use of short story material in *The Hamlet* would seem to account for the novel's episodic structure, but *The Hamlet* is clearly all of a piece. Faulkner's long and intense concern with the Snopeses is apparent in other novels, particularly *Sartoris* and *The Unvanquished,* and his assimilation of other Snopes stories in *The Town* and *The Mansion* contributes to the argument for a detailed consideration of all the Snopes material.

The origins and structure of *The Wild Palms* present another problem, for the best evidence indicates that its two narratives were separated only *after* the publication of the novel. Faulkner recalled the simultaneous composition of the two stories in the Jean Stein interview:

> I did not know it would be two separate stories until after I had started the book. When I reached the end of what is now the first section of *The Wild Palms,* I realized suddenly that something was missing, it needed emphasis, something to lift it like counterpoint in music. So I wrote on the "Old Man" story until "The Wild Palms" story rose back to

pitch. Then I stopped the "Old Man" story at what is now its first section, and took up "The Wild Palms" story until it began to sag. Then I raised it to pitch again with another section of its antithesis, which is the story of a man who got love and spent the rest of the book fleeing from it, even to the extent of voluntarily going back to jail where he would be safe. They are only two stories by chance, perhaps necessity. The story is that of Charlotte and Wilbourne. (*LIG*, 247-48)

Faulkner gave substantially the same account on other occasions.[5] An interview reported in the New Orleans *Item* in 1939, however, says that Faulkner "wrote one story and thought it was good but not good enough. So he wrote another and slipped the chapters of the two in between each other like shuffling a deck of cards, only not so haphazardly" (*LIG*, 36). Yet another version is provided by Irving Howe, who quotes Faulkner as saying "I did send both stories to the publisher separately and they were rejected because they were too short. So I alternated the chapters of them."[6] In any of these three versions we must be alive to the possibility that Faulkner was exercising his well-known prerogative of misinforming reporters and interviewers. He later emphatically denied the deck-of-cards analogy (*LIG*, 132), and the quotation attributed to him by Howe does not appear in any published interview. The manuscript evidence supports the version Faulkner gave Jean Stein. The probable conclusion is that *The Wild Palms* is not a conflation of shorter stories, though that is what it appears to be.

Nevertheless, Faulkner originally conceived of a single story, the story of Charlotte and Harry, and his decision to "counterpoint" it with the "Old Man" story suggests that *The Wild Palms* is, in a sense, a combination of two stories which Faulkner had not put on paper. Cowley separated them and used "Old Man" in the *Portable,* and Faulkner subsequently authorized separate printings of the two, as when he allowed "Old Man" to be published by itself in *The Faulkner Reader.*[7] For a time Faulkner was almost alone in his insistence on the primacy of "The Wild Palms," but the secondary character of "Old Man" has come to be recognized.[8] If the story of the tall convict is read by itself, its ironic cast is lost. The tall convict is one of Faulkner's memorable primitives, and his strength, patience, fortitude, and capacity for suffering seem heroic attributes when his story is read in isolation. But his refusal to accept the possibility of love, his refusal to accept the freedom which chance thrusts upon him, is clearly less rational, less heroic, and less human than Harry's choice of love rather than security, of prison life rather than suicide. *"Between grief and nothing,"* Harry says, *"I will take grief"* (*WP*, 324). The tall convict, faced with a similar choice, takes nothing.

"Old Man," however, is clearly superior to the title story in a number of ways. Read by itself, "The Wild Palms" is maudlin, melodramatic, and improbable. The tall convict's actions proceed from his direct response to the desperate necessitives of survival, and from the fierce consistencies of his own character, but Harry and Charlotte vacillate and temporize, depending heavily on chance and on their friends to determine and sustain their romantic course. They lack the money to live comfortably together and decide to terminate their affair, but at the right moment Harry finds a wallet containing $1278 in a New Orleans trash can. Their dependence on Charlotte's husband for his consent and encouragement is equally improbable. Sensitivity and wit characterize Faulkner's rendering of Roger Howes in "Artist at Home," and make credible his acquiescence in his wife's flirtation, and Roger Shumann in *Pylon* and Howard Rogers in "Honor" are wronged husbands whose behavior is grounded in coherent motivation, but "Rat" Rittenmeyer is foolish and unconvincing in his efforts to be "civilized" in his dealings with his wife and her lover. Harry and Charlotte similarly depend on McCord, the Chicago newspaperman, and on the young couple they befriend at the Utah mine. The tall convict, by contrast, survives by virtue of his own main strength. He makes do with what he has, taking six days to burn himself a crude paddle, and acting as midwife with a tin can for a scalpel and shoestring to tie off the umbilical cord.

The tall convict is a comic character in two different senses. He is Bergson's mechanical man, maintaining an inappropriate rigidity in a situation that demands spontaneity and elasticity. Thus he is repeatedly the victim of a society whose motives and character he cannot fathom. He is gulled by the detective magazines into thinking he can rob a train, twice he attempts to surrender and both times he is shot at for his trouble, and the reward for his voluntary return to Parchman is an additional ten-year sentence for an escape which he did not even attempt. In each situation he acts on the basis of manifestly incorrect assumptions: that the detective magazines are telling the truth, that his surrender will be understood and welcomed, that the prison authorities are just. He is also comic in that he is ultimately triumphant. He undertakes the perilous journey and succeeds in his quest for

> something, anything he might reach and surrender his charge to and turn his back on her forever, on all pregnant and female life forever and return to that monastic existence of shotguns and shackles where he would be free from it. (*WP*, 153)

The object of his quest differs absolutely from that of Harry and Charlotte, and in this opposition we may discern the superiority of their failure to the tall convict's success. Charlotte sets the standard for the couple on their first morning in Chicago:

> Listen: it's got to be all honeymoon, always. Forever and ever, until one of us dies. It cant be anything else. Either heaven, or hell: no comfortable safe peaceful purgatory between for you and me to wait in until good behavior or forbearance or shame or repentance overtakes us. (*WP*, 83)

The theme which emerges here is the familiar notion of Faulkner's that magnificent failure is preferable to limited success. The quest for failure, as Walter J. Slatoff calls it,[9] is a mark of Faulkner's heroes as well as the basis for his literary creed and narrative techniques, and it is recorded in a wide variety of contexts in the novels and short stories. Both Quentin Compson (in *The Sound and the Fury*) and Thomas Sutpen have grand designs, and both fail spectacularly, while Jason Compson and Flem Snopes, two of Faulkner's unquestionably mean characters, succeed in their aims. This is not to say that Quentin and Sutpen are unqualified heroes — both fail, in part, because they are aiming for the wrong thing — but that the sympathy and admiration they receive is a result of their dissipation of energy and talents in endeavors which are doomed to fail. This notion provides the rationale for Faulkner's often-discussed criticism of Hemingway, and for his preference of *The Sound and the Fury* to his other works. Literary precedent for this creed is in Melville's review, "Hawthorne and His Mosses," and the traditional metaphor for it is in Keats' "Ode on a Grecian Urn." It is a metaphor of which Faulkner availed himself repeatedly.[10]

This theme is unlikely to emerge from an isolated reading of "Old Man." Instead such a reading might well lead to the conclusion that Faulkner is inviting our approval of the tall convict's motives and his conclusion: "Women ——t" (*WP*, 339). Such a reading would be consistent with the notion that Faulkner was a misogynistic ogre.[11] The two stories of *The Wild Palms*, like the various chapters of *The Unvanquished* and *Go Down, Moses*, are less than satisfactory as independent narratives and, unlike the episodes of *The Hamlet*, there is no convincing argument for their separate origins. "Old Man" may be a better story when it is separated from *The Wild Palms*, but it is certainly a different story in that event.

When Faulkner incorporated a single story into a novel, the larger context almost always led him to make appreciable alterations in its meaning and effects, and his revisions sometimes help to clarify ambiguities in the original version. The assimilation of the Claude Jackson yarn into *Mosquitoes* shows how differently a Faulkner story may finally appear in novel form. The story is a tall tale, one of several Faulkner and Sherwood Anderson contrived during their association in New Orleans. The original version survives in an undated letter from Faulkner to Anderson, and it is one of a series the two intended to exchange.[12] It is a rough exercise in hyperbolic fantasy and burlesque, with touches of blasphemy. The story tells of a man who tries to raise sheep in a swamp, and of his son who tries to catch the sheep before they become alligators, until he himself turns into a shark. The first page of the letter is given over to a catalogue of notes on Al Jackson: he is "the only one of them left," a descendant of Andrew Jackson, an eccentric who never allows anyone to see him "wading or swimming or undressed. Something about his feet they say, but no one knows for certain" (*USWF,* 474). Jackson's mother was the tatting champion of her Sunday school and famous for her recipe for communion wine, which included "among other things, grain alcohol" (*USWF,* 474). His father was afflicted with brain fever after being forced to memorize one thousand verses of the New Testament.

Faulkner then begins the narrative of the sheep-farm, describing the ludicrous attempt to raise livestock in the swamp. After a dozen or more sheep drown, the old man devises life-jackets for them. Then the alligators begin attacking the floating sheep, so Jackson improvises horns for the sheep, to keep the alligators at bay. The sheep evolve rapidly into scaly, legless aquatic animals with tails like beavers. When Claude Jackson tries to save his "crops" by diving for them, he also adapts quickly to the water, finally disappearing altogether:

> About a year later they heard of him again. There was a single shark appeared off the coast that kept on bothering the blonde lady bathers, especially the fat ones.
> "That's Claude," said old man Jackson, "he was always hell on blondes."
> And so their sole source of income was gone. The family was in quite a bad way for years and years, until the Prohibition law came along and saved them. (*USWF,* 476)

Faulkner recalled that he and Anderson decided to preserve the Jackson saga because it "got so unwieldy and (so we thought) so funny."[13] In their collaboration on the saga Anderson insisted that Faulkner take the burlesque seriously, making it an object-lesson in the craft of fiction. It is thus fitting that the more polished versions of the Jackson stories in *Mosquitoes* are attributed to Dawson Fairchild, the equivalent of Anderson in Faulkner's *roman à clef.* The Jackson stories in *Mosquitoes* are not simply amusing for their own sake. Fairchild's immediate purpose in relating them is to demonstrate his own story-telling virtuosity at the expense of the credulous Major Ayres, who seems ready to believe any bit of gossip, no matter how preposterous, providing it concerns the acquisition of wealth. The Major's obtuseness is patent, and Fairchild realizes that he is indulging in a rather cheap form of humor. Thus, in their new context the Jackson stories help to define the rather pointless situation in which the characters of *Mosquitoes* find themselves, and it is one of several stories which contribute to the mixed characterization of Fairchild as raconteur, wit, and artist. In addition the stories underline the Major's density and are part of Faulkner's satiric portrait of the man who intends to make his fortune by marketing a new laxative.

The short story "Wash" and the novel *Absalom, Absalom!* provide a much more substantial instance of Faulkner's employment of short story materials in the construction of his novels. "Wash" was originally published in *Harper's* in February 1934 and was collected that same year in *Doctor Martino.* It was also included in *Collected Stories* and is thus one of the few stories Faulkner chose to collect after it had been assimilated into a novel. That he did so suggests both his own high regard for the story and his awareness that it is quite different from the novel version of the same events. "Wash" concentrates on the single eventful day on which Wash Jones kills Thomas Sutpen, his granddaughter Milly, and the infant daughter of Milly and Sutpen, and then commits virtual suicide by attacking the armed men who have come to take him into custody. At the beginning of the day Wash is happy and proud of his lackey's relationship to Sutpen, but on that same violent morning he asserts himself by killing Sutpen, because of his anger, frustration, and disillusionment at Sutpen's callous treatment of Milly and their newborn child. His murder of Milly and the child, and his suicidal attack on the men who have come to investigate proceed from the same revulsion.

In *Absalom, Absalom!* these events are related in much the same manner, order, and phrasing, but in the novel the life and death of Thomas Sutpen are viewed from a number of different perspectives, and Sutpen's cavalier treatment of Milly and the child is seen as a manifestation of the larger moral failure of his "design." In "Wash" Sutpen is but brutally indifferent to Milly and the child, while in *Absalom, Absalom!* it is his disappointment at not having fathered a son that causes his indifference to his new offspring. There are a number of notable changes in detail from story to novel. In both narratives Sutpen arises early to superintend the foaling of his mare, and is only incidentally informed that Milly is in labor. In "Wash" the mare is called Griselda, in *Absalom, Absalom!* she is called Penelope. Although it will not do to make too much of this change — though perhaps Faulkner was working in the novel for an ironic contrast between Sutpen and Odysseus — the alteration does point up the fact that Faulkner did not choose such names capriciously. Other changes in fact and emphasis are more significant. Sutpen's wife and son are not named in "Wash," nor do they figure in it. We are told only that "Sutpen's son had been killed in action the same winter in which his wife had died" (*CS*, 538-39). In the novel, of course, Sutpen's design raises the importance of Ellen Coldfield Sutpen and of Henry Sutpen, who is alive at the time his father is killed. The Sutpen of "Wash" is a defeated man, a near-alcoholic who is but a reeling shadow of his former greatness, while the Sutpen of *Absalom, Absalom!* returns from the war with the determination to rebuild his plantation and found his dynasty.

Some explanation for these and other changes between the story and the novel may be found in the fact that "Wash" is essentially concerned with Wash Jones, with the radical alteration in his consciousness which takes place on the violent morning, and with the fatal consequences of his revised comprehension. *Absalom, Absalom!*, by contrast, is essentially concerned with Thomas Sutpen, and with Quentin Compson's attempt to come to terms with Sutpen's story. "Wash" begins with a dramatization of the scene which shows Sutpen to

Wash for what he is, and proceeds with a section describing the character and relations of Wash and Sutpen. In this section Wash's foolish trust and admiration of Sutpen are emphasized, so that Wash's thoughts on the morning of Milly's delivery are perfectly consistent with what has come before:

> From the house, where the lamp shone dim beyond the warped doorframe, his granddaughter's voice came steadily as though run by a clock, while thinking went slowly and terrifically, fumbling, involved somehow with a sound of galloping hooves, until there broke suddenly free in mid-gallop the fine proud figure of the man on the fine proud stallion, galloping; and then that at which thinking fumbled, broke free too and quite clear, not in justification nor even explanation, but as the apotheosis, lonely, explicable, beyond all fouling by human touch: "He is bigger than all them Yankees that kilt his son and his wife and taken his niggers and ruined his land, bigger than this hyer durn country that he fit for and that has denied him into keeping a little country store; bigger than the denial which hit helt to his lips like the bitter cup in the Book. (*CS*, 542-43)

Sutpen's callous treatment of Milly abruptly shatters Wash's illusions. "Well, Milly," he tells the new mother, "too bad you're not a mare. Then I could give you a decent stall in the stable" (*CS*, 535). His final indifference to Milly and their daughter is reflected in his parting instructions to the black midwife: "Do whatever they need with whatever we've got to do it with" (*CS*, 536). The effect of this on Wash is immediate and profound: "He heard what Sutpen said, and something seemed to stop dead inside him" (*CS*, 544). After he kills Sutpen, his thoughts run to a revised understanding of himself and Sutpen and their relations:

> *Better if his kind and mine too had never drawn the breath of life on this earth. Better that all who remain of us be blasted from the face of the earth than that another Wash Jones should see his whole life shredded from him and shrivel away like a dried shuck thrown into the fire.* (*CS*, 548-59)

His remaining acts — the killing of Milly and the child, the setting of the fire, and the suicidal charge against the Major, the sheriff, and the assembled countrymen ("men of Sutpen's own kind ... symbols also of admiration and hope; instruments too of despair and grief" *CS*, 547) — all are but the logical application of his new knowledge.[14]

Though Quentin Compson recalls the killing of Sutpen in chapter VI of *Absalom, Absalom!* (181-87), the most extended treatment of the incident is to be found in the following chapter. Quentin tells the story to his Harvard roommate, Shreve McCannon, in the novel's characteristic compound of speculation, inference, hearsay, and eyewitness testimony. Quentin's narrative is based on the accumulated reports of his father, his mother, his grandfather, the midwife, and Major de Spain. The main difference between the order in which the events are related in the story and the novel is that Quentin, to

Shreve's exasperation, is so preoccupied throughout his historical monologue that he fails to mention that the child is a girl. Shreve, consequently, is mystified, and twice tries to interrupt Quentin to get an explanation:

> "Wait," Shreve said, "wait. You mean that he had got the son at last that he wanted, yet still he ——"
>
> "Wait," Shreve said, "for Christ's sake wait. You mean that he ——" (*AA*, 286, 289)

Quentin, however, is oblivious to his roommate until the very end of the narrative:

> *"Will you wait?"* Shreve said. "—— that with the son he went to all that trouble to get lying right there behind him in the cabin, he would have to taunt the grandfather into killing him first and then the child too?"
>
> "—— What?" Quentin said. "It wasn't a son. It was a girl."
>
> "Oh," Shreve said. "—— Come on. Let's get out of this damn icebox and go to bed." (*AA*, 292)

Faulkner once said that *Absalom, Absalom!* was originally conceived as the story of a man who wanted sons and destroyed them, and the finished novel develops this theme in the story of Henry Sutpen and Charles Bon, but in "Wash" there is no indication of any such "design" on Sutpen's part. The novel leaves the unmistakable impression that Sutpen would have acted differently towards Milly's child (and perhaps towards Milly) if it had been a boy, but in "Wash" Sutpen's use of Milly is merely the arrogant appropriation of a convenient body, the thoughtless act of an exhausted man who relies on Wash's consistent adulation and Milly's mindless acquiescence, not for the realization of a life's ambition, but for the casual satisfaction of a casual lust. The difference may be accounted for by the fact that *Absalom, Absalom!* is concerned with the reversal of Sutpen's fortunes, while "Wash" is concerned with the education of Wash Jones.

"Wash," I would suggest, is among the literal beginnings of *Absalom, Absalom!* and the place of the events of the story in the intricate structure of the novel is worth noting, for the various stylistic, factual, structural, and thematic alterations and affinities between the two texts serve to illuminate both. There is, for example, a slightly awkward passage in "Wash" (*CS*, 544) which seems to suggest that Wash tells Sutpen the child is a girl, but in the novel this difficulty is avoided, since Quentin fails to mention the sex of the child during his narration. In the story this passage also serves to reduce the psychological distance between Wash and Sutpen:

> ... an expression on his gaunt face almost imbecile with a kind of weary triumph, saying "Hit's a gal, Kernel, I be dawg if you ain't as old as I am ——" (*CS*, 544)

In "Wash," Jones' lyrical renunciation of Sutpen seems out of place in the mind of a character whose representative thoughts, speech, and actions are extremely crude and colloquial. In *Absalom, Absalom!*, however, the renunciation is one of several passages in which Wash's feelings are imagined and articulated by Jason Lycurgus Compson, and reported by his son Quentin for Shreve's benefit. Such alterations point up the differences of attitude and emphasis in the two works. The events in "Wash" have an objective existence of their own, established by the omniscient narrator, tending toward a single conclusion. The corresponding events in *Absalom, Absalom!* are fabricated by the several raconteurs, and are but parts of the larger work. It is the *story* of Wash and Sutpen which has objective existence for Mr. Compson and Quentin and Shreve, while the facts upon which the story is based are elusive, ephemeral, transitory. Wash's renunciation of Sutpen is what Mr. Compson imagines Wash might have been thinking, and his version of the murder tells, perhaps, as much about his own preoccupations as it tells about Wash. In the story we know that it *is* what Wash was thinking. In "Wash" the death of Sutpen, Milly, the child, and Wash are the end of the story, and "Wash" is the end of Sutpen. These deaths are the prehistoric events of *Absalom, Absalom!*, and they have significance and consequences far beyond the immediate moment of their occurrence.

It is perhaps not surprising, then, that Wash's part in *Absalom, Absalom!* is seldom discussed, for in the novel his actions are reported rather than observed firsthand, and his thoughts and feelings are guessed at, rather than shared. We are constantly reminded that the setting of the primary action is Quentin and Shreve's room at Harvard, and that the Sutpen's Hundred which they construct is as much fictive as actual. Wash is, for the most part, a shadowy figure on the landscape of nightmare. His killing of Sutpen is understood as the Easterner in Crane's "The Blue Hotel" understands the gambler's killing of the Swede:

> We are all in it! This poor gambler isn't even a noun. He is kind of an adverb.... that fool of an unfortunate gambler came merely as a culmination, the apex of a human movement, and gets all the punishment.

Miss Rosa Coldfield's description of Wash is similar. To her Wash is *"that brute," "brute instrument of that justice which presides over human events which, incept in the individual, runs smooth ... brute who was not only to preside upon the various shapes and avatars of Thomas Sutpen's devil's fate but was to provide at the last the female flesh in which his name and lineage should be sepulchered—"* (*AA*, 134)

That Miss Rosa is the author of this reading of Wash should make us suspicious of it. It is clear that she is repelled by Wash's crudity, as she was by Sutpen's, and in her diatribe Wash becomes "the brute" as Sutpen is "the demon." The occasion for her anger at Wash was that he embarrassed her publicly, *"yelling of blood and pistols in the street before my house"* (*AA*, 135), as Sutpen had earlier embarrassed her privately. Her notion of Wash should be compared with the intensely personal and particular rendering of his character that Mr. Compson gives. Neither view of Wash should be taken as the single correct one, and the correspondences between Mr. Compson's version and Faulkner's treatment in "Wash" do not prove that Mr. Compson is any closer to the truth than Miss Rosa is. The whole of *Absalom, Absalom!* suggests that Faulkner was less than satisfied with "Wash" as an explanation of Wash Jones, Thomas Sutpen, and why the South lost the war. In "Wash," Sutpen is a brave and ruthless Southern officer whose viciousness Wash comes to relate to the viciousness and corruption of the whole South. In *Absalom, Absalom!*, Sutpen is clearly differentiated from Southerners like the Compsons and the de Spains and the Coldfields, and his downfall proceeds from his "innocent" desire to imitate the forms of the Southern aristocracy without accepting its spirit, while the downfall of the South proceeds from its tolerance of Sutpen and men like him.

The comparison and relative simplicity of "Wash" contrast with the diffusion and complexity of *Absalom, Alsalom!* In the novel both the character of Wash and the episode of Sutpen's murder are obscured by the technical virtuosity of the narration and by Quentin's breathless reconstruction of Sutpen's effect on those who knew him. "Wash," however, is one of Faulkner's best stories, and it has merit and significance quite apart from its relations with *Absalom, Absalom!*

Faulkner's use of "Notes on a Horsethief" in *A Fable* is more difficult to analyze than his use of "Wash" in *Absalom, Absalom!*, partly because "Notes on a Horsethief" is more complex in style, theme, and technique than "Wash," and partly because "Notes on a Horsethief" is essentially an excerpt from a novel, rather than an independently conceived story. The story was published in three versions. In 1950 the Levee Press published it in a bound volume of limited edition, making no allusion to its part in the novel, which did not appear until four years later. In 1954, versions of the story, clearly labeled as excerpts, were published in *Vogue* and *Perspectives USA*. In basic incidents the story is the same in all three versions as it is in the novel. An English groom is hired by an American millionaire to look after an expensive racehorse. The groom takes advantage of a train accident to steal the horse. With the aid of an itinerant black preacher and his grandson, the groom manages to escape capture for over a year, though the trio is pursued by five groups of police, as well as by numerous amateurs after the large reward. During this period they race the horse at every opportunity, though it has only three good legs, and they are believed to have won a fantastic amount of money. Faced with capture, the groom kills the horse, rather than allowing it to be retired to stud. The groom is arrested, but he is soon spirited out of jail, and the body of the horse disappears, leaving no trace of the felon or the felony. The preacher and his grandson are also protected by a young man who resigns his position as federal deputy marshal out of sympathy for the thieves, by a successful lawyer hired by the ex-deputy, and by the inhabitants of the little towns where the trio races the horse, particularly those of the small Missouri village where the capture takes place.

In the Levee Press version of the story, and in the excerpt published in *Perspectives USA,* the "Notes" end with the scene in which the preacher is permitted to leave the small Missouri town. The *Perspectives USA* excerpt corresponds to pages 151 through 189 of the published text of *A Fable,* while the *Vogue* excerpt includes this material and a subsequent section of the novel, pages 189 through 204. Only the Levee Press version approaches the semblance of autonomy, and even it anticipates the novel in some particulars. The groom, for example, is introduced in the first line of the story as "the sentry" (*Notes,* 1), and an early passage announces that the American experience will allow the groom to become rich during the war:

> ... there happened to the groom the three things developing so directly and logically from one another as to seem bizarre, incongruous and paradoxical only to everyone save himself and which in the end enabled him to become (by more standards than just his) rich not only during the war but while actively engaged in the midst of it.... (*Notes,* 3)

This result, however, is not developed elsewhere, and thus the story's initial promise is unfulfilled. Since they are taken from the novel, the *Perspectives USA* and *Vogue* excerpts include a good deal of material extraneous to the story of the horsethieves, material not comprehensible outside the context of *A Fable.*

In *A Fable* the groom figures as Harry, a silent, brooding, vicious man, whose seemingly unprovoked attack on the runner is the occasion for much speculation among his superiors, just as the mysterious hold he seems to have over the other enlisted men in his company is variously explained as fear, terror, coercion, extortion, and love. Harry dies with the other British and German infantrymen who attempt to support the Private's rebellion against military authority by walking unarmed into No Man's Land. The British runner, who is in sympathy with the rebels, wishes to use Harry's influence over the other men in the company as a means of encouraging the rebellion. Rebuffed by Harry, the runner seeks out the Reverend Sutterfield (the preacher of *Notes*) who relates the story of the stolen racehorse.

In one sense the story of the horse and the groom is a conventional description of how a man in an extreme situation came to be there. More specifically, *A Fable* implies, Harry's American experience soured him, though he was sour already:

— the morose, savage, foul-mouthed, almost inarticulate (only the more so for the fact that occasionally a fragment of what he spoke sounded a little like what the valley knew as English) foreigner who moved, breathed, not merely in an aura of bastardy and bachelordom but of homelessness too, like a half-wild pedigreeless pariah dog: fatherless, wifeless, sterile and perhaps even impotent too, misshapen, savage and foul. (*FAB*, 189-90)

Harry's ultimate and futile participation in the rebellion may be understood as his grudging recognition of his place in the community of man, though to the very end he appears to be misanthropic. But his last words, uttered when he is caught with the other rebels between the German and British rockets, are his unconscious admission of his fellow-feelings. "No," he cries, "no! Not to us! They cant kill us! They cant! Not dare not: they cant!" (*FAB*, 321-22). The sustaining cause of the groom's actions in America is his love of the magnificent horse, the immediate and profound affinity between them. Their relationship is magical and strong, worthy of comparison with that of other fabled lovers, and his dedication to the horse finally affects those who observe him. Having once embarked on this magnificent quest for failure — the miracle is not that he was captured, but rather that he escaped it for so long — he can never completely resign himself from the ideals which inspired him. If there are altruistic motives in the vicious Sentry, Faulkner seems to be saying, men all men may be truly immortal. The story of the Sentry is reminiscent of an earlier Faulkner story, "Honor," in which a seemingly rootless and irresponsible veteran, Monaghan, is discovered to be motivated by the memory of a selfless and loyal friend. Finding no situation in postwar society which satisfies him, Monaghan appears, like the Sentry, to be excessively and conventionally "tough." In "Honor," as in *A Fable*, the opening scene shows the superficial toughness and meanness of the character, while the subsequent scenes explain how he came to be this way.

Notes on a Horsethief develops little of this material. The emphasis in the separate publication of the story is on the wildly improbable situation of the groom and his confederates, and on the influence which they have on their pursuers and captors. Here *Notes* provides something of a conventional success story, for the supposed wealth which the groom is thought to have accumulated during the flight is paramount in the minds of most who come in contact with the trio. The horse's owner offers a large reward, the townspeople of the village where the three are captured are fascinated by the amount of money they are supposed to have won, and even the turnkey who doggedly refuses to release the preacher finds himself affected by the putative wealth of his captive. The "federal ex-deputy" and the lawyer, however, make it plain that the significance of the horsethieves is not determined by the amount of money they did or did not win, nor by the value of the racehorse, nor by the size of the reward offered for their capture, but because theirs is "the doomed and glorious frenzy of a love story" (*Notes,* 15). The lawyer realizes that his participation in the case has significance beyond the size of his fee, and he toys with

> a picture of himself not engaged in just another mere petty — yes, monotonous too — legal victory but as a — perhaps the — figure in a pageant which would in reality be an histori- cal commemoration and in fact even more than that: the affirmation of a creed, the postu- lation even of a very life: the loud strong voice of America itself out of the soundless westward roar of the tremendously battered yet indomitably virgin continent where no- thing save the vast unmoral sky limited what a man could try to do nor even the sky his success and its adulation if he just thought of the right twist to do it with.... (*Notes,* 31)

So neither the groom nor his novelistic counterpart, the Sentry, are to be understood as mere mercenaries. In the story it is strongly suggested that the fortune the thieves are thought to have won is a figment of the imagination of their pursuers, who, like the turnkey, lose all sense of proportion when they begin to speculate on the quantity of ill-gotten wealth. The turnkey first believes it is $20,000, then $30,000, then $40,000, and finally $45,000 (*Notes,* 24, 36, 44). The lawyer tells him that there isn't any money, but the turnkey cannot accept this. The preacher tells the lawyer that there was more than $30,000, and in the final scene of the story he admits that "It was a heap" (*Notes*, 53, 71).

The groom, in the course of his American adventures, becomes a Mason, a Baptist, and a crapshooter, and each of these three unlikely roles is vital to the success he enjoys. The story version implies that it is his skill at crapshooting which enables him to become rich during the war, but in *A Fable* his wealth is acquired by a short-term lending operation based on the assumption that the men in his company will not be killed. To his superiors, this operation seems cruel and heartless, but, as Edmond Volpe points out, "his loan to each man constitutes an act of faith in that individual's survival."[15] This scheme recalls the early story "Thrift" and Flem Snopes' notorious loan-sharking in *The Hamlet,* but Harry is not avaricious like Flem, nor is he frugal and calculating like MacWyrglinchbeath. His lending operation in *A Fable* is like his theft of the racehorse; he is motivated by something beyond mere money.

The prose in both the story and the novel is for the most part what might be described as late Faulkner orotund, depending on seemingly interminable convoluted periodic sentences and incremental negative qualification. It pre- sents difficulties in both versions, and it may contribute to the belief that the horsethief story is only loosely related to the allegorical development of *A Fable.*[16] The obscurity of *Notes on a Horsethief,* however, is equally attrib- utable to the circumstances of its origin in the context of *A Fable.* Like "Wash" it is a different narrative when it is read outside the novel in which it was incorporated, but unlike "Wash" it is of mixed interest as a story in its own right, and Faulkner's choice of title for the Levee Press and magazine versions of the story indicates that he was aware of its limitations. Faulkner's habit of publishing excerpts from his novels points up the episodic character of his work in the longer form. Beginning with an excerpt from the first chapter of *Absalom, Absalom!*, continuing through the collaboration with Cowley on *The Portable Faulkner,* and ending with excerpts from *The Reivers,* these selections are occasionally of some use in discovering Faulkner's intentions in novels, in part because some of the excerpts bear little apparent relation to the novels from which they were taken.

Sartoris, the first of the Yoknapatawpha novels, includes Faulkner's first published treatments of many of the characters, incidents, and episodes which he was to develop in subsequent stories and novels. "There Was a Queen" focuses on three Sartoris women: Virginia De Pre, Narcissa Benbow Sartoris, and Elnora. The center of the story is Narcissa's mysterious trip to Memphis. This incident is first considered from Elnora's point-of-view, then from Miss Jenny's, then from that of Narcissa's son, Benbow, and finally from that of Narcissa herself. Narcissa, the story reveals, had once been the recipient of a series of obscene letters. Rather than destroying them or reporting them to the authorities, she kept them. Then they were stolen from her room. She makes the trip to Memphis to secure the return of the letters by giving herself to the Federal agent who found them when the thief fled. Miss Jenny, shocked by the fact that Narcissa had kept the letters and by the manner in which she secured their return, dies. In *Sartoris* the anonymous letters are mentioned on several occasions, but the Memphis trip and Miss Jenny's death are not treated.

"There Was a Queen" may be properly termed a sequel to *Sartoris,* but it is in no way dependent for its effects on the novel. Both the Sartoris family history and the current situation of the Sartoris women are described in the opening paragraphs of the story. There are a number of significant differences between the story and the novel, as many differences as there are similarities. In the story, Narcissa says that she told Miss Jenny only about the first of the letters, while in *Sartoris* she shows her several, and the two discuss them. In the novel, the bank clerk who writes the letters is identified as Byron Snopes, one of the first of the Snopes clan to run into trouble in Jefferson, but the author of the letters in the story is identified only as "that book-keeper in Colonel Sartoris' bank" (*CS,* 739). Faulkner here declines an obvious opportunity to connect "There Was a Queen" with *Sartoris* and the other works in the chronicle, but it appears that he did not wish to call attention to the bank clerk in the story. Elnora, by contrast, is a minor figure in *Sartoris,* and in the novel the blacks' comments on the Sartoris vagaries are often comically inadequate, and a good deal of attention is devoted to seemingly ridiculous behavior of the Sartoris blacks. In *Sartoris* the white family must rescue them from their own foolishness — Old Bayard repays the church money which Simon has taken to bankroll Melony's beauty parlor; Caspey is chided for his anachronistic black militancy — but in "There Was a Queen," as in *The Sound and the Fury,* it is the black family which does all the work, and Elnora is fully conscious of her vital role in the household. This is related to another major difference between the story and the novel: in "There Was a Queen" Elnora is identified as Old Bayard's half-sister, while in the novel this explicit joining of the white and black families is barely suggested.[17] The story adds a new dimension to the Sartoris family in this rendering, since Elnora is seen to be both "family" and "quality," in contrast with Narcissa, who is neither. The final major difference between the story and the novel is that "There Was a Queen" is almost devoid of Sartoris men. All of them except young Benbow are dead. In *Sartoris* considerable attention is directed toward young Bayard's unsuccessful attempts to come to terms with his family's past. In "There Was a Queen" primary attention is directed toward Narcissa's attempt to repudiate the Sartoris traditions and values and her own past.

Whether her attempt is successful is moot. Returning from Memphis, she takes young Benbow with her for a ritual cleansing in the creek. "In Jordan," Miss Jenny chides her. "Yes, Jordan at the back of a country pasture in Missippi" (*CS*, 741). Narcissa argues that her conduct was necessary, and Miss Jenny seems to agree:

> "I had to get them back. Don't you see that?"
> "Yes," the old woman said. "Yes." She sat bolt upright in the wheel chair. "Well, my Lord. Us poor, fool women....' (*CS*, 741)

Miss Jenny retains her composure throughout this interview, but it is clear that Narcissa's revelation hastens her death. Though by her own admission she is "a bedridden old woman," though she claims that she is not dependent on Narcissa, and though she understands that Narcissa is no kin to the Sartoris family, it is clear that Narcissa has twice violated the rigid code of the Sartoris aristocracy, first by keeping the letters, and second by retrieving them as she did. This second violation, the one with which the story is immediately concerned, is seen as a direct consequence of the first. "There Was a Queen" expresses conflicting and unresolved judgments of Narcissa. Against Miss Jenny's seeming acquiescence we are offered Elnora's assertion that Narcissa is "Trash. Town trash" (*CS*, 729). She observes of Narcissa to Miss Jenny, "She won't never be a Sartoris woman" (*CS*, 730). "Born Sartoris or born quality of any kind ain't *is*, it's *does*," Elnora maintains (*CS*, 732). By this standard Narcissa clearly lacks quality, but the limitations of the Sartoris "quality" are shown in novel and story alike. They are, Miss Jenny says, "a lot of fool proud ghosts" (*CS*, 736, 738). Unable to cope with life's disgusting alternatives, they take to themselves, while Narcissa goes out into the world to do what she feels she has to do. Her trip to Memphis ostensibly secures her safety, and Benbow's, while the ritual cleansing and her confession to Miss Jenny constitute her expiation and absolution.[18]

Faulkner was to return again and again to the characters and incidents of *Sartoris* for story and novel material. The stories which went into *The Unvanquished* are obvious examples, and "My Grandmother Millard," which apparently derives from *The Unvanquished* itself, is anticipated in some details in *Sartoris*.[19] Stories like "The Tall Men" and "Mule in the Yard" may ultimately be traced to passages in *Sartoris,* while incidents in the lives of the Sartoris twins, John and Bayard, are treated in "All the Dead Pilots" and "Ad Astra," and are touched on briefly in the novel."[20] Also of interest are the early notices in *Sartoris* of Flem Snopes and his clan, whose symbolic opposition to the Sartorises is a staple of criticism since George Marion O'Donnell, and whose literal opposition to the Sartorises is portrayed in *The Unvanquished.* In the later stories, however, Faulkner invariably altered tone, emphasis, and fact from the *Sartoris* version. "Mule in the Yard" becomes a comic story, and there are comic aspects of John Sartoris' rivalry with Spoomer in "All the Dead Pilots." In a different kind of development, Old Bayard of *Sartoris* is the young Bayard whose coming to manhood is described in *The Unvanquished,* but the earlier Sartoris novel suggests little or nothing of this aspect of his life. The relations between "There Was a Queen" and *Sartoris* show that Faulkner's conception of his principal family was not a static one. To deny the autonomy of any of the texts featuring the Sartoris family violates the integrity of that text and obscures the dynamics of Faulkner's development.

Faulkner's famous criticism of Hemingway — that Hemingway learned very early in his career the kind of writing he could do well, and simply continued to repeat his success[21] — has a kind of parallel in Faulkner's own work, for he repeatedly returned to the same kinds of characters, situations, and incidents in his fiction. He was always fascinated by hunters and by fugitives. The individual who clings to standards and values which are no longer operative is common to many of his works. In developing such characters and situations, Faulkner seems naturally to have elaborated on previously created analogues. The parallels between "Dry September" and *Light in August* illustrate his use of both analogous characters and situations. Both Will Mayes and Joe Christmas are pursued and murdered for their alleged breaches of the color line. McLendon and Percy Grimm, the self-appointed vigilantes, are similar in a number of respects. Both act on what they assume are unimpeachable motives, both act outside the sanctions of the law, both enact excessive and vicious punishment on their quarry. In both the story and the novel the offended white woman is of questionable reliability or character.

The similarities between the story and the novel, however, are no more noteworthy than the differences. Christmas is only putatively black, while Will Mayes certainly is. Christmas has actually committed the crime with which he is charged, while Mayes has not. Christmas has a reputation for violence, while Mayes has not. Christmas runs and fights until the ultimate moment, never denying his guilt, while Mayes is a tractable victim who solemnly protests his innocence. Christmas is the object of a long and intense search, during which the community arms itself against him, while Mayes is caught before he knows that he is wanted, and the vigilantes work in secrecy, extracting their vengeance almost before the community has been informed of the "crime."

Both "Dry September" and *Light in August* present devastating indictments of Southern racial attitudes. Christmas dies because he cannot escape the society's demand that he declare himself white or black and behave accordingly. The people of Jefferson consider his murder of Joanna Burden a vindication of their beliefs in racial separation. His act not only conforms to their expectations of black behavior, it also constitutes a just punishment for Joanna, who had isolated herself from the community in her attempts to help blacks. Her "help," however, is condescending, based on her assumption that "the Negro" is the white man's curse.

> I had seen and known Negroes since I could remember. I just looked at them as I did rain, or furniture, or food or sleep. But after that I seemed to see them for the first time not as people, but as a thing, a shadow in which I lived, we lived, all white people, all other people. I thought of all the children coming forever and ever into the world, white, with the black shadow already falling upon them before they drew breath. And I seemed to see the black shadow in the shape of a cross. (*LIA*, 239)

She forms a liaison with Chrismas out of charity, out of pity, and out of a feeling of obligation to his race. She derives excitement and satisfaction from living with a member of the "doomed" race.

Like Joanna Burden, Miss Minnie Cooper uses the volatile prejudice against blacks to compensate for an inadequate love-life. Mayes is not the first black, the barber Hawkshaw recalls, whom Miss Minnie has accused of being attracted to her. Miss Minnie is even more pitifully ignorant of the reality of Will Mayes than Joanna Burden is of the reality of Joe Christmas. Having stirred up the fatal trouble, Miss Minnie collects herself and goes to the movies, where she is the object of pity and sympathy. She becomes hysterical and is taken home, where her friends minister to her. "Do you suppose anything really happened?" one of them wonders (*CS*, 182). Neither Miss Minnie nor her friends give any thought to Will Mayes. For them, he simply does not count. Only Hawkshaw makes any attempt to thwart the vigilantes, but he, like Horace Benbow in *Sanctuary*, is too weak to be effective. Against his repeated protest, "I know Will Mayes" (*CS*, 169, 170), there is McLendon's persuasive argument: "Happen? What the hell difference does it make? Are you going to let the black sons get away with it until one really does it?" (*CS*, 171-72). The same kind of response to the racial shibboleth is made by the white sheriff in

Light in August, who is not prepared to believe that Christmas killed Joanna Burden until Brown diverts suspicion from himself by identifying Christmas as a "nigger."

> "That's right," he says. "Go on. Accuse me. Accuse the white man that's trying to help you with what he knows. Accuse the white man and let the nigger go free. Accuse the white man and let the nigger run."
>
> "A nigger," the marshal said. "I always thought there was something funny about that fellow." (*LIA*, 91)

Though the characters and situation in the story and the novel are similar in a number of respects, and though the thematic implications are similar, it is incorrect to assume that the two are essentially identical. Will Mayes is a pathetic victim, while Joe Christmas is in some sense a tragic one. "Dry September" lacks the mitigating and affirmative characters who figure prominently in *Light in August,* and is closer to *Sanctuary,* both chronologically and thematically.[22] Like Will Mayes, Lee Goodwin is the innocent victim of a mob, and like Hawkshaw, Horace Benbow lacks the strength and conviction to save him. Both Mayes and Goodwin are unjustly accused of sexual offenses by women who give no thought to the consequences of their accusations. Again, the differences between the two narratives are at least as striking as the similarities. Horace Benbow is the center of attention in much of *Sanctuary,* but Hawkshaw plays only a minor part in "Dry September." Goodwin, on the other hand, has a relatively minor role in *Sanctuary,* and the mob which destroys him is not differentiated into personalities such as McLendon and Grimm. Goodwin is found guilty in court, while neither Mayes nor Christmas is accorded the formality of a trial. Finally, though there are some parallels between Joanna Burden, Miss Minnie Cooper, and Temple Drake, each is a distinct character with a distinct pattern of behavior and motivation.

Though Faulkner returned again and again to certain types of characters and situations, he took pains to avoid simple repetition, and his stories are more than mechanical exercises in a proven form. When he chose to refer overtly to previously developed characters and events, however, it is more difficult to discover his precise intentions. The characters of Yoknapatawpha, he said, had an existence in his own mind quite apart from their individual avatars in stories and novels.

> I think that after about ten books, I had learned enough of judgment to where I could pick and choose the facet of the character which I needed at that particular time to move the story I was telling, so that I can take a facet of one character in one story and another facet of that character in another story. To me it's the same character, though sometimes to the reader it may seem as though the character had changed or had developed more — to me he hasn't. (*FIU*, 24)

The qualification "after about ten books" suggests that in the earlier Yokna-patawpha fiction individual characters had not received full definition. The danger of assuming an absolute correspondence between successive versions of the same characters and incidents can be seen in the problems raised by the yok-ing together of "That Evening Sun" and *The Sound and the Fury.* In other cases, the characters are so different in conception from one appearance to the next that they are hardly recognizable. The practical-joking Ratliff of "A Bear Hunt" is a much different character from the mild, affable salesman of *The Hamlet.* Gavin Stevens is obtuse when he attempts to explain the behavior of Joe Christmas in *Light in August,* but he is ingenious and perceptive in some of the detective stories, such as "An Error in Chemistry."

The changing of characters' names from one story to the next can be understood as a kind of deliberate carelessness on Faulkner's part. In such cases Faulkner is not trying to confuse the reader, nor is he consciously altering the historical "facts" of Yoknapatawpha. He is concerned with the immediate fictional situation and he tells the story with the most readily available tool.

> Those characters to me are quite real and quite constant. They are in my mind all the time. I don't have any trouble going back to pick up one. I forget what they did, but the charac-ter I don't forget, and when the book is finished, that character is not done, he is still going on at some new devilment that sooner or later I will find out about and write about. (*FIU,* 78)

Not only did Faulkner sometimes forget what individual characters did, he also seems to have forgotten the names which he had originally assigned to them. The conscious altering of names is undertaken sometimes to meet new fictional needs, as when the behavior of Cotton in "The Hound" is transferred to Mink Snopes in *The Hamlet,* and sometimes to meet extraliterary conditions, as when Surratt becomes Ratliff.[23] If, as he claimed, Faulkner imagined his char-acters as existing independently of the fiction, he did not always assume that he knew everything there was to know about them, and he felt no responsibility to tell all that he knew at any given time. In discussing the change between Nar-cissa Benbow in *Sartoris* and in *Sanctuary,* Faulkner agreed with the suggestion that he was merely taking a different look at the same character, but he also admitted that he had no notion of Temple Drake's adventures in *Requiem for a Nun* when he wrote *Sanctuary.* "The writer," he said in explaining his new conception of Temple, "is learning all the time he writes, and he learns from his own people ... they teach him, they surprise him, they teach him things he didn't know, they do things and suddenly he says to himself, Why yes, that is true, that is so" (*FIU,* 9, 96). This comment, like the warning in the headnote to *The Mansion,* is Faulkner's way of acknowledging that his conception of his characters was dynamic.

To sum up the nature of the various kinds of relations between specific

Faulkner stories and novels, it may be useful to consider a story and a novel which have several different connections. "A Name for the City," published in *Harper's* in October 1950, was rewritten for *Requiem for a Nun,* published in the following year. So, like "Wash," it is a story worked into a novel. "A Name for the City" involves many of the principal families and characters of the Yoknapatawpha chronicle — Gavin Stevens, Compson, Grenier, Holston, Habersham, Peabody, Ratliffe. It involves a return to the earliest period of Faulkner's fictional history. There are a number of characters and analogues with characters and situations in other Faulkner texts. Pettigrew, the zealous mail-rider, is similar to the turnkey of *Notes on a Horsethief* and *A Fable.* Gavin Stevens stands in the same relation to the unnamed narrator of "A Name for the City" as he does to Chick Mallison in *Intruder in the Dust* and in some of the *Knight's Gambit* stories. The frantic efforts of the founding fathers of Jefferson to avoid paying Alexander Holston for his stolen lock recall the chicanery of Flem Snopes in "Centaur in Brass," as well as Res Grier's futile attempt to outwit Quick in "Shingles for the Lord." The story also extends and develops bits and pieces of Yoknapatawpha lore. Ikkemotubbe's mother is named for the first time in the chronicle, and it is revealed that the founder Habersham's son married one of Issetibbeha's heirs and emigrated with the Indians to Oklahoma. The whole story purports to explain a previously unmentioned portion of Yoknapatawpha history — how Jefferson got its name.

Requiem for a Nun also demonstrates the two other kinds of connections between Faulkner's stories and novels, since "The Jail" was printed as an excerpt in *Partisan Review* in October 1951, and since the novel is in part a construct of and a sequel to material developed in earlier stories and novels, particularly *Sanctuary* and "That Evening Sun." The best approach to "A Name for the City" and *Requiem for a Nun,* however, is to treat the former as an autonomous short story and the latter as an autonomous novel. The short story contains no references to either Nancy Mannigoe or Temple Drake, the central characters in *Requiem for a Nun,* nor is Temple's husband, Gowan Stevens, a character in the story. Gavin Stevens, also a major figure in the novel, appears in "A Name for the City" as the authority and the interpreter of the narrator's story. The relations between the story and the principal action of the novel are obscure at best, and the section of the novel, "The Courthouse," which corresponds to "A Name for the City" shows a number of significant revisions in the story material. Faulkner removed all traces of Gavin Stevens from the prose section of the novel, which is rendered in omniscient voice. Had he retained Gavin in the prose parts of the novel, the relationship between "A Name for the City" and the situation of Temple and Nancy would be more apparent than it is, but in *Requiem for a Nun,* as in *The Wild Palms,* Faulkner emphasizes the contrapuntal effect by making the contrasts sharp. Michael Millgate has examined the parallels between the main action, the *Harper's* story, and the prose interchapters of the novel, and he concludes that Gavin Stevens "is effectively the controlling intelligence throughout the whole of *Requiem for a Nun.*" The theme of the novel, he argues, is that "man yields up first his responsibilities and ultimately his rights to impersonal institutions: flexibility and humanity disappear and human lives are increasingly dominated by abstract and often arbitrary principles and laws."[24]

Though this is a clear implication of *Requiem for a Nun,* it is not the basic idea of "A Name for the City." The story is an exercise in primitive social comedy, fondly recalled from a distant and sophisticated perspective. Pettigrew, the mail-rider, is bribed to forget the "impersonal institution" of Federal postal regulations, and he and the other early settlers of Jefferson demonstrate both their flexibility and their humanity in the situation. The town of Jefferson is created under the most improbable set of circumstances, but the atmosphere is one of hope and pride. "We're going to have a town," Peabody tells Pettigrew. "We already got a church — that's Whitfield's cabin. And we're going to build a school, too, soon as we get around to it. But we're going to build the courthouse today.... Then we'll have a town. We've already even named her" (*Harper's,* 213-14). The naming of Jefferson in this story is more a comic tribute to Pettigrew's individuality and fierce responsibility to himself than it is a yielding up to an impersonal institution. The story emphasizes the individuality and eccenticity of the early settlers, Holston and his mammoth lock, Compson's furious and futile search for the lock, Peabody's sardonic humor, Ratliffe's ingenious sophistries.

No one in the story seems to think that the men are making a mistake in founding the town and naming it Jefferson. In the prose section of *Requiem for a Nun* Faulkner added a twenty-page section to the narrative in which the "mistake" theme is developed. The consciousness of the mistake is demonstrated by Ratliffe, and the omniscient narrator goes to some pains to describe the dissipation of the bright dream in "the electricity and gasoline, the neon and the crowded cacophonous air" (*REQ,* 47). There is a suggestion of this futility in "A Name for the City" when the narrator reveals that the town would, after a hundred years

> ...wake frantically from its communal slumber in a rash of Rotary and Lions Clubs and Chambers of Commerce and City Beautifuls. a furious beating of hollow drums toward nowhere, but simply to sound louder than the next tiny human clotting to its north or south or east or west, dubbing itself city as Napoleon dubbed himself emperor, and defending the expedient by padding its census roles — a delirium in which it would confound forever seething with motion and motion with progress.... (*Harper's,* 201)

This is an early observation in "A Name for the City," and it is included parenthetically in the initial statement of the problem of the lock, so it colors the reading of all the subsequent events, but the sardonic comment on the modern boosters is essentially a satiric view. There is no hint in the story of the particular evil which will develop in the town of Jefferson, no hint of Temple and Nancy. *Requiem for a Nun* is concerned with making clear the connection between the past and the present, specifically with making clear to Temple the connection between the sins of her youth and the murder of her child. But to imply that the murder is implicit in the comic machinations of Peabody and Compson and Ratliffe and Pettigrew is to assume a thorough determinism, which would in effect deny Temple's responsibilities.

"A Name for the City" might also be read as an exploration of the familiar Faulkner theme, articulated most clearly in *Go Down, Moses,* that man's attempt to assert domination over the land is his Original Sin. The presence of Ikkemotubbe in the story provides some encouragement for this reading, and further support can be found in Pettigrew's apparently cynical conclusion that the Federal government would accept a fifty-dollar debit to provide axle grease for the Indians' exodus to Oklahoma. This theme is developed only tentatively in the story, where the Chickasaws are primarily observers of the white man's follies. The theme receives a more detailed exploration in *Requiem for a Nun,* which includes a sweeping history of the community of Jefferson, and of the state capital at Jackson, "the golden dome, the knob, the gleamy crumb, the gilded pustule" (*REQ*, 110). The story is basically a comic legend which, though it contains echoes and reverberations of more serious Faulkner themes, is first and finally a demonstration of the lengths to which men will go to compound one harmless folly with another.

When Faulkner incorporated story material into a novel, he seems always to have approached the later work as a new creation, sufficient unto itself. In creating the new work he characteristically altered the tone, fact, and emphasis of the original situation. The stories out of which the novels grew are not to be read as mere notes for the longer works, nor are they "replaced" by the fiction which followed them. If his characters had a constant existence in Faulkner's mind, they have, by his own admission, no such constant existence in his texts. In the stories which followed novels, the same kinds of change and development can be observed. Refusing to be bound by what he had previously written, Faulkner created new situations for old characters, creating a new and independent set of characters in the process. Though he spoke of his ambition to write an encyclopedic treatise on the principal families of Yoknapatawpha County, there is no indication that he had that purpose in mind in any of the fiction he actually published. Rather, he took a kind of pride in exercising his prerogative to move his characters around in place and time. His reuse of characters and incidents he explained as the craftsman's choice of the most readily available tools and materials, but the tools and materials were always employed in the creation of a new object.

"Optimism," says Bertrand Russell, "assumes, or attempts to prove, that the universe exists to please us, as pessimism that it exists to displease us."[25] Faulkner's development from pessimism to optimism can be observed in almost every case in which he reconsidered characters and situations which he had previously delineated. Faulkner's pessimistic fiction is characterized by a number of related themes and forms: the outcome of human action is suffering and futility; most individuals act from base motives, while the few who are prompted by ideals are ineffective, easily dissuaded, or corrupted by vicious characters; those who suffer are incapable of understanding the cause of their misfortune, or if they sense the cause they are unable to articulate it; their suffering issues in self-destructive violence, denial, and repudiation, and their actions are incomprehensible to those who observe them; the narrative is heavily ironic, with few actions interpreted or defended, for the first-person narrators are incapable of correctly assessing the events they have seen and participated in, while the omniscient narrators seem too disgusted to comment on or defend the pathetic and grotesque actions which they describe. The more optimistic fiction, on the other hand, describes characters who act with some success from some nobility of purpose. They can understand what they see, they can offer some explanation of its significance, and they can act on that understanding. The first-person narrators are both self-conscious and articulate, the omniscient narrators are didactic. In the development from pessimism to optimism, Faulkner's fiction moves in emphasis from ignorance to knowledge, from frustration to fulfillment, from senseless destruction to hopeful creation, from despair to hope, from denial to affirmation.

This pattern of development is not peculiar to Faulkner — the same general movement may be seen in Shakespeare and Joyce, while the opposite development takes place in Mark Twain — but in few other writers is the transformation accomplished in successive renderings of the same characters and incidents. One of the consequences of Faulkner's transformation has been the tendency of critics to belittle his later fiction, everything that appeared after *Go Down, Moses.* His reconsideration of characters and incidents which he first treated savagely and ironically is felt by many to be contrived and sentimental. "Most recently," says Leslie Fiedler, "Faulkner seems to have repented many of his blasphemies against women and to have committed himself to redeeming one by one all his anti-virgins, but his attempts at redemption somehow do not touch the level of acceptance reached by his original travesties."[26] A continuing problem for Faulkner criticism is to describe the specific nature of this transformation, rather than to guess at the reasons for it or to condemn it. In such an effort, the short stories are extremely useful, for they are of sufficiently various form, subject, and quality to preclude overly simple assessment.

Faulkner's first published story, "Landing in Luck," is an exercise in irony. An inexperienced and incompetent aviation cadet, Thompson, attempts his first solo flight, in spite of the misgivings of his instructor, Bessing.

Thompson loses a wheel on the takeoff, forlornly circles the field until he is almost out of fuel, and finally, paralyzed with fear, crashes the plane. Miraculously, he escapes injury. He does not, however, receive the dressing-down which he might have expected from Bessing, who congratulates him on a brilliant piece of flying. Thompson, who had formerly despised Bessing, accepts this judgment, and spends the evening bragging of his accomplishment to his fellow cadets. Thompson has learned nothing from his experience, and Bessing, who had only allowed him to try the solo because he believed Thompson would either break his neck or do so poorly that he would be recommended for a discharge, mistakenly gains a new respect for his pupil. Thompson is a willfull, childish bumbler. He succeeds through no fault of his own and then takes advantage of his luck to display his unearned superiority to his fellows. What kind of a world is it, Faulkner seems to be asking, which allows people like Thompson to succeed?

The other characters in "Landing in Luck" are hardly more admirable than Thompson. Bessing is primarily concerned with avoiding criticism from his superiors, the commanding officer is miffed by criticism he has received from *his* superiors, and the other cadets are alternately envious and contemptuous of Thompson's luck. The only accurate judgment of Thompson comes from the omniscient narrator, who, in his selection, ordering, and phrasing of the narrative incidents, shows us what Thompson and his acquaintances cannot see or will not express. The vital contrast in the story is that between Thompson's thoughts and behavior in the crippled plane, and his behavior after the crash:

> For Thompson's nerve was going as he neared the earth. The temptation was strong to kick his rudder over and close his eyes. The machine descended, barely retaining headway. He watched the approaching ground utterly unable to make any pretence of levelling off, paralyzed; his brain had ceased to function, he was all staring eyes watching the remorseless earth. He did not know his height, the ground rushed past too swiftly to judge, but he expected to crash any second. Thompson's fate was on the laps of the Gods. "—and so, when my petrol gave out, I knew it was up to me. I had already thought of a plan — I thought of several, but this one seemed the best — which was to put my tail down first and then drop my left wing, so the old bus wouldn't turn over and lie down on me. Well, it worked just as I had doped it out...." (*EPP*, 48-49)

Given what we know of Faulkner's descriptions of his largely imaginary exploits as an aviation cadet, it is possible to read "Landing in Luck" as a veiled confession on Faulkner's part, but the narrative voice is reserved and distant, and the implied author goes to extreme lengths to dissociate himself from the central character. In one of Faulkner's last stories, "Race at Morning," the tone and emphasis are completely reversed. "Race at Morning" is the story of an epic Yoknapatawpha hunting chase, featuring familiar characters such as Will Legate, Roth Edmonds, and Ike McCaslin, as well as the young boy who narrates the story, and "Mister Ernest," who has informally adopted him. Mister Ernest and the boy pursue a magnificent buck for almost thirty miles through the bayou, but when they seem to be closing in for the kill, Mister Ernest empties his gun. The boy understands why. The joy of the hunt is in the chase, not in the kill. If the buck goes free, he will be there again to be chased the following year. The hunt is a privilege which must be earned, and it must express the same qualities of character which are essential in the more prosaic business of making a living:

> ... all of a sudden I thought about how maybe planting and working and then harvesting oats and beans and hay wasn't jest something me and Mister Ernest done three hundred and fifty-one days to fill in the time until we could come back hunting again, but it was something we had to do and do honest and good during the three hundred and fifty-one days, to have the right to come back into the big woods and hunt for the other fourteen.... (*USWF*, 309)

The hunters in "Race at Morning" are competent, generous, and properly humble. They are in control of their destinies, and they are aware of their responsibilities toward others and toward themselves. The story is a celebration of a significant experience rightly understood and honestly expressed.

None of this is meant to imply that "Race at Morning" is a better story than "Landing in Luck." Both have serious deficiencies. The hunting story taxes credibility in a number of respects. We are told early in the story that the boy cannot write his own name — though he knows "every cuss word in the dictionary, every poker hand in the deck, and every whisky label in the distillery" (*USWF*, 296), but he is the narrator of the story. The length of the chase is staggering, and it is hardly likely that Mister Ernest and the boy could have escaped serious injury in the grapevine accident. Both the narrator and Mister Ernest display capacities for insight and expression far greater than those ordinarily expected of them, and the moral of the chase is much too neatly dovetailed with Mister Ernest's decision that the boy should begin his formal schooling. "Landing in Luck" has similar weaknesses. The essential difference between the two stories is the difference between oversimplified irony and oversimplified romance. Thompson is a uniformly despicable character, Bessing's reversal of attitude is mechanical, the C.O.'s indifference is a cliché, the omniscient narrator's ironic distance is as obtrusive as the boy's artificial naiveté. Neither story shows Faulkner at anything like his best, but in juxtaposition the two stories indicate the vast change in the characteristic mode of his fiction.

The same differences in emphasis and attitude may be seen in a comparison of *Soldiers' Pay* and *The Reivers*. In *Soldiers' Pay* Donald Mahon is passive, pathetic, helpless, and moribund. He is the victim of the war, of his heartless and mindless fiancé, and of the little Georgia town which regards him as a horrific curiosity rather than as a human being. In *The Reivers* Lucius Priest is an active, sensitive, responsible boy. He is the trusted darling of his family and he is looked after by benevolent and colorful caretakers such as Boon Hogganbeck, Ned McCaslin, Miss Reba Rivers, Everbe Corinthia, and Uncle Parsham Hood. *The Reivers* imports a comic world, while *Soldiers' Pay* imports an ironic world. Mahon is powerless to affect his fate. He has to depend on his father, on Gilligan, and on Margaret Powers for pity and protection. Lucius is constantly asserting himself. He requires no pity and little protection. It is particularly significant that *The Reivers* is narrated in retrospect by an older Lucius Priest who is transmitting the lessons he learned to his grandchildren. Through long reflection on his experiences he has come to understand them. What he has learned is summarized in his conversation with Boss. "You can live with it," Boss tells Lucius:

> You will. A gentleman always does. A gentleman can live through anything. He faces anything. A gentleman accepts the responsibility of his actions and bears the burden of their consequences, even when he did not himself instigate them but only acquiesced to them, didn't say No though he knew he should. (*REV*, 302)

Such an insight is completely lacking in *Soldiers' Pay*. Donald Mahon seems to survive only until he recalls the moment of his wounding, "leaving a darkness he did not remember for a day he had long forgot" (*SP*, 203). All the relationships between men and women in *Soldiers' Pay* seem doomed to frustration or to tawdry fulfillment. Cecily Saunders reluctantly marries George Farr, Januarius Jones conquers the pathetic Emmy, Margaret Powers refuses the devoted Gilligan, and Julian Lowe's once-passionate attraction to Mrs. Powers is dissipated in letter-writing. None of the characters faces anything, none accepts the responsibility of his actions, none bears the burden of consequences. The two villains of *The Reivers*, Butch Lovemaiden and Otis, are respectively thrashed and banished, but Januarius Jones has his way with Emmy, and Mrs. Saunders arranges her daughter's marriage to her own satisfaction, giving Donald Mahon's father a gratuitous insult in the process. Injustice, indifference, and malice are the norms of behavior in *Soldiers' Pay*, and they determine the result of almost every impulse and the outcome of almost every incident.

If a hero is an individual who is capable of acting positively and does so, and if a victim is incapable of positive action, Faulkner's earlier fiction describes a world in which all men are victims, while his later fiction describes a world in which some men (and women) can occasionally achieve heroism. The difference between these two worlds can be seen by comparing *Sanctuary* and *Intruder in the Dust*. In both novels an innocent man is accused of a crime. In *Sanctuary* Lee Goodwin is a victim of his own fear and ignorance, and he is convicted by a spiteful community. In *Intruder in the Dust* Lucas Beauchamp is saved by two young boys and an old woman. Lucas Beauchamp is a proud man who refuses to give his attorney the information which will clear him, while Goodwin is afraid, rather than too proud, to allow his attorney to employ similar information. In the world of *Sanctuary* justice is impossible, for many oppose it, and no one is strong enough to defend it. In the world of *Intruder in the Dust* justice is possible because many believe in it and are able and willing to work for it.

Faulkner's consecutive novels dealing with Civil War material, *Absalom, Absalom!* and *The Unvanquished,* also demonstrate strikingly different tendencies. Sutpen learns nothing. He is eternally innocent of moral scruples. Bayard Sartoris learns a significant lesson, acts on it, and explains it. To be sure, Bayard's action is a denial, a repudiation of the familial and communal codes of honor, but it is nevertheless a wise and courageous action, as both Redmond and Drusilla acknowledge. The war itself is remote in most of *Absalom, Absalom!,* but it becomes progressively more immediate and sordid in *The Unvanquished.* The latter novel is among Faulkner's most simple and direct — he once suggested that it was the easiest of his works for beginning readers — while *Absalom, Absalom!* is among his most complex, indirect, and difficult works. The many differences between the two books, combined with the knowledge that they were written at nearly the same time, suggests that the changes in Faulkner's attitudes and techniques did not take place all at once.

In describing the changes from Faulkner's earliest and most ironic and pessimistic works to his latest and most optimistic fiction, the short stories are extremely useful. Virtually all the *New Orleans Sketches* emphasize irony and pathos, while virtually all stories published after 1940 are comic in one sense or another. There is a grand mixture in the stories published in the thirties. The minor comedy "Thrift," and the richly tragic "Red Leaves" both appeared in the *Post* in 1930. "Pennsylvania Station" and "Lo!" were both published in 1934, and "That Will Be Fine" and "Golden Land" were both printed in 1935. There is as much fluctuation between pessimism and optimism in the stories of the thirties as there is in the novels of that period. General terms such as "pessimism" and "optimism" are, of course, slightly misleading and ultimately reductive, but they are nevertheless indicative of the major pattern of Faulkner's development.

This pattern of Faulkner's technical and thematic changes is clearly demonstrated in three different versions of the episode in which Boon Hoggenbeck shoots at a black man on the streets of Jefferson. First described by Quentin in "Lion," retold by the omniscient narrator of *Go Down, Moses,* and finally recalled by Grandfather in the opening chapter of *The Reivers,* this episode shows the metamorphosis of Boon from a murderer into a clown.[27] The same pattern of transformation can be observed in numerous other Faulkner characters and incidents. Temple Drake is literally and figuratively redeemed in

Requiem for a Nun. Gavin Stevens appears in *Light in August* as a pseudo-intellectual patrician, but he becomes progressively more astute in the stories that make up *Knight's Gambit,* and he emerges in the later novels as a quixotic champion of humanity and social justice. Suratt appears as a typical hard-drinking countryman in *Sartoris,* becomes (as Ratliff) a committed opponent of Flem Snopes in *The Hamlet,* and finishes as a shrewd and humorous observer, participant, and raconteur in *The Town* and *The Mansion.* The changes in each case may be attributed both to Faulkner's concern for the integrity of each story or novel and to his evolution toward a qualified optimism. Such alterations in characterization and narrative "fact," tone, and emphasis are accompanied, invariably, by alterations in narrative voice and point-of-view, and they illustrate, repeatedly, the autonomy and interdependence of Faulkner's stories and novels.

3

Collections, Cycles, and Apocrypha

Collected Stories

A complete edition of Faulkner's short fiction would include (in addition to the authoritative *Collected Stories*) the magazine versions of the stories which went into *The Unvanquished, Go Down, Moses,* and *The Hamlet,* the magazine versions of stories revised or reprinted in *Knight's Gambit* and *Big Woods;* various uncollected stories such as the early fiction collected by Carvel Collins in *Early Prose and Poetry* and *New Orleans Sketches,* "Thrift," "Once Aboard the Lugger," *Miss Zilphia Gant, Idyll in the Desert,* and posthumously published pieces such as "Mr. Acarius" and *The Wishing Tree.* In the absence of such an edition we must keep in mind that our response to a given story is determined in large part by the place Faulkner assigned it in his published volumes, and that his decision *not* to collect a large number of stories was partly determined by the exigencies of publication and partly by his own canons of taste. It is also important to remember that Faulkner wrote his stories with his eye on the immediate object, and later imposed unity on his short story collections by revision and by contrapuntal arrangement of previously published material. What happened to the stories after they were published individually in magazines, then, is of secondary importance.

Faulkner's rationale for the careful organization of his volumes of short stories is explained in a letter to Cowley concerning the arrangement of *Collected Stories.*

> The only book foreword I ever remembered was one I read when I was about sixteen I suppose, in one of Sienckewicz (maybe that's not even spelled right), which, I dont even remember: Pan Michael or what, not the actual words either: something like "This book written in ... travail (he may have said even agony and sacrifice) for the uplifting of men's hearts." Which I believe is the one worthwhile purpose of any book and so even to a collection of short stories, form, integration, is as important as to a novel — an entity of its own, single, set for one pitch, contrapuntal in integration, toward one end, one finale.[1]

Collected Stories is the major volume of Faulkner's period of consolidation. Coming on the heels of *Intruder in the Dust* and *Knight's Gambit,* it was his first published volume following the Nobel award. Its organization gave him a respite from *A Fable,* and it practically marks the end of his work in the short story form. Fewer than half a dozen stories followed it. Although Faulkner revised some of his earlier stories extensively for the *Big Woods* volume, *Collected Stories* shows little evidence of revision. *Collected Stories* is at once an index to Faulkner's judgment of his previously published short story texts, and an original text in its own right, organizing a diverse body of material in contrapuntal and thematic patterns.

The emphasis on counterpoint was by no means a new one for Faulkner. His first book of short stories, *These 13,* was organized in a fashion which anticipated the arrangement of *Collected Stories.* In the summer of 1931 Faulkner expressed the view that "a book of short stories should be linked together by characters or chronology" (*LIG,* 13). *These 13* was divided into three groups. The first division included stories which appear in "The Wasteland" section of *Collected Stories.* The second division included stories set in Yoknapatawpha, some of which were placed in "The Village" and two of which appear in "The Wilderness." The third section consisted of three stories which were included in the "Beyond" section of *Collected Stories.* Other instances of Faulkner's experiments with contrapuntal arrangement are *The Wild Palms, Requiem for a Nun,* and *Big Woods.* While *The Wild Palms* consists of alternating chapters of distinctly separate narratives, *Requiem for a Nun* alternates sections of prose history and legend with sections of dialogue concerning the plight of Temple Drake Stevens and Nancy Mannigoe, and *Big Woods* is a connected series of hunting stories separated by expository passages which Faulkner called "interrupted catalysts" (*LIG,* 83). A related method is basic to novels like *The Sound and the Fury, As I Lay Dying, Absalom, Absalom!, The Town,* and *The Mansion,* in which the narrative is developed through contrasting points of view and articulated by contrasting voices.

In arranging *Collected Stories* Faulkner drew on the two books of short stories published in the thirties, *These 13* and *Doctor Martino,* as well as on the large body of stories not previously collected. The stories he chose *not* to include tell almost as much about his aims as the stories he did include. First, *Collected Stories* contains none of the New Orleans pieces. Second, it contains nothing from *The Unvanquished, Go Down, Moses,* or *Knight's Gambit.* Third, the separately published *Miss Zilphia Gant* and *Idyll in the Desert* are missing, as are "Thrift" and "Once Aboard the Lugger." Fourth, none of the Snopes stories which went into *The Hamlet* are included, though several are among Faulkner's best and one, "Spotted Horses," must have been among his favorites. Finally, though about half the volume consists of stories never before collected, no previously unpublished stories are included. What remains is an astonishingly rich and varied collection, unified by Faulkner's grouping of the stories in seven related sections.

The sections of *Collected Stories* are ostensibly geographic, though the boundaries of the several regions are not always precise, and the section-designations have thematic implications as well. Each section encompasses a particular imaginative region, while individual stories chart explorations of that region. Faulkner deliberately avoided arranging the stories in chronological order of composition, publication, or historical setting. The section entitled "The Middle Ground," to take the most extreme example, consists of stories published over a period of thirteen years. The matter ranges in time from the Civil War ("My Grandmother Millard"), to the period immediately after the Civil War ("Wash," "Mountain Victory"), to the period immediately following World War I ("Honor"), to the Depression ("Pennsylvania Station," "Golden Land"). The stories are set in Yoknapatawpha County ("Wash," "My Grandmother Millard," "There Was a Queen"), in New York ("Pennsylvania Station"), in Hollywood ("Golden Land"), in Virginia ("Artist at Home"), in Tennessee ("Mountain Victory"), in an unnamed city ("Honor"), in St. Louis and the Mississippi resort town of Cranston's Wells ("Dr. Martino"), in an unidentified Southern state ("Fox Hunt"), and in an unnamed Mississippi hamlet ("The Brooch"). While no single apparent theme or tone is common to the stories of "The Middle Ground," the section can be understood as a series of investigations of the twin themes of sex and death. Most generally, however, the stories in this section demonstrate Faulkner's belief that "everyone is capable of almost anything — heroism or cowardice, tenderness or cruelty."

Similar diversity can be observed in the other sections of *Collected Stories*. "Beyond," the final group, includes stories from a wide variety of geographic and imaginative landscapes, concentrating on problems of psychological aberation. "The Wasteland" consists of five stories about World War I, and though they share the sense of despair which the section title implies, each is different in emphasis and texture. The four stories of "The Wilderness" range from the tragic doom of "Red Leaves" through the ironic comedy of "Justice" to the broad comedy of "A Courtship" and the historical travesty of "Lo!" The first two sections of the volume, "The Country" and "The Village," consist of stories set in Yoknapatawpha, but they were published over a thirteen-year period, and there is great variation among them in theme and technique. Within each section particular attention must be given to the arrangement of stories, for the effect of the volume is cumulative, beginning with the dramatic irony of "Barn Burning" and ending with the lyrical flight of "Carcassonne." The arrangement of *Collected Stories* is thematic and contrapuntal, but the themes and counterpoints are implicit rather than stated, and the general topics suggested by the section designations are best understood as indicative of

Faulkner's attitude toward his short stories at the end of the forties, and not as his conscious and invariable aim in individual works. Thus the arrangement of the stories tells us something about *Collected Stories* as an integrated volume, but it is of limited value in understanding and assessing particular stories. In the discussion that follows, I will examine representative selections from *Collected Stories,* to show something of the variety of technique and mode and the range of achievement of the works included in that volume.

"Barn Burning," the first story, describes the development of Colonel Sartoris Snopes, with his coming to manhood and his concomitant rejection of his father. "Barn Burning" is important for the close view it gives of a crucial incident in the Snopes saga, but it differs from the other Snopes stories in many ways. The story moves from an initial situation in which the boy is completely submissive to "the old fierce pull of blood" (*CS,* 3) to the traumatic conclusion in which he not only declines to aid his father, but also seeks out his father's enemy, leading to a denouement in which he believes that his father and brother have been killed. In describing this development, Faulkner places heavy emphasis on the sensational details which contribute to the boy's response. In the opening paragraph of the story the background of his father's trial for barn burning is combined with the boy's sharp awareness of his own physical danger:

> The store in which the Justice of the Peace's court was sitting smelled of cheese. The boy, crouched on his nail keg at the back of the crowded room, knew he smelled cheese, and more: from where he sat he could see the ranked shelves close-packed with the solid, squat dynamic shapes of tin cans whose labels his stomach read, not from the lettering which meant nothing to his mind but from the scarlet devils and the silver curve of fish — this, the cheese which he knew he smelled and the hermetic meat which his intestines believed he smelled coming in intermittent gusts momentary and brief between the other constant one, the smell and sense just a little of fear because mostly of despair and grief, the old fierce pull of blood. He could not see the table where the Justice sat and before which his father and his father's enemy (*our enemy* he thought in that despair; *ourn! mine and hisn both! He's my father!*) stood, but he could hear them…. (*CS,* 3)

This introduction, besides establishing the immediate scene and the essential situation, is noteworthy for the different levels of awareness implied and juxtaposed throughout the story. First, there is the essential physical fact, presented by the omniscient narrator, and there are the physical facts of which the boy is conscious. Then there is the sensation which the boy believes he feels, the smell of the meat. This is related to the feelings which he cannot express, but for which his conscious thoughts provide an inarticulate demonstration. At other crucial junctures in the story the same differentiations of awareness are made. When he first sees the de Spain house, the boy responds simply, but the narrative explication of his unexpressed and unconscious feelings is complex and sophisticated:

Hit's as big as a courthouse he thought quietly, with a surge of joy whose reason he could not have thought into words, being too young for that. *They are safe from him. People whose lives are a part of this peace and dignity are beyond his touch, he no more to them than a buzzing wasp: capable of stinging for a little moment but that's all; the spell of this peace and dignity rendering even the barns and stable and cribs which belong to it impervious to the puny flames he might contrive....* (*CS*, 10)

In this case, as in his instinctive understanding that Harris is his enemy, the boy is mistaken. Ab Snopes proves that he can "touch" de Spain, and that the de Spain buildings will burn. Even at the end of the story, when the boy has reason to believe that he is responsible for his father's death, he persists in a mistaken assessment of Ab's character:

Father. My father, he thought. "He was brave!" he cried suddenly, aloud but not loud, no more than a whisper. "He was! He was in the war! He was in Colonel Sartoris' cav'ry!" not knowing that his father had gone to that war a private in the fine old European sense, wearing no uniform, admitting the authority of and giving fidelity to no man or army or flag, going to war as Malbrouck did: for booty ... it meant nothing and less than nothing to him if it were enemy booty or his own. (*CS*, 24-25)

"Why," asks Wayne Booth in commenting on this passage, "should explicit judgment be banned from *The Sound and the Fury* and allowed in 'Barn Burning'?"[2] The answer is that explicit judgment is a constant technique in "Barn Burning," from the opening paragraph through the final scene. Booth maintains that the boy's final defense of Ab is more poignant to us because we are told that it is based on incorrect assumptions, but the above passage is not an isolated use of the technique. The final authorial aside is natural, perfectly consistent with the narrative viewpoint which is sustained throughout. These "intrusions" underscore the irony of Sarty Snopes' ignorance, and they increase the pathos of his situation. The narrator invites our sympathetic approval of the boy, and the asides express understanding and sympathy, rather than contempt, while the authorial comments, as well as the story's events, imply significant reservations about our *judgment* of Sarty.

"Barn Burning" also embodies one of Faulkner's favorite devices of characterization — the metaphoric description of a character's eyes to imply his attitude towards the world. Especially memorable are the descriptions of Popeye, whose eyes "looked like rubber knobs, like they'd give to the touch and then recover with the whorled smudge of the thumb upon them" (*SAN*, 5-6) and of Flem Snopes, whose eyes are "the color of stagnant water" (*HAM*, 22). Faulkner's fiction repeatedly implies a close correspondence between the appearance of a character's eyes and that character's vision of his own situation. Sarty's eyes are "gray and wild as storm scud" (*CS*, 4) as he prepares to testify at his father's trial. Ab's eyes are "pebble-colored," part of "the inscrutable face, the shaggy brows beneath which the gray eyes glinted coldly," and finally "cold eyes" (*CS*, 12, 16, 19). The brother's eyes are "muddy" (*CS*, 20). Ab's eyes are appropriate to the cold passion with which he beats his son and burns barns. He strikes his mules "savage blows ... but without heat" (*CS*, 6). His voice is "harsh like tin and without heat like tin," he speaks harshly to the de Spain servant "without heat," and he speaks to his other son "in breathless and frozen ferocity, the cold dead voice" (*CS*, 8, 11, 21). "Barn Burning" is, in part, an elaborate structure of visual metaphor and simile, some of which is expressed by the characters, some of which is overtly developed by the omniscient narrator, and all of which contributes to the developing conflict between father and son.

Sarty Snopes discovers that he cannot avoid choosing between the irreconcilable ideals of loyalty to his father and loyalty to his own sense of justice. At first he accepts his expected role in spite of his frustration. *"He aims for me to lie,* he thought, again with that frantic grief and despair. *And I will have to do hit"* (*CS*, 4). At this point he intends to do what is expected of him, though he knows it is wrong. Until the final break, he tries to be a dutiful son, working "with an industry that did not need to be driven or commanded twice" (*CS*, 16). He shares his father's resentment of de Spain, and he even volunteers to help burn de Spain's barn. But Ab foresees his son's treachery. He knows that Sarty was "fixing to tell them" (*CS*, 8), and he refused to acknowledge the boy's subsequent attempts to regain his favor. When he sets out with the older son to consummate his revenge on de Spain, he takes the precaution of having Sarty tied up. Thus Ab makes Sarty see what he must do, though he has intended for the boy to learn another lesson: "You got to learn to stick to your own blood or you ain't going to have any blood to stick to you" (*CS*, 8). This proves literally true. Sarty unties himself, escapes from his mother and sisters, runs furiously to warn de Spain, and then runs just as furiously to warn his father and brother that de Spain is coming after them:

> ... running again, knowing it was too late yet still running even after he heard the shot and, an instant later, two shots, pausing now without knowing he had ceased to run, crying "Pap! Pap!," running again before he knew he had begun to run, stumbling, tripping over something and scrabbling up again without ceasing to run, looking backward over his shoulder at the glare as he got up, running on among the invisible trees, panting, sobbing, "Father! Father!" (*CS* 24)

Sarty cannot go home again. He has denied the most basic of family ties, in spite of his determined efforts to adhere to it. The story is effective because his instinctive choice is made between alternatives which have positive theoretical bases and negative practical consequences. Sarty's choice, in other words, is a difficult one because Ab Snopes is not a complete villain. His use of fire, for example, is explained as a kind of moral act:

... the element of fire spoke to some deep mainspring of his father's being, as the element of steel or of powder spoke to other men, as the one weapon for the preservation of integrity, else breath were not worth the breathing, and hence to be regarded with respect and used with discretion. (*CS*, 7-8)

Ab always behaves in a fashion consistent with his own notion of how he can best preserve his integrity. He is a stern father and husband, but he becomes violent only when he believes that he has been threatened. There is something admirable in his spirit:

... something about his wolflike independence and even courage when the advantage was at least neutral which impressed strangers, as if they got from his latent ravening ferocity not so much a sense of dependability as a feeling that his ferocious conviction in the rightness of his actions would be of advantage to all whose interest lay with his. (*CS*, 7)

Using the only means available to him — force and fear and rude eloquence — Ab endeavors to convince Sarty that their interests are identical. Though Sarty's final defense is based on an incorrect assumption about the nature of Ab's "service" to Colonel Sartoris, his summation — "He was brave!" is not a totally inaccurate assessment of his father's character.

Over and against "the old fierce pull of blood," Sarty offers the vain hope that the opposites can be reconciled. *"Maybe he will feel it too,"* he thinks after seeing the de Spain mansion. *"Maybe it will even change him now from what maybe he couldn't help but be"* (*CS*, 11). But Ab is what he is, while Sarty is in the process of becoming. Again, after the judgment against Ab for ruining de Spain's rug, Sarty hopes his father will change his ways, and that de Spain will not collect his award:

Maybe it will all add up and balance and vanish — corn, rug, fire; the terror and grief, the being pulled two ways like between two teams of horses — gone, done with for ever and ever. (*CS*, 17)

In the violent conclusion to the story the conflict is indeed resolved for ever and ever, but not because of any change in Ab. Of all the characters in "Barn Burning," only Sarty is ever aware of alternatives to his own and his father's choice of action. Trying to encompass both alternatives, he brings about the result he had most sought to avoid. When Ab sends him to the barn for the can of oil, he responds readily in "the old habit, the old blood which he had not been permitted to choose for himself" (*CS*, 21). He realizes that he could keep on running and never come back: *"I could run on and on and never look back, never need to see his face again. Only I can't. I can't."* But at the end of the story he is going on and on, knowing that he will never see his father again. In the last line we are told "He did not look back" (*CS*, 25).

Earlier passages, however, make clear that he will look back many times over the perspective of later years, and he will come to understand why he did what he did.

> Later, twenty years later, he was to tell himself, "If I had said they wanted only truth, justice, he would have hit me again." But now he said nothing. (*CS*, 8)

Another early passage differentiates three distinct levels of awareness and perception beyond Sarty's present condition. As he eats beside the fire which Ab has built, he does not remark the smallness of the fire. If Sarty were older, the narrator tells us, he might have wondered why the fire were not larger, in view of Ab's "inherent voracious prodigality with material not his own." Then he might have speculated that Ab's small fires were the result of his experience as a Civil War fugitive, and finally he might discern the respect which Ab accords to all fires (*CS*, 7-8). Such an understanding, however, must needs be based on facts which Sarty does not possess and on a reflective maturity he has not yet attained. He does not know the exact nature of his father's war service. The narrator has this information, and gives it to the reader in a number of places. The first descriptive passage regarding Ab, in fact, shows him "walking a little stiffly from where a Confederate provost's man's musket ball had taken him in the heel on a stolen horse thirty years ago" (*CS*, 5). Because this information is not dwelt upon, but is presented in what seems to be an incidental description, its significance cannot be fully understood until the end of the story.

"Barn Burning," like much of Faulkner's fiction, is a story which depends on the subtle manipulations of time and point-of-view. It is not necessary to infer a detailed time-scheme for the story, though Ab's wounding "thirty years ago" implies a setting in the early 1890s, nor is it necessary to sort out all the different variations of point-of-view. The primary interest of "Barn Burning" is not in its development of the abstract theme, Time, nor in the technical manipulation of narrative conventions. Similarly, though the story is, in its main outlines, a classic of the initiation pattern, or, from another perspective, a classic fictional rendering of the Oedipal crisis, "Barn Burning" succeeds because it portrays with feeling and directness the difficult situation of a sensitive young boy who is a memorable individual in a particular environment, and who is in conflict with other memorable individuals.

"Shingles for the Lord," the second story in the collection, is similar enough to "Barn Burning" and at the same time different enough from it to indicate the deliberate counterpoint of *Collected Stories*. Both texts describe a close relationship between a young boy and his farmer-father, and both fathers set fire to a symbolic building. Whereas Ab Snopes is an arsonist by vocation, Res Grier is an inadvertent arsonist. "Shingles for the Lord," unlike "Barn Burning," is a comic story, one of Faulkner's better exercises in that vein. The story deals with the hubris of Res Grier, who, in an attempt to outwit his neighbor Solon Quick, accidentally sets fire to the country church they are supposed to be repairing. Because he is unable to borrow a froe and a maul from a neighbor, Grier is two hours late for his appointment to begin making new shingles for the church. Quick and Bookwright have refused to begin working until Grier arrives, and Quick reasons that Grier now owes the church six additional hours of labor, basing his computations on the WPA system of work-units. Quick then offers to make up the six hours for Grier, in exchange for Grier's half-share of a dog which Quick has coveted for some time. Grier agrees to the offer, but only after purchasing the other half-interest in the dog, in exchange for doing half a day's work removing shingles for the dog's co-owner, Tull. So Quick will have to work six additional hours and will still own only half of the dog.

But this is not enough for Grier. Wanting revenge on Quick and his work-units, he determines to work out his payment to Tull by removing the shingles at night:

> "I don't aim to have nothing on my mind tomorrow but watching Mr. Solon Work-Unit Quick trying to get a bill of sale for two dollars or ten dollars either on the other half of that dog. And we'll do it tonight. I don't want him jest to find out at sunup tomorrow that he is too late. I want him to find out that even when he laid down to sleep he was already too late." (*CS*, 37-38)

Grier and his son, who narrates the story, undertake to remove the shingles at night without being observed, hanging their lantern from the decking. Grier accidentally pulls the decking loose with a crowbar, the lantern falls, and the church burns. Grier is knocked unconscious trying to carry a water barrel up the steps of the church. He is chagrined when the other members of the congregation assemble at the scene, and when the Reverend Whitfield chastises him, calling him "arsonist."

> "If there is any pursuit in which you can engage without carrying flood and fire and destruction and death behind you, do it. But not one hand shall you lay to this new house until you have proved to us that you are to be trusted again with the powers and capacities of a man." (*CS*, 41)

In the sanctity of his home, comforted by liniment and a hot toddy, Grier vows to return to work on the church:

> "I Godfrey, if him and all of them put together think they can keep me from working on my own church like ary other man, he better be a good man to try it." He taken another sip of the toddy. Then he taken a long one. "Arsonist," he said. "Work units. Dog units. And now arsonist. I Godfrey, what a day!" (*CS*, 43)

The comedy of "Shingles for the Lord" has identifiable elements of slapstick, broad farce, witty provincial horse-trading, and grim humor. There is also an element of subdued violence, particularly in the manner in which Grier wields the froe, maul, and ax while he is haggling with Quick. The burning of the church is comic rather than horrible, for Grier and his son are not seriously endangered, and there is the immediate promise of a new church. The caustic asides directed at the WPA, the grandiose rhetoric of the Reverend Whitfield, and Grier's description of Old Man Killigrew and his deaf wife all contribute to a tolerant view of the class of characters who are treated with grim irony in *As I Lay Dying* and *The Hamlet*. There is even a church-going Snopes in the story, who appears as one of the poor, hard-working farmers willing to build the church again. It is as though Faulkner were deliberately reversing the emphasis on meanness and sullen violence which is so apparent in the lives of the country people in *The Hamlet* and in "Barn Burning."

The narrative voice of the story belongs to Grier's son, a young boy who is never named. Grier himself is simply "Pap" in most of the story. His last name is not mentioned until over halfway through, and that reference is oblique. He is named only once after that, when the story is almost completed. The narrative voice presents a number of problems, for though the boy speaks in dialect throughout the story, and though he uses many nonstandard idioms, he is given to the use of metaphor and simile which reflect a sensibility far more articulate than that which might be expected of him.

Most of his metaphors are natural and fresh. Whitfield's watch, for example, "looked as big as a full-growed squash" (*CS*, 28). The boy sees Whitfield "thundering down at Pap like a cloudburst," "his eyebrows looking like a big iron-gray caterpillar at the edge of a cliff" (*CS*, 28, 29). Some of his figures are predictably prosaic. Quick's knife is "sharp as a razor," and the men at work "set flat on the ground in a kind of circle" (*CS*, 30,31). Quick and Bookwright work "light and easy as two clocks ticking," but Grier makes "every lick of hisn like he was killing a moccasin" (*CS*, 31). When Grier splits a shingle, it goes "whirling past Solon's shin like a scythe blade," and the coveted dog "would ease through the woods without no more noise than a hant" and "tiptoe that trail out jest like a man" (*CS*, 32). When Grier is removing the shingles, he appears to be in danger of tilting "up that whole roof at one time like a hinged box lid," and he snatches the whole section of roof around the lantern "like you would shuck a corn nubbin" (*CS*, 38, 39).

The boy's descriptive and metaphoric tendencies come into sharpest focus in the passage detailing the burning of Whitfield's baptizing shirt:

> There was a special nail where he would keep a old long nightshirt he would wear to baptize in. I would use to watch it all the time during church and Sunday school, and me and the other boys would go past the church sometimes jest to peep in at it, because to a boy of ten it wasn't jest a cloth garment or even a iron armor; it was the old strong Archangel

> Michael his self, that had fit and strove and conquered sin for so long that it finally had the same contempt for human beings that returned always to sin as hogs and dogs done that the old strong archangel his self must have had.
>
>   For a long time it never burned, even after everything else inside had. We could watch it, hanging there among the fire, not like it had knowed in its time too much water to burn easy, but like it had strove and fit with the devil and all the hosts of hell too long to burn in jest a fire that Res Grier started, trying to beat Solon Quick out of half a dog. But at last it went, too, not in a hurry still, but jest all at once, kind of roaring right on up and out against the stars and the far dark spaces. (*CS*, 40)

This passage indicates a much more sophisticated perception than we would expect from the Grier boy, but it is rendered in the linguistic mode that determines the reader's initial assessment of his capabilities. The theological and symbolic commentaries are just, though only Whitfield, of all the characters, would seem capable of such insights and expressions. The same problem arises in the passage in which the boy describes Whitfield

> ... standing there with his hat on, too, like he had strove too long to save what hadn't ought to been created in the first place, from the damnation it didnt's even want to escape, to bother to need to take his hat off in any presence. (*CS*, 40-41)

The Grier boy, like Sarty Snopes, has an experience which reveals to him his father's true character, but unlike Sarty, he is his own recorder and commentator. The careful distinctions so apparent in "Barn Burning" between what the boy observes, what he can understand, and what he can express are missing in "Shingles for the Lord." This disparity between the narrator's perception and his situation, rather than the few details in the story which do not conform to the requirements for sociological realism,[3] is the chief weakness of "Shingles for the Lord." But the story is, after all, comedy, and the clearly artificial manner of exposition is no more a debilitating weakness here than it is in *Huckleberry Finn,* another text distinguished by a semiliterate narrator who uses semicolons properly.

Res Grier, like Ab Snopes and Sarty, is an overreacher, but the consequences of his attempt to extend beyond his limits are neither fatal nor harmful, and he accepts them with something approaching equanimity. The experience shows the boy his father's fallibility, as it shows him the true significance of the church:

> It was jest a shell now, with a red and fading core, and I had hated it at times and feared it at others, and I should have been glad. But there was something that even that fire hadn't even touched. Maybe that's all it was — jest indestructibility, endurability — that old man that could plan to build it back while its walls was still fire-fierce and then calmly turn his back and go away because he knowed that the men that never had nothing to give toward the new one but their work would be there at sunup tomorrow, and the day after that, and the day after that, too, as long as it was needed, to give that work to build it back again.

So it hadn't gone a-tall; it didn't no more care for that little fire and flood than Whitfield's old baptizing gown had done. (*CS*, 42)

Res Grier, though the boy does not say so, is similarly indestructible and durable. "Shingles for the Lord" is his celebration of these qualities. Res Grier's comic flaw is his desire for more than justice, for revenge on Quick. This desire leads to his downfall, but it is rather more a pratfall than total destruction. His dealings with Quick show his wit, imagination, and sense of fair play, but his attempt at revenge proves that his talents are unsuited to his hopes. The story recalls Samuel Johnson's definition of comedy — "a dramatick representation of the lighter faults of mankind" — but in "Shingles for the Lord" the lighter faults of Grier, Quick, and Whitfield are more than compensated for by their virtues.

The third story in "The Country," "The Tall Men," is one of Faulkner's most overtly didactic stories. Perhaps for that reason it is also one of his least successful. The vehicles of the message, which is a celebration of the fierce independence of the McCallum family, are Mr. Pearson, the state draft investigator, and Gombault, the county sheriff. Pearson has come to arrest two of the McCallum boys for failing to register for the draft, and Gombault accompanies him to the McCallum farm. Pearson is convinced that Gombault has warned the boys so that they can escape, and in his fury he sententiously types Gombault, the McCallums, and their kind: "... *this doddering, tobacco-chewing old man is one of them, too, despite the honor and pride of his office, which should have made him different*" (*CS*, 46). But Pearson's expectations are not fulfilled. The boys have not run away, and at their father's instructions they pack their bags to go to Memphis to enlist. This frustrates Pearson, who wants to arrest them for failing to register. The senior McCallum's leg has been mangled that same afternoon, and it is amputated while Pearson and Gombault wait outside. After the amputation, the two bury the leg in the McCallum family cemetery.

Pearson's grievances against "these people" prove to be without foundation. One by one, they are almost mechanically rebutted in Gombault's recitation of the McCallum family history. Pearson believes that people like the McCallums resort to subterfuge to gain relief jobs, but Gombault points out that the McCallums have farmed their land without help or advice from the government agents. Pearson believes that they try to cheat the government, but Gombault shows that they have no intention of doing any business at all with the government, and they accept their loss when they find that they cannot sell their cotton crop. Pearson thinks they are bitter and vindictive when they are caught cheating, but Gombault shows that they abide by the rules without resentment. Finally, Pearson is convinced that they deliberately deny the government's generosity by evading the draft, but Gombault shows him that the boys' failure to register is perfectly consistent with their other actions with respect to the government.

The refutation of one cliché by another is not particularly effective in Gombault's presentation, but since he has at least the advantage of the facts, his narrative demonstrates the fallacies of Pearson's shallow stereotyping. Still, his insistence on underlining the morals of the situation — things are not always what they seem, Depression farm policies are pernicious, the McCallums are honest and heroic — is rather too pointed, unnecessarily overt and strident. Like most fictional polemics, Faulkner's is too one-sided. Virtually all of Pearson's assumptions are shown to be incorrect by Buddy McCallum's treatment of his sons and of Pearson, and the morals of the story are sufficiently apparent in Buddy's behavior during the amputation. Gombault is an unnecessary lecturer, preeminently aware of his role. "I been trying to tell you something," he tells Pearson early in the story, "but I reckon it will take these McCallums to impress that on you" (*CS*, 46). The behavior of the McCallums is, or ought to be, sufficient to impress Pearson, but Gombault is determined that he will not miss the point. Buddy, it is discovered, was a hero in World War I, and his father walked all the way to Virginia to enlist in the Confederacy. The meaning of these discoveries is explained in Gombault's final speech to Pearson:

> Yes, sir. We done forgot about folks. Life has done got cheap, and life ain't cheap. Life's a pretty durn valuable thing. I don't mean just getting along from one WPA relief check to the next one, but honor and pride and discipline that make a man worth preserving, make him of any value. That's what we got to learn again. Maybe it takes trouble, bad trouble, to teach it back to us, maybe it was the walking to Virginia because that's where his ma come from, and losing a war and then walking back, that taught it to old Anse. Anyway, he seems to learned it, and learned it good enough to bequeath it to his boys. Did you notice how all Buddy had to do was to tell them boys of his it was time to go, because the Government had sent them word? And how they told him good-by? Growned men kissing one another without hiding and without shame. Maybe that's what I'm trying to say. (*CS*, 60)

The obvious parallels between this speech and the Nobel address show Faulkner, as early as 1941, expressing in fiction the themes he was to articulate at Stockholm. "The Tall Men" supports the contention that Faulkner's art diminished in power in direct proportion to the degree that his themes were made explicit, either by his characters or in his own voice. Though a number of other stories written after 1940 tend to substantiate this view, some of Faulkner's earlier fiction fails because of his apparent reluctance to moralize. "Pennsylvania Station," a story from the late twenties or early thirties, illustrates the latter phenomenon.

The heavy ironies of "Pennsylvania Station" result from the contrast between the two speakers, an old man and a young man, both out of work and trying to keep warm in the temporary refuge of Penn Station. The old man tells the story of Danny, his sister's son, who is an obvious scoundrel and probably a murderous thug. Danny accepted his mother's attention and affection, and then cheated her out of the money she had carefully saved for her own burial. The old man does not understand any of this, remembering Danny as a good boy who was just a little wild. The young man makes a number of ironic comments on the story, but makes no attempt to show the old man that his interpretation of the facts is incorrect. The story ends when the two are forced to leave the sanctuary of the station by the night watchman assigned to disperse loiterers.

The ironies implicit in the old man's story are compounded by the other voices heard in "Pennsylvania Station": the omniscient narrator's, the young man's, Sister's, Danny's, and Mr. Pinckski's. The omniscient narrator provides the essential details of the immediate scene in Penn Station and suggests the general tone of the piece. Particular attention is paid to the station itself, to the railroad's employees, and to the cold, impersonal treatment of indigents like the old man and the young man. The arcade of the station is filled with "a stale chill like that which might lie unwinded and spent upon the cold plains of infinity itself" (*CS*, 609). The subway trains passing beneath the station seem to be "two green eyes tunneling violently through the earth ... as though of their own unparalleled violence creating ... lighted niches in whose wan and fleeting glare human figures like corpses set momentarily on end in a violated grave yard leaned in one streaming and rigid direction and flicked away" (*CS*, 613-14. The voice of the railway agent has "a quality at once booming, cold, and forlorn, as though it were not interested in nor listening to what it said" (*CS*, 620). The loiterers respond to the agent "with that identical neatness of indigence, with that identical air of patient and indomitable forlornness," and they move toward the exit "in a monstrous and outrageous analogy to flying fish before the advancing prow of a ship" (*CS*, 621). Though the station is a squalid sanctuary, it still is preferable to the world outside:

> Beyond the doors lay a thick, moribund light that seemed to fill the arcade with the smell of snow and of cold, so that for a while longer they seemed to stand in the grip of a dreadful reluctance and inertia. (*CS*, 624)

The comments and observations of the omniscient narrator are uniformly austere, presenting the whole scene as though it were a counterpoint to the airplane in the rotunda of the station, "motionless, squatting, with a still, beetleing look like a huge bug preserved in alcohol" (*CS*, 624).

The young man is equally ironic and detached. He listens with apparent contempt to the old man's story, and his comments are of the wise-guy variety, though he refrains from wounding the old man when he has a chance. The old man is capable of a certain kind of inference, but unlike his impatient young auditor, he always takes the charitable attitude toward the perfidious Danny. He repeatedly insists that Danny was not bad, "just wild, like any young fellow" (*CS*, 611). In his view Danny proved his concern for his mother by sending a \$200 wreath to her funeral. This act, which the old man refers to no fewer than four times in the story, is convincing proof for him of the boy's goodness. He does not realize that the wreath could mean nothing to the dead woman, from whom Danny had taken the money she spent years accumulating in order to have a decent burial.

Danny's mother emerges as a long-suffering, selfless woman. She is an illiterate charwoman whose only interests in life are her undeserving son and her burial money. She comes to understand that Danny has cheated her, but when it becomes apparent that Danny has forged a note to get the burial money from Mr. Pinckski, she lies for him. "I signed it," she maintains. Pinckski is the typical money-grubbing undertaker. He gives Danny \$130 in exchange for a forged receipt absolving him of any obligations to Danny's mother. He pretends to know nothing of Danny's trick. "Should I know," he asks, "if she can't write or not when her own son brings me a note signed with her name?" (*CS*, 622).

All the characters, from the ingenuous old man to the wise-cracking young man, are shallow, cast in the model of sentimental and melodramatic stereotypes. The only sense of an individual, articulate personality comes from the omniscient narrator, who was a late addition to the story. "Pennsylvania Station" was written in dramatic dialogue and later made into a story.[4] Faulkner's experiment with dramatic form in an early draft of "Pennsylvania Station" is useful in understanding his method in novels like *Absalom, Absalom!* and *Requiem for a Nun*, both of which it anticipates. In *Absalom, Absalom!* the part of the cynical young man is taken by Shreve McCannon, who may be closer to the truth about Sutpen, Faulkner remarked, than anyone else in the story (*FIU*, 39). The parallels between "Pennsylvania Station" and *Requiem for a Nun* are more obvious, particularly since *Requiem* features long passages of dramatic dialogue, and was eventually produced as a play.[5] In both cases the presented scene is merely the location of a recitation of significant events long since past. In both cases there is an apparently disinterested listener in the drama — the young man in "Pennsylvania Station," the Governor in *Requiem*. In the story, however, the old man gives no indication that he is in the least cognizant of the meaning of the past events, and the young man is not disposed to inform him. In *Requiem* Temple ultimately recognizes and expresses her responsibility for her past conduct, largely through the persistent agency of Gavin Stevens.

Like many of Faulkner's storytellers, the old man is passing time, instructing, he thinks, his audience. Like many of Faulkner's audiences, the young man is possessed of worldly insight and experience beyond that of his supposed instructor. The moral judgment of Danny which the old man cannot reach is the most obvious and the least conclusive of the story's results. Danny combines more villainous traits than a credible character can stand. He is a liar, a cheat, a forger, a racketeer, an ungrateful child, a murderer. Yet Danny's crimes call forth the stoic fortitude and perseverance of his mother and uncle. Danny's deceit and ingratitude are the qualities against which the others' courage and moral conduct are defined. What is wanting in the story is a genuine conclusion to the melodrama. The old man's telling of the story is the merest accident of Depression circumstances, and neither the omniscient narrator nor the young man comment in other than indirect ways. The contrast between the narrative and dramatic voices is technically interesting, but the story as a whole is inconclusive. The ironic reticence of "Pennsylvania Station" is as unsatisfactory as the rhetorical sentimentality of "The Tall Men."

In "Artist at Home" Faulkner presents, through the medium of another ironic narrator, a wry parable of the process of creative inspiration. Roger Howes, a moderately successful novelist, his wife, Anne, and the poet-*manqué* John Blair make the three sides of a rather special triangle. None of the three is given more than a line or two of physical description; Howes is fat and bald and smokes a pipe, Anne has hair long enough to cover her face, Blair wears a coat which resembles a sky-blue dressing gown. The three are defined almost exclusively by their particular responses to their mutual experiences. Anne, at the outset of the story, is unhappy with Howes' habit of allowing outsiders like Blair to intrude upon them, presuming upon Howes' unoffered hospitality. Art, she seems to think, is not worth all this fuss and bother. When Blair arrives, uninvited, at their Virginia home, she is infuriated. Her indignation increases when Blair tells her she has "neither intelligence nor imagination," and that she is "not intelligent enough to get my poetry at first hand" (*CS*, 633-34). But when Blair treats her to a firsthand example of his poetry, a precious image of herself in relation to his own life, she is immediately won over. Subsequently she and Blair are provoked by Howes' exasperatingly civilized refusal to play the wronged husband. Blair refuses to accept Howes' continued offers of hospitality and leaves the house. He returns one night to speak to Anne and catches pneumonia standing in the rain outside. Before he dies, he writes one superb poem, which Howes has published. Howes, it is revealed, has been writing furiously throughout the entanglement:

> And what was it he had been writing? Him, and Anne, and the poet. Word for word, between the waiting spells to find out what to write down next, with a few changes here and there, of course, because live people do not make good copy, the most interesting copy being gossip, since it mostly is not true. (*CS*, 644)

The narrative is distinguished by the ironic, intrusive narrator, who constantly shifts his verb tenses from past to present to subjunctive, and by the number' of literary allusions and echoes which crop up. The narrator alludes to Pope, Roger alludes to Shelley, and the scene in which Blair contracts pneumonia is a clear parallel to the visit of Michael Furey to Gretta in "The Dead." The whole story might also be read as a gentle takeoff on Henry James, for Howes' behavior seems often to be a deliberate inversion of James' conventions of conduct. It is as though Mrs. Newsome had *insisted* that Strether pursue Mme. de Vionnet. Too, though the story includes two artists, and though there are several scenes and details which demonstrate the aesthetic sensibilities of the characters, both the narrator and Howes repeatedly undercut the tendency to romanticize the life and feelings of the artist. The creative impulse is forced into a burlesque equation with the stock market, and there are many references in the story to the money artists can make.

An especially obvious device in "Artist at Home" is the narrator's use of pointed and coy comments to the reader. Among the earliest of these is the passage describing the first conversation between Anne and Blair:

> She looks at him, holding the flowers and the scissors. Then she tells him to come on into the house and live there forever. Except she didn't say exactly that. She said, "You walk? Nonsense. I think you're sick. You come in and sit down and rest." Then she went to find Roger and tell him to bring down the pram from the attic. Of course she didn't say exactly that, either. (*CS*, 630)

This scene shows Anne's lack of understanding of her own feelings, and it markedly affects the reader's response to her subsequent diatribes against Blair. The image of Poet-as-Child is fixed here, and is expanded when Blair describes his unhappy childhood in declaring himself to Anne. The scene further emphasizes Blair's physical delicacy, and it prepares the reader for his eventual demise. From the beginning Howes recognizes that Blair has the makings of a poet, and he accepts his guest's several eccentricities. "There's a lot of wear and tear to just being a poet," he tells Anne, "I don't think you realize that" (*CS*, 631). Special consideration must be given to Blair, if he is to write the poem that is in him. When he sees Anne is concerned for Blair's health, he "went and put another cushion in the pram" (*CS*, 634). He not only acquiesces in his wife's flirtation, he seems to encourage it.

The point of the story is not the flirtation itself, nor the clinch which proves the mutual affection of Anne and Blair. "That can be seen in any movie," the narrator comments (*CS*, 636). The point is that both Blair and Howes are inspired to write by their experience. The narrator puts it bluntly:

> Now get this. This is it. He came back down to the office and put some paper into the typewriter and began to write. He didn't go very fast at first, but by daylight he was sounding like forty hens in a sheet-iron corn-crib, and the written sheets on the desk were piling up.... (*CS*, 638)

As the story continues, Howes writes when there is a new development in his personal situation, and he writes nothing while he waiting for something else to happen. He is by no means completely cold and calculating in his exploitation of Anne and Blair, for he is obviously deeply affected by the thought that he might lose his wife. He allows himself one passionate outburst at Blair, and he continues to woo Anne himself. His love for her is genuine, but he is too sophisticated to allow himself to express it in the obvious romantic clichés.

Howes' conversation shows that he is trying to employ the same detached, cynical attitude adopted by the narrator. Particularly significant in this connection are the financial metaphors used to express the condition of artistic health. The Howes are comfortable as a result of Roger's earlier writing. His current lack of productivity is a source of irritation for Anne. The visiting poets and writers disrupt the pleasant life which Roger's previous work has made possible. Anne thinks that the parade of guests interferes with Roger's writing. She knows, however, that money is not the ultimate aim of an artist, and that Blair is wrong to ask his host, "will this sell?" Howes has enough sense of the literary market to advise Blair about his sales, and he has enough artistic sense to know that such potboiling is not Blair's real work. Appropriately, when Blair's one great poem is finally published, "the magazines that don't have any pictures took the poem, stealing it from one another while the interest or whatever it was ate up the money that the poet never got for it" (*CS*, 643-44). But Roger himself benefits financially from the experience, for his novel sells. With some of his royalty money he buys Anne a mink coat, which she refuses to accept, so she will not have to remember that Blair died "to dress me in the skins of little slain beasts" (*CS*, 645). Thus the financial rewards of art are finally denied, and the narrator's repeated ironic references to Howes' bullish and bearish literary market are put into proper perspective.

There are some awkward aspects in "Artist at Home." Some relationships are initiated but dropped, such as Blair's interest in the cook, Pinkie. The inclusion of parenthetical commentary in what is supposed to be dialogue is arresting, but the unnecessary uncertainty over the extent of Blair's intimacy with Anne is troublesome. Finally, it is not really necessary for the narrator to state directly that Howes' novel concerns the three of them. All of these imperfections, however, proceed from the narrative voice, and we must ultimately be suspicious of it. The narrator's interpretation of events is less than completely trustworthy, though it is often amusing:

> And here we are again. the bald husband, the rural plute, and this dashing blade, this home-wrecking poet. Both gentlemen, being artists: the one that doesn't want the other to get wet; the other whose conscience won't let him wreck the house from inside. Here we are, with Roger trying to hold one of these green silk, female umbrellas over himself and the poet too, jerking at the poet's arm. (*CS*, 642)

This passage implies that both Roger and Blair are shallow fools who have allowed themselves to appear ridiculous. Howes, the narrator seems to be saying, should not worry about Blair's getting wet, while Blair should not scruple to come inside the house. There is clearly no necessary connection between artists and gentlemen. But the narrator does not do justice to the pathos of the scene, the dramatic high-point of the story. Anne responds to it with hysterical laughter, but her laughter is quite different from the narrator's.[6]

"Artist at Home" is a relative rarity in Faulkner's fiction because it deals explicitly with the subject of artistic creation and because it deals with liberated and sophisticated characters. Further, it has no connection with Yoknapatawpha County and its inhabitants. More representative of *Collected Stories* are two stories included in "The Wilderness." "Red Leaves," one of Faulkner's earlier stories, illustrates the characteristics of the ironic mode of the earlier fiction. "A Courtship," the last of the stories in the volume to be published, is a tall tale illustrating the comic and romantic character of the later fiction. Both stories concern the Chickasaws who inhabit the Mississippi wilderness, and both stress the primitive virtues of strength and courage.

"Red Leaves" describes the inexorable pursuit of a black slave who has served the Man, Issetibbeha, for twenty-three years. Issetibbeha is dying, and tribal custom dictates that his horse, his dog, and his servant be buried with him. The slave, aided occasionally by the other blacks, hides from his pursuers for five days before he is captured. The pursuit and capture are carried out with all the solemnity of ritual, but the Indians have little stomach for the chase. The slave's actions are incomprehensible to them. In life he has been privileged to serve the Man, and has thus escaped the ignominy of sweating in the fields. "Why should he not wish to die," Three Basket asks, "since he did not wish to sweat?" (*CS*, 326). The slave resists the inevitable with all the strength and cunning at his disposal. On the fourth day of his pursuit, however, he is suddenly struck by a cottonmouth moccasin:

> "Olé, grandfather," the Negro said. He touched its head and watched it slash him again across his arm, and again, with thick, raking, awkward blows. "It's that I do not wish to die," he said. Then he said it again — "It's that I do not wish to die" — in a quiet tone, of slow and low amaze, as though it were something that, until the words had said themselves, he found that he had not known, or had not known the depth and extent of his desire. (*CS*, 335)

The slave hides one more night in the swamp, and then submits to capture. He is complimented by the Indians for his conduct: "You ran well. Do not be ashamed" (*CS*, 338). He is treated with courtesy and respect, and he is allowed · to try to eat and drink before he is killed.

The title of the story, Faulkner explained, "was probably symbolism." The red leaves are the Indians, whose normal deciduation "suffocated, smothered, destroyed the Negro" (*FIU*, 39). To the Indians, "the Negro" is a curse. Work must be found for the slaves, and the Indians must sweat to pursue the runaway. A few Indians are aware of the curse of slavery, but they are powerless to change the tradition or the fact, for they own unquestioning loyalty to the Man, even so gross and dyspeptic a Man as Moketubbe. The long second section traces the coming of the blacks into the Indians' domain. The villains are Doom, the father of Issetibbeha, and his white companion, the Chevalier Soeur Blonde de Vitry. The Chevalier teaches Doom the white man's ways in New Orleans, and Doom returns to his people, murders his uncle and his cousin, and becomes the Man. He then begins to "acquire more slaves and to cultivate his land, as the white people did" (*CS*, 318). There is not enough work for the slaves to do, and Doom uses them to entertain his guests by coursing them with dogs. The problem is compounded during the reign of Issetibbeha, Doom's son, when there are five times as many blacks and nothing for them to do. The tribal council settles "the Negro question" by determining to raise more blacks for the slave trade.

Against this background the drama of Issetibbeha's slave is played out. The slave is superior to his pursuers in energy, intelligence, and virtue. He is the victim of a society and a tradition over which he has no control, a society governed by ridiculous men with great vanity and small worth. In their slavish imitation of the white men's "civilization," Doom, Issetibbeha, and Moketubbe inadvertently bring about the degeneration of their people. Doom makes his palace from a steamboat which has gone aground in the river. Issetibbeha cannot sleep in the huge gilt bed which he imports from Paris. Moketubbe faints when he wears the red slippers which are, besides eating, his only apparent joy. There is a kind of wisdom and dignity in Three Basket and Louis Berry, but in deferring to a vicious authority and a brutal tradition they show their limitations. The clear image of the Indians' current position is developed in the passage describing the obese Moketubbe being carried through the swamp to the place where his father's slave will be captured:

> ... the supine obese shape just barely alive, carried through swamp and brier by swinging relays of men who bore steadily all day long the crime and its object, on the business of the slain. To Moketubbe it must have seemed as though, himself immortal, he were being carried rapidly through hell by doomed spirits which, alive, had contemplated his disaster, and dead, were oblivious partners to his damnation. (*CS*, 335)

Moketubbe's inheritance is a pair of red slippers he cannot wear and a people he cannot lead, bound by a tradition which has little meaning for them and none at all for him. The world of "Red Leaves" is a world of despair, in which the only dignified response is the stoic acceptance of the inevitable. The slave is doomed to death, and Moketubbe is damned to death-in-life. By adopting the institution of slavery, the Indians have destroyed the primitive innocence of their society. "I do not like slavery," one of them observes. "It is not the good way. In the old days, there was the good way. But not now" (*CS*, 314). They mistakenly attribute to the blacks the same stereotyped faults which the white man attributes to Indian and black alike. The slave's desire to live makes trouble for them, and, as they see it, this can only be explained as his legacy from a people "without honor and without decorum," and his clinging to life is the predictable response of a "savage" who "cannot be expected to regard usage" (*CS*, 316). The Indians deny the humanity of the slave and of his whole people.

The world of "A Courtship" is explicitly pre-lapsarian. The story takes place during the time before Ikkemotubbe is corrupted by the white man's ways, before the coming of the slaves, and before the discovery of the enmity between the whites and the Indians. A description of Ikkemotubbe early in the story makes a clear differentiation between the younger and the older Man:

> But he was not Doom yet. He was still just Ikkemotubbe, one of the young men, the best one, who rode the hardest and fastest and danced the longest and was loved the best, by the young men and the girls and the older women too who should have had other things to think about. (*CS*, 363)

"A Courtship" explains why Ikkemotubbe decided to leave the tribe for the civilization of New Orleans. He leaves because he has failed in his courtship of Herman Basket's sister. The courtship itself consists of a series of epic and mock-epic demonstrations of physical courage and accomplishment. Ikkemotubbe's rival for the attentions of the girl is the white steamboat pilot, David Hogganbeck. In the course of their rivalry the two learn to love and respect one another, and they finally value their friendship above the girl, who will have nothing to do with either of them. Ikkemotubbe and Hogganbeck develop the same bond that holds between Ishmael and Queequeg and Huck and Jim, the shared experience and affection which transcend heterosexual desire. The two are courteous and principled in their conduct towards each other, but in their behavior towards Herman Basket's sister they are juvenile and grotesque.

The humor of the story is often Rabelaisian, emphasizing the gross physicality of the two rivals. But this is only part of the humor, which is importantly related to the disparity between the exertions and the girl's response. She is utterly indifferent to both of them, and while they are exhausting themselves and risking death in a 130-mile race to a dangerous cave, she marries the placid, harmonica-playing nonentity Log-in-the-Creek. Herman Basket's sister has the same appeal to men that Eula Varner has:

> ... who is to say what age a man must reach or just how unfortunate he must have been in his youthful compliance, when he shall no longer look at the Herman Basket's sisters of

this world and chew his bitter thumbs too, aihee. Because she walked in beauty. Or she sat in it, that is, because she did not walk unless she had to. (*CS*, 362)

David Hogganbeck and Ikkemotubbe ignore the reality of Herman Basket's sister in the same way that the Indians in "Red Leaves" ignore the humanity of the slave. Neither makes a genuine attempt to understand the person they are pursuing. Herman Basket's sister, however, is free, and she exercises her choice by marrying Log-in-the-Creek, thus denying the significance of Ikkemotubbe and Hogganbeck's gargantuan feats.

Her choice "sours" Ikkemotubbe, as Ab Snopes' defeat by Pat Stamper in *The Hamlet* sours Ab. Though the narrator does not dwell on the fact, the girl's repudiation of Ikkemotubbe is the direct cause of his leaving the tribe. When he returns, he is Doom, bringing slaves and the arsenic with which he murders his uncle and cousin in order to become the Man. The narrator, an Indian descendant of one of Ikkemotubbe's contemporaries, is primarily concerned with celebrating the feats of the unsuccessful rivals. It would be easy for Ikkemotubbe to kill David Hogganbeck, but he would prefer to defeat him honorably. Hogganbeck recognizes this, and he acknowledges that Ikkemotubbe must be satisfied. The two agree to settle their dispute by means of an eating contest. Hogganbeck wins, but Ikkemotubbe cannot reconcile himself to the loss:

> "I had you beat before we started," David Hogganbeck said. "We both knew that."
> "Yes," Ikkemotubbe said. "But I suggested it."
> "Then what do you suggest now?" David Hogganbeck said. And now my father said how they loved David Hogganbeck at that moment as they loved Ikkemotubbe, that they loved them both at that moment while Ikkemotubbe stood before David Hogganbeck with the smile on his face and his right hand flat on David Hogganbeck's chest, because there were men in those days. (*CS*, 373)

By these standards, Log-in-the-Creek is not a man. "He raced no horses and fought no cocks and cast no dice," the narrator tells us, "and even when forced to, he would not even dance fast enough to keep out of the other dancers' way, and disgraced both himself and the others each time by becoming sick after only five or six horns of what was never even his whisky" (*CS*, 363-64). He is, however, patient and persistent, continuing to play his harmonica in spite of the entreaties and strategies of the others. The harmonica suggests that Log-in-the-Creek is a kind of artist, and the story is as much a record of his success as it is a record of Ikkemotubbe and Hogganbeck's failure. Ikkemotubbe sheds tears for himself at the end of the story, and ridicules both Log-in-the-Creek and Herman Basket's sister. He and Hogganbeck exchange proverbs of their respective traditions concerning the inconstancy of women, and they conclude that there is one wisdom for all men, one heartbreak. There is no heartbreak for Log-in-the-Creek, however, and his successful wooing of Herman Basket's sister may be taken as an ironic commentary on the antics of the rivals. In this story, at least, the artist wins the girl, while the athletes are left to chew their bitter thumbs. "Red Leaves" ends in death, and "A Courtship" ends in marriage. Both the slave and Ikkemotubbe learn from their failures, but only in "A Courtship" is there any hint that a semblance of justice has been achieved.[7]

The most uniformly bleak group of stories in *Collected Stories* is "The Wasteland," five stories about World War I. Of these, "Turnabout" is perhaps the best-known, and it is worth noting since it received the imprimatur of Hemingway, who included it in his anthology *Men at War.* "Turnabout" describes the experience of an American pilot who befriends two young British midshipmen, and, through them, learns the meaning of the waste and futility of war. The American, Bogard, takes one of the young men on a bombing mission with him. The boy, Hope, enjoys the experience and is very impressed when Bogard lands the plane with a bomb hanging dangerously from it. Bogard, however, had not known that the bomb was there. Like Cadet Thompson's, his is a landing in luck. Bogard then accepts Hope's invitation to accompany him on a torpedo mission. He is frightened at the danger which the Britons face and becomes sick in the boat. The story, up to this point, consists of a neat series of reversals, the contrast between Hope's enthusiasm and Bogard's squeamishness, between Bogard's blind luck and the Britons' confident execution of dangerous maneuvers, between the Americans' swagger and rudeness and the Britons' courtesy and modesty. These contrasts are underscored when Bogard learns that Hope and his crew have been killed. In an effort to avenge them he dive-bombs a château deep behind enemy lines. In his furious rage at the moment of the dive he thinks, "God! God! If they were all there — all the generals, the admirals, the presidents and the kinds — theirs, ours — all of them" (*CS*, 509).

"Turnabout" begins with the self-controlled Bogard taking charge of the drunken Hope, who appears to him and to the other American flyers as a mere child who looks upon the war as a grand game. His boyish enthusiasm for the game he and his mate Ronnie play in sighting German ships is received with contempt by the Americans, who obviously believe that their own flying assignments are far more dangerous than anything Hope has encountered. For this reason, Hope's praise of the aviators falls on deaf ears. They have no respect for such childish ranting. The aviators, including Bogard, are condescending towards him during the flight, though Bogard is impressed with his ability to handle a machine gun. When Bogard lands the plane with the bomb hanging from the undercarriage, Hope is ecstatic in his admiration. "Frightened, myself," he admits. "Tried to tell you. But realized you knew your business better than I. Skill. Marvelous. Oh, I say, I shan't forget it" (*CS*, 492).

Each of these points is turned about when Bogard accompanies Hope and Ronnie on their torpedo mission. Hope treats Bogard with respect, Bogard is petrified, and he tries to tell the two boys how to operate their craft. The boys face an emergency comparable to Bogard's fouled bomb, but unlike Bogard, they are instantly aware of the nature of their problem and they solve it by means of their own skill. Bogard becomes sick in the boat, whereas Hope had not, as the aviators had predicted, been sick in the plane. Out of this experience Bogard develops a profound respect for the two young seamen, and he sends Hope a case of Scotch after the trip.

The differences between Bogard and Hope, Faulkner explained at West Point, are the fundamental differences in age. The superficial differences in manners are national traits and are not very important.[8] They have in common a forced involvement in a war which is, like all wars, both inefficient and devastating. Bogard and his crew, like Hope and Ronnie, nearly lose their lives because of the malfunction of the machinery of war. Hope accepts this as part of the game, but to Bogard it is appalling. The deaths of Ronnie and Hope, the story implies, are the result of another such malfunction. Bogard's final fury is directed at the forces, transcending national alignments, which are responsible for the war and its waste. He is decorated, like Yossarian in *Catch-22* for a successful mission for which, had it failed and had he survived it, "he would have been immediately and thoroughly court-martialed" (*CS*, 509). Like the other stories in "The Wasteland," "Turnabout" shows the horror and futility of impersonal combat, and demonstrates the impotent rage to which it drives its participants. Above the wasteland rises the voice of the wounded man in "Crevasse," "meaningless and unemphatic and sustained" (*CS*, 474) . "Victory" ends on a similar note. "My God," Walkley says, after seeing the pathetic Gray, "I think I am going to vomit" (*CS*, 464).[9]

"Turnabout" was the last of the five stories of "The Wasteland" to be published, the other four having appeared the previous year in *These 13*. The tone of the war stories is consistent with that of *Sanctuary,* with which they were roughly contemporary. During approximately this same period, however, Faulkner was writing an entirely different group of stories, placed together in the final section of *Collected Stories,* "Beyond." These stories have a wide variety of settings, but each describes a protagonist in profound conflict with his environment, and each character, as a result of the conflict, moves into an imaginative world strikingly different from the one to which he has been accustomed. Allison, in the title story of the section, passes at the moment of his death into a kind of limbo where he searches for his dead son. Wilfred Midgleston in "Black Music" steps out of his role as a timid architect's drafts-man and spends an afternoon as a faun. Davy, the seemingly pleasant young

narrator of "The Leg," has hallucinations and acquires sinister and super-
natural capabilities. The two young travellers of "Mistral" are gradually drawn
into the violent romantic intrigue of a small town in northern Italy. Carl, the
"innocent" young deck hand of "Divorce in Naples," has a traumatic fling
with a woman. And the young man in "Carcassonne," sleeping in a roll of
tarred roofing paper above a cantina in Puerto Rico, lives in his imagination as
a medieval knight.

Because of its placement at the end of *Collected Stories,* "Carcassonne" is
worthy of special attention. The physical action in the story is the slightest of
any in Faulkner's fiction. A young man lies down to go to sleep, allowing his
mind to wander. From this apparently trivial bit of action Faulkner develops
one of his clearest statements of the will of man to endure and prevail by means
of his imaginative achievement of immortality. The young man imagines
himself *"ON A BUCKSKIN PONY with eyes like blue electricity and a mane
like tangled fire, galloping up the hill and right off into the high heaven of the
world (CS, 895).* The young man wants to perform something *"bold and
tragical and austere" (CS, 899).* One possible implication of the story is that he
is in fact performing something bold and tragical and austere by maintaining
his hopes that he will do so. There is a vivid contrast in "Carcassonne" between
the young man's squalid surroundings and the brilliant world of his imagination, between his skeleton and his soul. This contrast is made explicit in the
brief passages describing the poverty of his surroundings — the siren from the
docks, the music from the cantina — in juxtaposition with the bright achievement of his imagination. The contrast between the physical and the imaginative
worlds is articulated in the dialogue between the man and his skeleton:

> Living, as it did, a retired life, his skeleton could know next to nothing of the world. Yet it
> had an astonishing and exasperating way of supplying him with bits of trivial information
> that had temporarily escaped his mind. "All you know is what I tell you," he said.
> "Not always," the skeleton said. "I know that the end of life is lying still. You haven't
> learned that yet. Or you haven't mentioned it to me, anyway."
> "Oh, I've learned it," he said. "I've had it dinned into me enough. It isn't that. It's that
> I don't believe it's true."
> The skeleton groaned.
> "I don't believe it, I say," he repeated.
> "All right, all right," the skeleton said testily. "I shan't dispute you. I never do. I only
> give you advice." (*CS,* 899)

The young man, Faulkner said in speaking of his fondness for the story, is
"in conflict with his environment" (*FIU,* 222). By refusing to be bound by its
limitations, he achieves freedom. This is especially apparent in the elaborate
conceit in which he relates the roll of roofing paper to the spectacles of the
imagination. The roofing paper is rolled up and stood on end in a corner of the
garret every morning:

> It was like those glasses, reading glasses which old ladies used to wear, attached to a cord
> that rolls into a spindle in a neat case of unmarked gold, a spindle, a case, attached to the
> deep bosom of the mother of sleep. (*CS*, 895)

The young man savors this image and extends it, "... and he thought of his tarred paper bed as a pair of spectacles through which he nightly perused the fabric of dreams (*CS*, 896). The substance of his dreams is his own personal heroic immortality, his denial of death, like the riderless Norman horse, severed by a single blow "thundering on through the assembled foes of our meek Lord, wrapped still in the fury and the pride of the charge, not knowing that it was dead" (*CS*, 896).

There are several parallels between the severed horse and the man who imagines it. Both are cut in half, both deny the significance of the separation, and both achieve a kind of glory in the denial. Faulkner also used the phrase "failed poet" in speaking of this story, though it is unclear whether he was referring to himself, to his character, or to both. The young man is an image-maker, and he is familiar with literary history and personalities and allusions. His landlady thinks of him as a poet because "With her, if you were white and did not work, you were either a tramp or a poet. Maybe you were" (*CS*, 897-98). The rats in the garret remind him that Mrs. Widdrington "didn't expect the rats to pay for using her darkness by writing poetry" (*CS*, 898). This leads him to associate the rats with Byron, and then with the killing of Polonius by Hamlet, and all are bound up with his vision of the horse:

> Something of the rat about Byron: allocutions of stealthful voracity ; a fiery patterning of
> little feet behind a bloody arras *where fell where I was King of Kings but the woman with
> the woman with the dog's eyes to knock my bones together and together.* (*CS*, 898)

"Carcassonne" has been treated briefly and gingerly by a number of critics who seem to feel that it is important, without knowing quite what to make of it. Michael Millgate expresses the tentative conclusion that it "perhaps represents an attempt to capture in words the anguish and ecstasy of the creative experience, or at least of the creative ambition," and that it "should perhaps be regarded as expressing a commitment to an ultimately tragic vision of life."[10] William Van O'Connor says that it is "hardly a story, in that it has no development or plot, but it is interesting for what appears to be an autobio-graphical assertion."[11] Dorothy Tuck calls it "less a story than a prose poem of a postmortal flight of consciousness," and she identifies the protagonist of the story with the central character of "Black Music."[12] Walter J. Slatoff refers to the story as "an allegory of the body and soul or of the struggle of the artist."[13] Austin McGiffert Wright classifies it as an episode of romantic discovery, a "direct depiction of a character's state of feeling in a situation whose objective nature is only vaguely suggested."[14] The complex texture of the story, and the deliberate fusion of symbols would seem to account for the critical uncertainty about the story. Another of Faulkner's comments, however, suggests that "Carcassonne" is susceptible to a clear interpretation. In explaining the so-called Southern Renaissance, he observed "I myself am inclined to think it was because of the bareness of the Southerner's life, that he had to resort to his own imagination, to create his own Carcassonne" (*FIU*, 136). The most comprehensive reading of the story is that of Noel Polk, who argues that "Carcassonne" was written to unify *These 13*, confirming that volume's patterns of irony and despair, "the most complete portrait of a waste land that Faulkner was ever to draw."[15]

The young man in the story lives a bare life, and he creates in his imagination his own version of the timeless French city. Faulkner has denied a literary influence for the story, but it is clearly analogous to the situation in Gustave Nadaud's poem of the same title:

> I'm growing old, I've sixty years,
>   I've labored all my life in vain,
> In all that time of hopes and fears
>   I've failed my dearest wish to gain.
> I see full well that here below
>   Bliss unalloyed there is for none.
> My prayer will ne'er fulfillment know, —
>   I never have seen Carcassonne!
>   I never have seen Carcassonne.[16]

The young man, however, spends no time bemoaning his fate, but creates his own kind of "bliss unalloyed," his own realm of heroic pursuit of the ideal:

> Still galloping, the horse soars outward; still galloping, it thunders up the long blue hill of heaven, its tossing mane in golden swirls like fire. Steed and rider thunder on, thunder punily diminishing: a dying star upon the immensity of darkness and of silence within which, steadfast, fading, deepbreasted and grave of flank, muses the dark and tragic figure of the Earth, his mother. (*CS*, 899-900)

There is, then, a development, a plot to "Carcassonne," and though the text may be read as an allegory, a parable, or a prose poem, it remains, at base, a conventional prose narrative, in which the protagonist's initial frustration and despair are resolved in the hope of the dream. If "Carcassonne" indeed represents Faulkner's commitment to a tragic view of life — especially if we share Polk's reading of the protagonist as a dead or dying man as well as a failed poet — it should nevertheless be remembered that tragedy is of the highest order of literary and personal experience. The achievement of "Carcassonne," as well as that of the volumes (*These 13* and *Collected Stories*) which it concludes, demonstrates that Faulkner himself was something more than a "failed poet" or a "mere" writer of short stories.

The Unvanquished and *Go Down, Moses*

Collected Stories is unified by Faulkner's mature and retrospective vision of the relations among his short story texts. He made few revisions of stories for that volume, choosing rather to follow the texts of stories printed in *These 13, Doctor Martino,* or individual issues of periodicals.[17] *The Unvanquished* and *Go Down, Moses,* however, show numerous and radical changes between the magazine versions of individual stories and the corresponding material in the published volumes. Both *The Unvanquished* and *Go Down, Moses* have been treated as collections of stories, as unified "cycles" of related stories, and as novels. The ultimate determination of the exact nature of the two books depends on whether the separate parts of each are coherent in themselves, on whether they may be read individually without significant loss or alteration in the story's meaning. The number of important variations between the separately published stories and the final volumes, Faulkner's own comments on his "final intention," and the serious difficulties which attend the reading of excerpts, all tend to support the conclusion that the two books are best approached as novels.

The publishing history of *The Unvanquished* suggests that there were at least two, and perhaps three, distinct stages of composition. "Ambuscade," the first chapter in *The Unvanquished,* or the first story in the cycle, was published in the *Saturday Evening Post* on September 29, 1934. It describes how Bayard and Ringo shoot at the Yankee and then take refuge under Granny's skirts. It is a story of discovery, Bayard's first direct experience of the war which he and Ringo have imagined to be a romantic game. An editorial note following the conclusion of the story announced, "This is the first of a series of stories in which these same two boys will appear" (*Post,* 81). The second story in the series, "Retreat," appeared in the *Post* on October 13, 1934. This story concerns the abandonment of the Sartoris home in the face of an impending Yankee invasion, the loss of the silver, mules, and house, and the desertion of Loosh. On November 3, 1934, the *Post* published "Raid," which describes the adventures of Granny, Bayard, and Ringo on their expedition to recover the mules and the silver. The series of stories announced by the *Post* editor seems to have been completed with the publication of "Raid," the third story to appear in the magazine in as many months. Almost two years elapsed before "The Unvanquished" and "Vendée" were printed there.

In the meantime, "Skirmish at Sartoris" appeared in *Scribner's,* in April 1935. "Skirmish at Sartoris," the second-to-last chapter in *The Unvanquished,* describes the immediate postwar period during which Colonel Sartoris and Drusilla Hawk unite against the Federal commissioners who have come to superintend the election of a black marshal in Jefferson. Colonel Sartoris rides into town, shoots the Burdens, and returns to Sartoris where he and Drusilla are married. Thus the order of the publication of the stories differs from their order in *The Unvanquished*. "The Unvanquished," published in the *Post* on November 14, 1936, is very different in tone and substance from its predecessors. The *Post* editors supplied a synoptic note at the head of "The Unvanquished," identifying the characters and describing the manner in which Granny got into the business of requisitioning mules and selling them back to the Yankees. There is no indication in any of the first three *Post* stories that this development will take place. "Raid" describes how Granny's request for her own mules, "Old Hundred" and "Tennie," and a single chest of silver is answered by a written authorization for 110 mules and ten chests of silver, but Granny scrupulously objects to receiving more than her original loss, and at the end of the story demands that Ringo and Bayard join her in praying for forgiveness because they brought back more mules than the authorization stipulates. "The Unvanquished," called "Riposte in Tertio" in the book, also introduces Ab Snopes as Granny's partner in the mule business. By forging orders similar to the one she received from Colonel Dick, Granny obtains mules from the Yankees, and Ab Snopes sells them back to them. The money is distributed to the poor people of the hill country around Sartoris. Granny is finally caught, partly because Ab Snopes convinces her to go against her better judgment and requisition another batch of mules. Since the business is over, Granny is disappointed that she has not achieved her goal of raising enough money to provide Colonel Sartoris a chance to rebuild after the war. With this in mind she makes one more sortie. She tries to requisition stolen horses from Grumby's Independents, a ruthless band of terrorists and scavengers. They kill her.

The comic tone of the first three *Post* stories is conspicuous by its absence in "The Unvanquished," though there is some grim humor in Ab's dialogue, and there is a light moment when Granny insists that Ringo have his mouth washed out with soap. But "The Unvanquished" is the first story in the *Post* series which directly involves a death, and it is the first in which the Sartorises are permanently thwarted. Granny's initial suspicion of Ab's plan anticipates the grim denouement, and the threat of danger is constant in the story. "Vendée," published in the *Post* on December 5, 1936, describes Bayard and Ringo's revenge on Grumby. The boys are men now, completely different characters from the innocents who drew the map of Vicksburg in the dust and shot hopefully at the Yankee in "Ambuscade." Patiently they pursue Grumby, kill him, and nail his severed hand to Granny's grave as a sign that she has been avenged. Bayard's narrative is consistently grim and understated throughout "Vendée," and the full implications of his quest are not revealed until Uncle Buck McCaslin describes, in the last paragraph of the story, what has happened to Grumby.

> "The proof and the expiation," Uncle Buck hollered. "When me and John Sartoris and Drusilla rode up to that old compress, the first thing we see was that murdering scoundrel

pegged out on the door to it all except the right hand. 'And if anybody wants to see that, too,' I told John Sartoris, 'just let them ride into Jefferson and look on Rosa Millard's grave!' Ain't I told he is John Sartoris' boy? Ain't I told you?" (*USWF*, 117)

This episode completes the story of Bayard in the Civil War, and it represents his violent coming of age.

In writing *The Unvanquished* Faulkner made a number of changes in the five *Post* stories and in "Skirmish at Sartoris," and added "An Odor of Verbena," which describes Bayard's ultimate rejection of the code of violent revenge. The nature of Faulkner's revisions has been discussed by a number of critics, the consensus being that the additions unify the material of the stories. The individual chapters of *The Unvanquished* make only partial sense when they are separated from the volume, or they make a different kind of sense when they are extracted from the surrounding context. Reading *The Unvanquished* text of "Skirmish at Sartoris," for example, could be a mystifying experience for the reader previously unacquainted with Grumby. The *Scribner's* text of the story is also more satisfactory in that Bayard's naiveté is more credible there than in the novel. In "Skirmish at Sartoris" a good deal is made of Bayard's innocence. This can be accepted at face value in the *Scribner's* text, but it takes on an ironic cast in *The Unvanquished* when we recall that the "poor suffering child" is actually the man who has murdered and dismembered Grumby. Similarly *The Unvanquished* text of "Skirmish at Sartoris" presumes on information developed in earlier parts of the book. In the *Post* text of "Raid," for example, Drusilla tells young Bayard, "When you go back home and see Uncle John, ask him to let me come there and ride with his troop. Tell him I can ride, and maybe I can learn to shoot. Will you?" (*USWF*, 47). For the sake of exposition, this instruction is repeated in the *Scribner's* text of "Skirmish at Sartoris," with a few slight changes in the phrasing (*USWF*, 59-60). The same material is repeated in the "Raid" section of *The Unvanquished*, in the same phrasing as the *Post* text, while the addition made for the *Scribner's* "Skirmish at Sartoris" is deleted (*UNV*, 115, 217). Though *The Unvanquished* text of "Skirmish at Sartoris" refers to Drusilla's request in a manner which would serve to enlighten a reader unfamiliar with "Raid," the effect of the reference is to recall a previously developed incident rather than to introduce obliquely a new one.

The vast majority of the changes made for *The Unvanquished* are in the form of elaborations, explanations which emphasize the perspective of the articulate and mature Bayard. The narrator of the first three *Post* stories presents his material simply and directly, without detailed interpretation, while the narrator of *The Unvanquished* is, from the opening paragraph of the story, a sophisticated expositor. "Behind the smokehouse," the *Post* text begins, "we had a kind of map. Vicksburg was a handful of chips from the woodpile and the river was a trench we had scraped in the packed ground with a hoe, that drank water almost faster than we could fetch it from the well" (*USWF*, 3). Compare the opening of *The Unvanquished*:

> Behind the smokehouse that summer, Ringo and I have a living map. Although Vicksburg was just a handful of chips from the woodpile and the River a trench scraped into the packed earth with the point of a hoe, it (river, city, and terrain) lived, possessing even in miniature that ponderable though passive recalcitrance of topography which outweighs artillery, against which the most brilliant of victories and the most tragic of defeats are but the loud noises of a moment. To Ringo and me it lived, if only becuase of the fact that the sunimpacted ground drank water faster than we would fetch it from the well, the very setting of the stage for conflict a prolonged and wellnigh hopeless ordeal in which we ran, panting and interminable, with the leaking bucket between wellhouse and battlefield, the two of us needing first to join forces and spend ourselves against a common enemy, time, before we could engender between us and hold intact the pattern of recapitulant mimic furious victory like a cloth, a shield between ourselves and reality, betwen us and fact and doom. (*UNV*, 3-4)

This passage introduces themes and establishes expectations which are not satisfied until the conclusion of "An Odor of Verbena," and one implicit task of Bayard's narrative is to describe the process by which the simple boy of the story — Bayard and Ringo's actions and dialogue are identical in story and novel — becomes the complex man who can be extrapolated from the narrative voice. If we accept the generalization that a short story reveals character while a novel shows a character in development, the consecutive chapters of *The Unvanquished* describe the several stages of Bayard's development.

The notion that *The Unvanquished* is a unified cycle of stories rather than a collection of separate pieces or a novel is a reputable one in that it has support in several of Faulkner's own comments. An interview in the Memphis *Commercial Appeal* in 1937 mentions that Faulkner "announced the publication of a new book, *Unvanquished* [sic], a collection of short stories to appear in February" (*LIG*, 33). Faulkner's description of the origin of *The Unvanquished* may also be glossed to support the "cycle" notion, but the passage is ambiguous (*FIU*, 252). Malcolm Cowley refers to *The Unvanquished* and *Go Down, Moses,* as "a hybrid form between the random collection and the unified novel,"[18] and Olga W. Vickery calls *The Unvanquished, The Hamlet, Go Down, Moses,* and *Knight's Gambit* "story-novels," and she uses the term "fused novel" to describe what she contends is Faulkner's "most original and certainly most misunderstood" form.[19] While the metaphors of hybridization and fusion are useful in describing the process by which *The Unvanquished* and *Go Down, Moses* were written, the hybrid cannot be separated into its genetic parents, the fusion cannot be reversed, without a significant loss to the reader.

There is a considerably better case for regarding *Go Down, Moses* as a collection or cycle of stories than there is for *The Unvanquished,* but the parts of *Go Down, Moses* are even more difficult to comprehend outside the context of the volume into which they were gathered. The textual history of *Go Down, Moses* is a fascinating one, and it shows clearly the ways in which Faulkner changed his mind about his works. The book was originally published as *Go Down, Moses and Other Stories,* but the title was shortened, at Faulkner's request, in subsequent printings. It seems highly unlikely that Random House would have made such an expensive mistake — Cowley notes that books of short stories are thought to have only about a third of the sales of a novel by the same author — and Faulkner's own statements are contradictory. One interview at the University of Mississippi reports that Faulkner described the book as "simply a collection of short stories,"[20] but in response to Cowley's queries he replied, "I always *thought* it was a novel."[21] In his later years he insisted that the book was a novel. Asked to explain the difference between Part IV of "The Bear" and the remainder, he said:

> "The Bear" was part of a novel. That novel was — happened to be composed of more or less complete stories, but it was held together by one family, the Negro and white phase of the same family, the same people. *The Bear* was just a part of that — of a novel.

It is "all right" for Ike McCaslin to think ahead to his thirty-fifth year, Faulkner continued, "because the rest of the book was part of his past too. To have taken that story out to print it alone I have always removed that part, which I have done. As a short story, a long short story, it has no part in it, but to me 'The Bear' is part of the novel, just as a chapter in the novel."[22]

As anyone who has ever tried to teach "The Bear" to a student unfamiliar with the background of *Go Down, Moses* can testify, the story is less than fully coherent on a first reading. Part of the problem, of course, comes from the convolutions of the prose, but not all. Again, the opening lines are instructive:

> There was a man and a dog too this time. Two beasts, counting Old Ben, the bear, and two men, counting Boon Hogganbeck, in whom some of the same blood ran which ran in Sam Fathers, even though Boon's was a plebian strain of it and only Sam and Old Ben and the mongrel Lion were taintless and incorruptible.
>
> He was sixteen. For six years now he had been a man's hunter. (*GDM,* 191)

This passage marks a smooth transition from the previous story or chapter, "The Old People," which describes Ike's killing of his first buck, and also deals with Sam Fathers and Boon Hogganbeck. But to the reader who lacks this information, this and subsequent passages of "The Bear" can be exasperating. The same kind of mutual dependence obtains between those stories which are more easily understood outside of the *Go Down, Moses* context. "Was" seems complete in itself, and it has been reprinted as a short story — though it is the only episode in *Go Down, Moses* which was not published as a short story prior to the publication of *Go Down, Moses*. But "Was" takes on significance in the remainder of the book as the story of the "romance" of Ike's parents, and as the initial exposition of the symbolic relations among whites and blacks, and between the hunting and the land which unites them all. The irony of "Delta Autumn" is increased by the knowledge of L.Q.C. McCaslin's role in "The Bear," and the title story is much more effective at the end of the McCaslin history than when it is separated from it.

The original versions of the short stories which were transformed into *Go Down, Moses* bear the same relation to that volume that the magazine stories do to *The Unvanquished*. They are self-contained, simple, and direct in the magazine versions, whereas they are interdependent, complex, and oblique in the novels. Together the two volumes support Edwin M. Holmes' observation that Faulkner's revisions tend toward "extended complexity, increased intensity, and evocation of mood."[23] A major difference between *The Unvanquished* and *Go Down, Moses* is that Faulkner apparently did not discern the connections among the stories in *Go Down, Moses* until after they had been written and published in magazine form. There is no continuity among the magazine versions of the *Go Down, Moses* stories, no Bayard Sartoris to connect them. The identity of the protagonist was not clearly established until *Go Down, Moses* itself was published. Ike McCaslin's role in "Lion," the first of the group to be published, is that of the proficient hunter who instructs the young boy, Quentin, in the same way that Sam Fathers instructs Ike in *Go Down, Moses*. It is tempting to identify the Quentin of "Lion" with Quentin Compson, for the boy of "Lion" resembles the narrator of "A Justice," the even earlier story, published in *These 13*, which also introduces Sam Fathers. Yet another early story, "A Bear Hunt," is set in Major de Spain's hunting camp and involves Uncle Ike McCaslin as a minor character. Neither "A Justice" nor "A Bear Hunt," however, is properly understood as a source of *Go Down, Moses*. One indication of this is that Faulkner included both in *Collected Stories,* while neither the magazine nor novel versions of any of the *Go Down, Moses* stories appear there. "Lion," "The Old People," "A Point of Law," "Pantaloon in Black," "Go Down, Moses," and "Delta Autumn" were all published in magazines and revised considerably for *Go Down, Moses*.

"Lion," "The Old People," and "The Bear," in their appearance as separate short stories, have a number of common features. Each centers on the experience of a sensitive youth. Each concerns the lessons of the hunt. Each ends with the youth's articulation of the significance of his experience. Each involves the youth's father in the development of the plot. Each is a self-contained short story. There are a number of differences among the three stories, and each differs considerably from the corresponding material in *Go Down, Moses*. "Lion" and "The Old People" are first-person narratives of the youthful protagonist, named Quentin in "Lion" but unnamed in "The Old People."

"The Bear" features an omniscient narrator and a nameless protagonist. The tone of "Lion" is ironic, and the lessons of the courageous dog are implied rather more frequently than they are expressed by the narrator. "This is how Lion's death affected the two people who loved him most," Quentin announces near the end of the story, "— if you could have called Boon's feeling for anything, love. And I suppose that you could, since they say you always love that which causes you suffering. Or maybe Boon did not consider being clawed by a bear suffering" (*USWF*, 197). Major de Spain, Quentin relates, would not return to the hunting camp after Lion and Old Ben were killed. But Boon returned to the camp and the story closes with the scene in which Boon rages over his inability to shoot the squirrels trapped in the gum tree. "He was living, as always, in the moment; nothing on earth — not Lion, not anything in the past — mattered to him except his helpless fury with his broken gun" (*USWF*, 200). Boon, unlike Major de Spain and Quentin, has apparently learned nothing from Lion. By ending the story with this incident, Quentin completes the description of his sense of loss. He can no longer share Boon's fierce concentration on the shooting of squirrels. He has tried to go back to the scene of the heroic struggle of Lion and Old Ben and Boon, but it has all changed:

> ... I entered the woods. They were changed, different. Of course it was just the summer; next fall they would be again as I remembered them. Then I knew that that was wrong; that they would never be again as I remembered them, and I, a boy, knew now why Major de Spain knew that he would never return and was too wise to try to. I went on. (*USWF*, 199)

"The Old People" concerns a different kind of discovery, the discovery of the meaning and value of the hunt. The frame of the story is the narrator's shooting of his first deer, which signifies his coming to manhood. The kill is more than the boy's demonstration of his competency as a woodsman; it is the occasion for his realization of the related values of human and animal life. Sam Fathers, the boy's tutor, knows and lives by the code of his Indian and black ancestors, choosing to reside in the wilderness. The boy's father understands and respects Sam's way of life, but the boy fails to comprehend Sam's love of the wilderness until he has shot his first deer. The blood of the deer with which Sam marks him symbolizes his initiation into the brotherhood of the hunters. Afterwards, he recalls:

> ... the wilderness watched us passing, less than inimical now and never inimical again since my buck still and forever leaped, the shaking gun-barrels coming constantly and forever steady at last, crashing, and still out of his moment of mortality the buck sprang, forever immortal, that moment of the buck, the shot, Sam Fathers and myself and the blood with which he had marked me forever, one with the wilderness which had now accepted me because Sam had said that I had done all right. (*USWF*, 207)

The end of the story is obscured by a discussion between the boy and his father of an incident which occurred the evening after the killing of the deer. The hunters surprise another buck and wait for it to return to its resting place. Sam and the boy see the buck, but the boy chooses not to shoot it, and they do not tell the others in the party of the incident. Having made his first kill, this scene implies, the boy no longer needs to kill. When he is talking with his father, however, the second buck becomes confused with the first, so that it seems as though the first buck is still alive. The father accepts the experience as genuinely mystical, for Sam had taken him into the same thicket when he shot *his* first deer, and he had had an experience similar to his son's. The incident of the second buck is credibly established, and it is a perfect expression in action of the lessons the boy has learned, but the total identification of the two bucks leaves the story with a troublesome ambiguity. "The Old People" has several echoes of other Faulkner works, in addition to the obvious carry-over of characters. Sam Fathers greets the second buck as the Negro in "Red Leaves" hailed the moccasin, "Oleh, Chief, Grandfather" (*USWF,* 210). The story of Ikkemotubbe is told again, to the effect that Sam Fathers is Ikkemotubbe's grandson, which differs from the story of Sam's parentage related in "A Justice." In the final dialogue between the boy and his father there is a clear anticipation of the last lines of Harry in *The Wild Palms.* "And even suffering and grieving is better than nothing," the father says, "there is nothing worse than not being alive" (*USWF,* 211).

"The Bear" was published in the *Post* on March 9, 1942, only two days before the publication of *Go Down, Moses.* This text is closer to "Lion" and "The Old People" in its structure and effects than it is to the famous section of the novel. One essential difference is that the young protagonist of the *Post* story is nameless, while *Go Down, Moses* develops the story of Old Ben and Lion as the experience of that most particular individual, Isaac McCaslin. There is a universality to "Lion," "The Old People," and the *Post* text of "The Bear" which is in large part the result of Faulkner's decision to leave his chief character (except for the single reference to Quentin in "Lion") nameless. Isaac McCaslin in *Go Down, Moses,* however, is a character with a very definite past, and his past has significant bearing on the material of "The Bear." The protagonists of the three magazine stories could be any young boy, but there are important ways in which Isaac McCaslin is uniquely himself, and he is treated with rather less sympathy and affection than are the boys of the stories.[24]

Like the boy in "The Old People," the boy in the *Post* text of "The Bear" learns something which is expressed in a concluding conversation with his father. The boy has seen a small, fierce mongrel dog attack Old Ben, and he has passed up a shot at the bear in an effort to save the dog. His father understands the action, and he gives the boy the "Ode on a Grecian Urn" to read. The boy is mystified. "He's talking about a girl," he objects. "He had to talk about something," the father explains:

> "Courage, and honor, and pride," his father said, "and pity, and love of justice and of liberty. They all touch the heart, and what the heart holds to become truth, as far as we know truth. Do you see now?"
> *Sam, and Old Ben, and Nip,* he thought. And himself too. He had been all right too. His father had said so. "Yes, sir," he said. (*USWF*, 295)

Old Ben does not die in the *Post* text; there is no hint of Lion, and there are only two brief, noncommittal references to Boon. The situation is very close to that of "The Old People," though the boy in "The Bear" does not tell his own story. Thus, the *Post* "Bear" is very different in its effects from the corresponding section of *Go Down, Moses,* though many of the details are the same, including the conversation about Keats' poem. But Isaac McCaslin does not see the point of the poem in relation to his refusal to shoot Old Ben:

> *He didn't know. Somehow it had seemed simpler than that, simpler than somebody talking in a book about a young man and a girl he would never need to grieve over because he could never approach any nearer and he would never have to get any further away.* (*GDM*, 297)

Ike recalls this conversation in his discussion of his repudiation of his inheritance with his cousin, McCaslin Edmonds. Ike, unlike the three young protagonists of the magazine stories, is finally unable or unwilling to accept the heritage of the wilderness, of Sam Fathers and Old Ben and Lion. He believes that his inheritance is tainted by the crimes of his grandfather, Lucius Quintus Carothers McCaslin, the slaveowner who compounded miscegenation with incest. By refusing to accept his grandfather's land, Ike hopes to atone for his ancestor's crimes. In the *Post* "Bear," as in "Lion" and "The Old People," there is no hint of this theme, nor does it figure in specific relation to Ike McCaslin in the magazine version of "Delta Autumn," the first of Faulkner's stories in which Ike is a central character.

In *Go Down, Moses,* "Delta Autumn" shows Ike's failure to escape his family's complicity in the degradation of blacks. His shrill reaction against the young woman who has borne Roth Edmonds' child is met with the succinct rebuttal: "Old man, have you lived so long and forgotten so much that you dont remember anything you ever knew or felt or even heard about love?" (*GDM*, 363). The same line is delivered, even more tersely, in the version of "Delta Autumn" published in *Story* (May-June 1942), but the situation in the short story is entirely different, for neither of the principals is related to McCaslin. In *Go Down, Moses* Ike is childless, a direct result of his repudiation of his inheritance, while the *Story* version says, "he had had a wife and children once though no more" (*USWF*, 274). References in the *Story* text to Ike's ownership of the land are not complicated by the reader's knowledge of Ike's repudiation. The *Go Down, Moses* text of the episode demonstrates the folly of Ike's attempt at repudiation, while the short story is primarily concerned with Uncle Ike's discovery that he and men like himself are responsible for the destruction of the wilderness. In *Go Down, Moses* Faulkner takes some pains to make explicit the connection between Ike's conveyance of the land to McCaslin Edmonds, and Roth's treatment of the woman who is his cousin. "You spoiled him," the woman tells Ike, "when you gave to his grandfather that land which didn't belong to him, not even half of it by will or even law" (*GDM*, 370). There is no corresponding statement in the short story, for there are no family ties among the participants. *Go Down, Moses* also shows the woman to be familiar with the earliest parts of the family history, including the incident described in "Was":

> "His great great — Wait a minute — great great *great* grandfather was your grandfather. McCaslin. Only it got to be Edmonds. Your cousin McCaslin was there that day when your father and Uncle Buddy won Tennie from Mr. Beauchamp for the one that had no name but Terrel so you called him Tomey's Terrel, to marry. But after that it got to be Edmonds." (*GDM*, 359)

Another addition to *Go Down, Moses*, Ike's gift to the woman of the silver hunting horn, also connects "Delta Autumn" with earlier material.

The short stories relating to the McCaslin blacks are also much different in emphasis from the related episodes in *Go Down, Moses*. "A Point of Law," the story of Lucas Beauchamp and George Wilkins' whisky stills, and "Gold is Not Always," the story of Lucas Beauchamp's venture into the gold-hunting business, are both exercises in minstrel comedy, but in "The Fire and the Hearth" they are developed in the context of Lucas' family ties with the Edmondses, particularly that with Zack Edmonds.[25] Both the short story "Pantaloon in Black" and the novel-section of the same title mention that Rider rents from Carothers Edmonds, and that Rider's fire is like the one Lucas Beauchamp lighted on his hearth forty-five years ago, but, again, the more complicated allusions of *Go Down, Moses* are missing from the story. The title story separated from the material which precedes it in *Go Down, Moses* is essentially a demonstration of Gavin Stevens' *noblesse oblige*, while in the novel the depth of Stevens' ignorance of the true situation is apparent.

Every short story in *Go Down, Moses* is altered by the McCaslin-Edmonds-Beauchamp relationships, and all of *Go Down, Moses* is related to Ike's futile attempt to repudiate the legacy of his grandfather. L.Q.C. McCaslin never appears in any of the short stories and is only a shadowy figure in *Go Down, Moses,* but he may be, as John L. Longley has written, "Faulkner's most monumental villain, the person who most nearly approaches the Shakespearean and Miltonic scale."[26] His absence from the earlier short stories is crucial to an understanding of the ways in which *Go Down, Moses* was unified, for it is his crimes which spoil the lessons of the wilderness for Ike. The *Go Down, Moses* structure contains one of the few clear cases in which Faulkner chose to develop tragic implications from material which was originally comic and affirmative.

Knight's Gambit and *Big Woods*

Two lesser volumes of stories gathered during his period of consolidation show Faulkner's tendency to impose a definite order on what would at first glance appear to be unrelated material. The collections are interesting in different ways. *Knight's Gambit* is arranged in the order in which the separate stories were published. Read consecutively, these stories provide some insight into Faulkner's developing conception of Gavin Stevens, a character whose relation to his creator has proved crucial for readers of the novels from *Light in August* on. *Big Woods*, while important in considering Faulkner's treatment of the experience and metaphor of the hunt, is perhaps even more important in that it calls attention to the characteristic changes in the later style, which in turn reflect the difference between Faulkner's earlier and later attitudes. In *Collected Stories,* as in *These 13* and *Doctor Martino*, Faulkner made few changes between the magazine and collected versions of stories, and he chose not to arrange them in the order in which they were written or published. In *Knight's Gambit*, though there are few differences between the magazine versions and those of the collections — the title story had not been previously printed — their order of appearance in the volume follows the order of publication and the approximate chronology of fictional events. In *Big Woods* Faulkner made drastic alterations in stories which had been published before, but he made no attempt to arrange them in the order of composition or publication. *Knight's Gambit,* then, shows several stages of Faulkner's attitude toward a single character, while *Big Woods* represents his attempt to impose a single attitude on a body of material.

Knight's Gambit, however, does not include anything like all the Gavin Stevens material Faulkner had composed through 1949.[27] Stevens figures in "Hair" and "The Tall Men," both of which Faulkner saved for *Collected Stories,* and he appears also in *Light in August*, "Go Down, Moses," *Go Down, Moses,* and *Intruder in the Dust.* The *Knight's Gambit* stories all feature Stevens the detective-lawyer as the major figure. In other stories and novels he is generally a minor character, an observer and commentator who is neither particularly astute nor reliable and who is in fact often myopic or wrong-headed. Consider his dissertation on Joe Christmas in *Light in August*:

> But his blood would not be quiet, let him save it. It would not be either one or the other and let his body save itself. Because the black blood drove him first to the Negro cabin.

And then the white blood drove him out of there, as it was the black blood which snatched up the pistol and the white blood which would not let him fire it. And it was the white blood which sent him to the minister, which rising in him for the last and final time, sent him against all reason and all reality, into the embrace of a chimera, a blind faith in something read in a printed book. Then I believe that the white blood deserted him for a moment. (*LIA*, 393)

This passage, Faulkner later observed, "is an assumption, a rationalization that Stevens made" (*FIU*, 72). Stevens is one of the people who helped destroy Christmas and rationalized their act by deciding what he was. It is not a flattering picture of the lawyer, who here reveals his intellectual kinship with Joe Brown and Percy Grimm.

The detective story is essentially a comic form which proceeds from mystery to knowledge, from crime to punishment, by means of deliberate manipulation of conventions by the artist, and through the persistent exercise of reason by the detective. The *Knight's Gambit* stories show that Faulkner was quite familiar with the conventions of detective fiction, though he chose to manipulate them through a character who lacks both the consummate rationality of C. Auguste Dupin and Sherlock Holmes, and the superficial toughness of Perry Mason and Mike Hammer.

"Smoke," the first story in *Knight's Gambit,* was probably the first story Faulkner wrote about Gavin Stevens, though "Hair," probably written about the same time, marks his first published appearance. "Smoke" gives only the vaguest indications of Gavin's appearance and character. The essential interest in the story is in the leisurely way Stevens sets his trap for the murderer, and in the way Faulkner sets his trap for the reader. Virtually all the shopworn tricks of detective/courtroom fiction are plied in the story. Stevens points us toward an obvious suspect, young Anselm Holland, and to a devious suspect, Virginius Holland, before encouraging the seemingly extraneous character, Granby Dodge, to incriminate himself. There is a false confession by young Anse, a reliable witness in Old Job. The murder was apparently committed in a locked room, and the murderer is surprised by an ingenious but simple trick. Among the vital ingredients of superior detective fiction is the presentation to the reader of the crucial evidence within a sufficiency of appearances from which the reality of the situation may be adduced. Faulkner virtually ignores this requirement, for Stevens withholds almost every piece of evidence which has led him to suspect Granby Dodge. It is not until the very end of the story that we are told of the confession of the Memphis thug hired by Dodge, of Dodge's purchase of the rat poison, of Dodge's inquiries to Stevens about wills.

It would of course destroy the mystery if all these things were known from the beginning. There would be no surprise and no story. The withholding of this information helps Faulkner fulfill the expectation that the detective will display an astonishing ability to interpret the facts, to separate appearance and reality. The proceedings in "Smoke" all seem to point to the guilt of Virginius Holland, but all of Stevens' descriptions of the murderer apply equally to Granby Dodge. Since Dodge is but a minor character, a reader is likely not to think much about him, and may simply assume the guilt of Virginius. "Smoke" is, therefore, at least satisfactory in the surprise of the discovery:

> As one we leaned across the table and looked down upon the sandy and hopeless mediocrity of Granby Dodge's head as he knelt on the floor and flapped at the fading smoke with his hands. (*KG*, 33)

"Smoke" does not present a particularly favorable picture of Gavin Stevens. His discovery of Granby Dodge's guilt, when the reader is told what Stevens knows, seems unremarkable, and the device of putting smoke in the brass box is nothing more than a questionably ingenious ruse. The lawyer in "Smoke" is no more admirable than the lawyer in *Light in August*, and he is even less interesting as a character. More favorable is the lawyer Stevens of "Hair," a story which also depends on the withholding of vital information, though it is not concerned with the discovery of a crime. "Hair" tells of the enduring devotion of the barber Hawkshaw to his dead fianceé and her family, and to the girl, Susan Reed, whom he eventually marries. Stevens is a minor but significant figure in "Hair." He observes with the nameless narrator the mystifying actions of Hawkshaw, and manages to surprise the narrator with the news that the barber and Susan have been married. All the evidence the narrator presents, up to the last lines of the story, prepares us for an unhappy ending. Hawkshaw's love seems to have been wasted on two women, one weak and the other untrustworthy. But Hawkshaw finally gets the girl, and Stevens realizes that Hawkshaw's reward is sufficient to compensate for Susan Reed's supposed promiscuity. "Hair" shows the narrator telling a story on himself, a story which suggests that he has been mistaken in his assessment of Hawkshaw, of Susan Reed, and of the human condition. Though it is not clear to what extent Stevens shares the narrator's initial pessimism, he obviously respects Hawkshaw:

> "Maybe he'll just go off and die," I said.
> "Maybe he will," Stevens said.
> "Well," I said, "he wont be the first man to tilt at windmills."
> "He wont be the first man to die, either," Stevens said. (*CS*, 144)

"Hair" describes Stevens as "a smart man: not like the usual pedagogue lawyer and office holder" (*CS*, 144), and it shows that he has the respect of men like the travelling salesman who narrates the story. Other details of his background are sketched in *Light in August*:

He is the District Attorney, a Harvard graduate, a Phi Beta Kappa: a tall, loosejointed man with an untidy mop of irongray hair, wearing always loose and unpressed dark gray clothes. His family is old in Jefferson: his ancestors owned slaves there and his grandfather knew (and also hated, a publicly congratulated Colonel Sartoris when they died) Miss Burden's grandfather and brother. He has an easy quiet way with country people, with the voters and the juries; he can be seen now and then squatting among the overalls on the porches of country stores for a whole summer afternoon, talking to them in their own idiom about nothing at all. (*LIA*, 388-89)

As he would later do for Samuel Worsham Beauchamp in "Go Down, Moses," Stevens arranges for the body of Joe Christmas to be returned to the family, but in both texts it is apparent that he has little understanding of either the murderer or his family. *Light in August* describes a Gavin Stevens who has achieved the objective symbols of intelligence. He fancies himself a simple and knowledgeable countryman, but he is neither as intelligent or as knowledgeable as he thinks.

"Monk," the second story in *Knight's Gambit*, is narrated by Gavin Stevens' nephew. The story shows Stevens' accidental success as a detective and his failure as a reformer. A young moron named Monk is arrested for murder, and the evidence against him is sufficiently damning to result in a conviction and a sentence of life imprisonment. Later the real murderer confesses, and Stevens secures Monk's pardon. Monk, however, refuses to leave the penitentiary, where he is quite happy. A short time later Monk brutally murders the prison warden, for whom he had previously shown a good deal of affection. The mystery is not *what* happened, but *why* it happened. Stevens eventually discovers quite by accident that Monk had been gulled by another prisoner who had convinced the moron that the warden must be killed. Stevens does not reveal the other prisoner's culpability, and he never tells the story to anyone except his nephew.

The second prisoner, Terrel, is pardoned incidentally to the current Governor's campaign, and Stevens makes no effort to persuade the parole board that Terrel is responsible for the deaths of both the warden and Monk. Stevens, the Governor makes plain, is an anachronistic "gentleman," "trying to bring the notions of 1860 into the politics of the nineteen hundreds" (*KG*, 54). He has never quite given up the hope that he can change the business of politics. Stevens is disturbed by his own conduct, and by the world of the Governor and Terrel:

It was in the middle of the morning, and hot, but he started back to Jefferson at once, riding across the broad, heat-miraged land, between the cotton and corn of God's long-fecund, remorseless acres, which would outlast any corruption and injustice. He was glad of the heat, he said; glad to be sweating, sweating out of himself the smell and the taste of where he had been. (*KG*, 59-60)

Stevens' abilities and limitations are clearly defined in "Monk." He is a capable observer and an astute judge of Monk's character, but he is unable to cope effectively with the likes of the Governor and Terrel. Thus, he is perceptive and weak, and he is glad to withdraw from a situation in which his ideals might be tested in action.

In "Hand Upon the Waters," the third *Knight's Gambit* story, Stevens acts. He shows perceptivity in deducing that Lonnie Grinnup was murdered, and he sets a successful trap for the murderer. Though he has suspected the wrong man, Stevens' actions nevertheless result in the solution of the case. In protecting the half-wit who avenges Lonnie's murder, Stevens again shows his devotion to an abstract, extralegal notion of justice. He shows some physical courage in facing the Ballenbaugh brothers unarmed, and he is wounded for his trouble. "Hand Upon the Waters" also develops the sense of Stevens as the inheritor of the Yoknapatawpha tradition, for he first becomes interested in the death of Lonnie Grinnup because Grinnup and Stevens are the last descendants of the county's founders.

The fourth *Knight's Gambit* story, "Tomorrow," shows Stevens investigating a mystery which arises not from the perpetration of a crime, but from the temporary and inexplicable delay in the achievement of justice. A man named Bookwright has killed, clearly in self-defense, a young hell-raiser named Buck Thorpe. Bookwright is acquitted, but only after his first trial ends in a hung jury. The man responsible for the hung jury is Stonewall Jackson Fentry, a poor farmer who, Stevens eventually learns, had loved Thorpe's mother and had cared for the boy after the mother died. "Tomorrow," like "Monk," is narrated by Gavin's nephew, here identified as "Chick." The story is the first in which Stevens manages to convey a positive lesson to his auditor. The patience, fidelity, and quiet devotion of Jackson Fentry to the memory of the woman and child he had loved recalls Hawkshaw's devotion to Sophy Starnes and Susan Reed in "Hair," and Byron Bunch's silent devotion to Lena Grove in *Light in August*. Fentry demonstrates the capacity, Stevens tells Chick, of "the lonely and invincible of the earth — to endure and endure and then endure, tomorrow and tomorrow and tomorrow. Of course, he wasn't going to vote Bookwright free" (*KG*, 104). Chick refuses to accept this, maintaining that he himself would have freed Bookwright. Stevens, in a speech which parallels the final scenes of "The Old People" and "The Bear" — he even puts his hand on Chick's knee as Quentin's father does in "The Old People" — completes his explanation and his lesson:

> "It was because somewhere in that debased and brutalized flesh which Bookwright slew there still remained, not the spirit maybe, but at least the memory, of that little boy, that Jackson and Longstreet Fentry, even though the man the boy had become didn't know and only Fentry did. And you wouldn't have freed him either. Don't ever forget that. Never." (*KG*, 105)

"An Error in Chemistry," the fifth *Knight's Gambit* story, won a prize in the *Ellery Queen's Mystery Magazine* contest for 1946. Like "Tomorrow," the story is narrated by Gavin's nephew, but the boy is not named, nor is he an important character in the story. "An Error in Chemistry" is concerned with the criminal hubris of Joel Flint, who, having murdered his wife and his father-in-law, disguises himself as the latter and flaunts his disguise at Stevens and the local sheriff. It is only when he tries to make a toddy by dissolving sugar in raw whisky, the "error" of the title, that Stevens, his nephew, and the sheriff penetrate the disguise. "An Error in Chemistry" shows Stevens at his best form as the ingenious detective, and his explanation of Flint's pride is masterful. The story, however, is improbable, and contains too many blatantly exploited mystery conventions, particularly in Stevens' ironic assumption of his own superiority to the sheriff, an obtuse type who might be an American cousin of Holmes' foils Lestrade and Gregson.

Detective stories, W.H. Auden has said, resemble Greek tragedy in that in both the decisive event has taken place before the story begins.[28] The title story of *Knight's Gambit*, however, shows Stevens accomplishing what Sherlock Holmes says is the greatest of all detective feats, the anticipation and prevention of an intended crime. The story demonstrates the progress of Gavin Stevens as detective and as his nephew's tutor, but it also recalls the Stevens of *Light in August*:

> ... that glib and talkative man who talked so much and so glibly, particularly about things which had absolutely no concern with him, that his indeed was a split personality: the one, the lawyer, the county attorney who walked and breathed and displaced air: the other, the garrulous facile voice so garrulous and facile that it seemed to have no connection with reality at all and presently hearing it was like listening not even to fiction but to literature. (*KG*, 141)

In "Knight's Gambit" Stevens mystifies his nephew, constantly talking of seemingly irrelevant matters while unravelling the mystery of Max Harriss. Harriss breaks in on Gavin and Chick, demanding that Stevens, as County Attorney, takes steps to deport Captain Gualdres, a house-guest of the Harriss family. Max's contention is that Gualdres has designs on the family fortune and has turned his attentions to their mother after jilting the sister. Stevens refuses the young man's demand, and gradually he discovers the truth. Young Harriss is insanely jealous of Gualdres, who has proved his superiority in riding and fencing, and who is in fact honorably in love with the sister. Stevens then learns that Max Harriss has purchased a wild stallion, and correctly guesses that Harriss is planning to murder Gualdres with it. The murder is prevented, Gualdres and Miss Harriss are married, and Max, at Stevens' suggestion, enlists in the army. Stevens, to complete the story, finally marries Mrs. Harriss with whom he has been in love for years.

"I have improved," Stevens tells Chick in the last line of the story, explaining how he got over the notion that he was too intelligent for Mrs. Harriss (*KG*, 246). Stevens does seem "improved," for he no longer smugly assumes the correctness of his own attitudes, he no longer resorts to mere trickery to win legal points, he is no longer afraid to act, and he no longer retreats from the occasionally sordid realities of the world. "Knight's Gambit" is Faulkner's most favorable treatment of Stevens, who again betrays his deficiencies in *Intruder in the Dust, The Town,* and *The Mansion.* The *Knight's Gambit* stories have been dismissed by Cowley as "examples of misapplied but impressive ingenuity."[29] Michael Millgate says the detective story form excited Faulkner's ingenuity "without calling out the full extent of his powers."[30] *Knight's Gambit,* he maintains, "must be seen primarily as a series of more or less deliberate exercises on the way to his final conception and characterization of Gavin Stevens." Though some stories, "Smoke" and "An Error in Chemistry," in particular, are deliberate exercises, they are not indicative of a long-range plan on Faulkner's part to "improve" Gavin Stevens. The changes in Stevens, rather, reflect the mellowing of Faulkner.

Big Woods includes revised versions of "The Bear," "The Old People," "A Bear Hunt," and "Race at Morning," and incorporates material from "Red Leaves," "Delta Autumn," "A Justice," *Requiem for a Nun,* and "Mississippi." Although it is customary to treat *Big Woods* as a lesser collection of previously published material, the substantial revisions Faulkner made in the separate stories, and the care with which the material is organized, suggest that it will bear examination as a unified volume, a new work. "The Bear," for instance, generally follows the *Go Down, Moses* text, but in it Ike is nearly always referred to as "the boy," and, with Part IV omitted, the complications of L.Q.C. McCaslin's legacy are avoided. "The Bear" in *Big Woods* represents the text of that narrative which Faulkner believed should be read as a short story. The fragment of "Delta Autumn" which concludes the volume omits the episode of Uncle Ike's encounter with the black woman, so both the impersonal treatment of miscegenation in the *Story* text and the personal treatment of *Go Down, Moses* are absent. The fragment concentrates on the killing of the doe, and Uncle Ike's final lament is understood as his conscious recognition of the passing of the big woods, debased by the men who hunt without honor. "A Bear Hunt" is revised to make Lucius Hogganbeck, a son of Boon, the victim of Ratliff's practical joke, and the story tells that Major de Spain's son supports Lucius Hogganbeck, as his father had supported Boon.

The major revisions for *Big Woods* are stylistic, rather than factual, and they are easily seen in two different versions of a passage from "Delta Autumn."

Soon now they would enter the Delta. The sensation was familiar to him. It had been renewed like this each last week in November for more than fifty years — the last hill, at the foot of which the rich unbroken alluvial flatness began as the sea began at the base of its cliffs, dissolving away beneath the unhurried November rain as the sea itself would dissolve away. (*GDM*, 335)

The old hunter said: soon we will enter the woods. It is not new to me, since I have been doing it each November for over seventy years — this last hill, at the foot of which the rich unbroken alluvial flatness begins as the sea begins at the base of the cliffs, dissolving away beneath the unhurried November rain as the sea itself dissolves away. (*BW*, 199)

The shift from omniscient to first-person narration establishes Uncle Ike as a more articulate character and encourages the natural identification of the reader with the narrator. The change from past tense to present tense is apparently intended to make the *Big Woods* version more immediate by eliminating the implied contrast between time past and time present. In *Big Woods* Uncle Ike's narrative illustrates the notion of time which Faulkner developed repeatedly. "There isn't any time," he told Loïc Bouvard:

In fact I agree pretty much with Bergson's theory of the fluidity of time. There is only the present moment, in which I include both the past and the future, and that is eternity. In my opinion time can be shaped quite a bit by the artist; after all, man is never time's slave. (*LIG*, 70)

The *Big Woods* fragment of "Delta Autumn" shows Uncle Ike conquering time in ways that he is unable to achieve in *Go Down, Moses,* where he is, in a sense, time's slave. The change in detail from fifty to seventy years in the woods also indicates a desire on Faulkner's part to show a final version of Uncle Ike as time's conqueror. The elimination of the limiting and local details of Isaac McCaslin's biography is also suggested by the change of the scene from "the Delta" to "the woods." Of course, there is no question that both versions are set in the Delta, but by omitting the explicit geographical reference Faulkner creates the impression that the incident could take place in any woods, and that Uncle Ike is no more bound by place than by time.

The reuse of material in *Big Woods* provides one more instance of Faulkner's desire to tell a story again, and to tell it better, and the entire volume shows him putting into practice his belief that form and integration are essential to a book of short stories. In the revision of the steamboat incident which had been part of the background of "Red Leaves" and "A Justice," Faulkner eliminated the references to the exploitation of the slaves by the Indians, and developed Ikkemotubbe's dissatisfaction with his absurd accomplishment. Similarly, the revised text of "Red Leaves" concentrates on Parts IV and V of the earlier story, omitting most of the explicit discussions of slavery, as well as the satiric portrait of Moketubbe and his red slippers. The opening section of *Big Woods*, revised from an article published in *Holiday* magazine in 1954, also eliminates many of the expressions of cynicism and disgust which appear in the article.[31] The entire *Big Woods* collection is elegiac in tone, a celebration of the land, a lament for its passing, and for the passing of the men who hunted it. In preparing his elegy, Faulkner was careful to eliminate the material which might have demeaned his hunters.

Apocrypha

In organizing *Collected Stories* Faulkner omitted several stories which had been published previously and which had not appeared in *The Unvanquished, Go Down, Moses,* or *Knight's Gambit,* and which had not been assimilated into any of the novels. None of the omitted stories is among his best, so Faulkner's failure to include them may well show his tacit recognition of their inferiority. The fact that he did not choose to collect any of these stories in either *These 13* or *Doctor Martino* would also support this interpretation. But since Faulkner's original outline of *Collected Stories* did not include four stories which eventually appeared in the collection, he may have omitted some deliberately, or he may have failed to remember some. But since several of Faulkner's better stories, already revised for novels, were also omitted from *Collected Stories,* it is legitimate to consider these "apocryphal" stories on their own merits.

The omission of "Thrift" from *Collected Stories* is regrettable. It is an amusing story of the mercenary Scot, MacWyrglinchbeath, who organizes his whole tour of duty in the First World War to maximize his monetary profit. He is a source of delight and consternation to his officers, and he imperturbably crashes a plane, deserts, and returns to fly dangerous missions in an ancient and cumbersome aircraft — all to make and save money. He refuses a promotion, not because of his contempt for officers, but because he concludes that it would cost him too much money to accept it. He excites the admiration and affection of such aviators as Robinson and Ffollansbye, and he avenges Robinson's death at considerable risk to himself. Returning home after the war, he resumes his old way of life, slightly chagrined that he is unable to make a profit on his cow, which has calved in his absence. "Thrift" provides numerous contrasts and connections with Faulkner's other stories of the First World War. There is a Ffollansbye in "All the Dead Pilots," for example, and MacWyrglinchbeath gets into the insurance business as Harry does in *A Fable.* The most obvious contrast, however, is between "Thrift" and "Victory," which also features a Scot, the pathetic Gray who is so affected by his war experiences that he cannot go home again. Here, perhaps, is the explanation of Faulkner's decision to exclude "Thrift" from *Collected Stories.* "Thrift" is undeniably comic and would not be at all compatible with the other stories grouped together in "The Wasteland," the only section in which it could conceivably be placed. Faulkner had earlier chosen not to include "Thrift" with the other war stories which constitute the opening section of *These 13,* and he was perhaps guided by the same principle of selection in both instances.[32]

The exclusion of "Once Aboard the Lugger," "Miss Zilphia Gant," and "Idyll in the Desert" from *Collected Stories,* is both less and more difficult to explain. Each would have fit rather neatly into the framework of *Collected Stories,* "Miss Zilphia Gant" in "The Village," and the other two in "The Middle Ground." Faulkner may have believed that the inclusion of these stories in the volume would do him no honor, tacitly accepting the judgment of the many editors who had rejected them. "Miss Zilphia Gant" was turned down by the *American Mercury, Scribner's Miscellany,* and the *Southwest Review* before it was published in a limited edition by the Book Club of Texas.[33] "Idyll in the Desert" was refused by the *American Mercury, Liberty,* the *Post, Scribner's, Harper's,* and *Woman's Home Companion* before Faulkner's agent, Ben Wasson, arranged for the limited edition published by Random House.[34] "Once Aboard the Lugger" is not listed in Faulkner's story-sending schedule and was probably "retired" by Faulkner before he began to keep meticulous records.

The obscure place of publication of "Once Aboard the Lugger" may indicate that Faulkner did not regard the story highly, for at the time it was published he could probably have commanded a high price for it had it been accepted by one of the national magazines. The story describes a bootlegging operation out of New Orleans, and is interesting for its combination of surface toughness and deeper lyricism, the stylistic equivalent of the narrator's rough exterior and sensitive consciousness. In action and speech he appears to be simply a young man who is making money by smuggling whisky, but the prose in which he tells his story is elegant in places. Having finished loading the whisky onto the boat, he tries to sleep, but he is too aware of his snoring companions and "the dark high breath of the sea in the pines":

> Out of this sound another sound grew, mounted swiftly, and I raised my head and watched a red navigating light and that pale wing of water that seemed to have a quality of luminousness of its own, stand up and pass and fade, and I thought of Conrad's centaur, the half man, half tugboat, charging up and down the river in the same higheared, myopic haste, purposeful but without destination, oblivious to all save what was immediately in its path, and to that a dire and violent menace. Then it was gone, and sound too died away, and I lay back again while my muscles jerked and twitched to the fading echo of the old striving and the Hush   Hush   of the sea in my ears.
> (*USWF,* 358)

As in the case of the young man in "Carcassonne," there is here a discrepancy between the central character's actions and his thoughts and feelings. Another variation on this theme can be found in "Miss Zilphia Gant" and "Idyll in the Desert," which both have protagonists whose actions and motives are completely misunderstood by those who observe them. Miss Zilphia Gant resembles Miss Emily Grierson in some important ways and the title character of "Elly" in others. All three women feel the debilitating consequences of sexual frustration, and all three are betrayed by men. Miss Zilphia Gant is the victim of her mother's hatred of men, just as Miss Emily is warped by her father's "protection," and as Elly is influenced by her grandmother's malevolence. Miss Zilphia's mother, deserted by her husband for another woman, hunts the pair down and kills them. She returns home and devotes her life to protecting Zilphia from male attention. Inevitably, Zilphia falls in love. Her mother breaks up the affair, and the young man leaves town. That night, the mother dies. Zilphia believes that the young man will return, but finally she learns that he is married to another woman. Zilphia has the couple watched by a detective and vicariously shares their marriage. The woman dies in childbirth, and the husband is killed in an automobile accident at the same time. Miss Zilphia leaves Jefferson and returns later with the couple's daughter, who is assumed by the townspeople to be her own. She then proceeds to raise the girl as her own mother raised her, carefully guarding the child from other children and by implication from the men who have betrayed them. The repetition of Mrs. Gant's desertion in Zilphia's life is rather too neat, and the whole story depends heavily on the improbable coincidence that Zilphia learns of the young man's marriage, and on the even more improbable coincidence that the young man is killed and the mother dies when the child is born. On the whole, the presence of "A Rose for Emily" and "Elly" in *Collected Stories* would make the inclusion of "Miss Zilphia Gant" a redundancy.[35]

"Idyll in the Desert" also concerns the perfidy of men and the thankless devotion of their women, and it also depends for its effects on coincidence and a neat reversal of fortune. A young tubercular man named Darrel Howes, or House, comes to a remote Arizona ranch to recuperate. When his strength seems to be failing, he sends for his lover, the wife of his former employer. The woman leaves her husband and nurses Howes back to health. She then contracts tuberculosis and Howes, apparently unaware of her condition, leaves. The woman's husband is notified, and he sends money to her in such a fashion that she believes it is from Howes. When she is about to die, her husband arranges for her to be moved to Los Angeles. On the same train are Howes and his new bride. Howes apparently does not recognize her, and she is dead when the train reaches Los Angeles. The primary interest in the story is in the manner of its narration. Like "Pennsylvania Station" and "Black Music," "Idyll in the Desert" evolves from a conversation between a young man who has had no direct contact with the central characters and an older man who has been directly involved with them. The older man, a mail rider named Crump, resembles some of Mark Twain's storytellers who have to be reminded constantly of the story they are supposed to be telling. Since Faulkner's own publisher owned the rights to the story, there would have been no problem in arranging for its publication in *Collected Stories,* and, in view of the perseverance Faulkner displayed in seeking to have the story published, there can be little question that he once had some regard for it, but it is possible that he felt it would not be a significant addition to "The Middle Ground," already the longest section of *Collected Stories.*

Several Faulkner stories have been published since his death, including texts from the earlier and later parts of his career. "The Wishing Tree" is a fantasy written for a young girl, a friend of Faulkner's family, and later copied by hand by Faulkner for his godson.[36] "Mr. Acarius," written in the early fifties, is apparently the one story written in the years of fame which Faulkner was unable to publish. "The Wishing Tree" is of only passing interest. It shows Faulkner's facility with the manipulations of a fairy tale in the service of a moral, and it contains echoes of *Alice in Wonderland* and of A.A. Milne's children's verse. Faulkner could be pleasant and sentimental when he chose to, even at the time he was writing *The Sound and the Fury.* "The Wishing Tree" also invites comparison with *Mayday,* another early narrative fantasy published posthumously.

"Mr. Acarius" shows Faulkner's later rendering of a personality type which had interested him from the beginning. Mr. Acarius is a failed martyr, a man who seeks to demonstrate his humanity by deliberately degrading himself. In co-operation with his skeptical doctor, Mr. Acarius gets devastatingly drunk and has himself committed to an alcoholics' hospital. His explanation of his behavior includes an admission that his attempt "to experience man, the human race," is doomed to failure:

> Mankind. People. Man. I shall be one with man, victim of his own base appetites and now struggling to extricate himself from that debasement. Maybe it's my fault that I'm incapable of anything but Scotch, and so our bullpen will be a Scotch one where for a little expense we can have peace, quiet for the lacerated and screaming nerves, sympathy, understanding ... and maybe what my fellow inmates are trying to escape from — the too many mistresses or wives or the too much money or responsibility or whatever else it is that drives into escape the sort of people who can afford to pay fifty dollars a day for the privilege of escaping — will not bear mention in the same breath with that which drives one who can afford no better, even to canned heat. But at least we will be together in having failed to escape and in knowing in the last analysis there is no escape, that you can never escape and, whether you will or not, you must reenter the world and bear yourself in it and its lacerations and all its anguish of breathing, to support and comfort one another in that knowledge and that attempt. (*USWF,* 437-38)

In the hospital Mr. Acarius cannot enter completely into the degradation of his fellow inmates. Rather, he is repelled by them, and he is appalled at the lengths to which they are willing to go in order to get more liquor. One inmate dies after a struggle with a nurse who has locked up the liquor, and Mr. Acarius takes advantage of the ensuing confusion to make his escape. He is arrested, released in his doctor's custody, and returns to his home, where he smashes all of his liquor bottles in the bathtub. "So you entered mankind, and found the place already occupied," his doctor observes. "Yes," Mr. Acarius cries. "You can't beat him. You cannot. You never will. Never" (*USWF,* 448).

Like Quentin Compson in *The Sound and the Fury,* Mr. Acarius wishes desperately to atone for a sin he lacks the courage to commit. Unlike Quentin, however, Mr. Acarius knows precisely what he is doing. Though he fails to experience pure penance in the hospital, his attempt is paradoxically successful, for through it he learns the folly of his behavior.[31]

The short pieces Faulkner wrote in New Orleans are so clearly inferior even to *Soldier's Pay* and *Mosquitoes* that it is little wonder Faulkner took no interest in collecting them. They anticipate a number of themes, characters, situations, and techniques which Faulkner was to employ in later fiction, but no one of them is of sufficient fictional merit to be accorded extended discussion. The chief deficiencies of these pieces are the mechanical exploitation of melodrama, an indulgence in easy irony, and flatness of characterization. The tone of the prose is that labored nonchalance dominant in Faulkner's early critical essays. His review of Edna St. Vincent Millay's *Aria da Capo,* for example, describes the play as "something new enough to be outstanding in this age of mental puberty, this loud gesturing of the aesthetic messiahs of our emotional Valhalla who have one eye on the ball and the other on the grandstand" (*EPP,* 84). The same strained, self-conscious rhetoric characterizes the sketch entitled "Mirrors of Chartres Street":

> Later, from a railed balcony — Mendelssohn impervious in iron — I saw him for the last time. The moon had crawled up the sky like a fat spider and planes of light and shadow were despair for the Vorticist schools. (Even those who carved those strange flathanded creatures on the Temple of Rameses must have dreamed New Orleans by moonlight.) (*NOS,* 16)

Another pose in the New Orleans pieces is that of belligerent and subliterate toughness, rendered through the narrative point-of-view and voice of a conventionally street-smart character. "Cheest," for example, is told by a self-impressed young jockey:

> "Listen, fellow," I says, "they can't nobody tell me nothing about the racing game."
> "Nor about nothing else: I already seen that."
> "Say," I says, looking him in the eye, "I'll quit you cold, see?"
> "That's fair enough; that's how I found you — cold and broke, too."
> "Say," I comes back, "you think you're smart, don't you?"
> "I got to be," he says, "or I'd been in the poorhouse ten years ago, with a stable full of beagles and clever children all eating their damn heads off."
> "Well, anyway we talked on back and forth, him not making nothing offa me — I been around, see? I have ridden the best in the land and I an't had enough mud in my face to

roon my complexion, neither. Ask anyone who's followed the game, suggest my name to them — Potter's the name, Jack Potter. Yeh. (*NOS*, 41-42)

Faulkner was eventually to make great fiction by adopting the narrative voice of an unsympathetic character like Jason Compson. Stories such as "That Will Be Fine" and "Honor" depend for their effects on the implicit rejection of the storyteller's cynicism, but "Cheest" is merely an obvious exercise in literary slumming.

Similarly, Faulkner's shifting point-of-view in "New Orleans" was apparently his first experiment with a technique which was to be crucial in *The Sound and the Fury, As I Lay Dying,* and other novels, though the speakers in this sketch are sentimentally conceived types, rather than particular and problematic individuals. The vast majority of the characters in *New Orleans Sketches* are victims. They are victims of their own ignorance, like the gullible black in "Sunset," the pretentious beggar in "Chance," the violent Antonio in "Jealousy." Others are victims of other people's malice, or of their own physical and moral weaknesses. The New Orleans world which Faulkner describes is dominated by misery, pathos, and obvious irony. It is only in the story set in what might well be rural Mississippi that Faulkner finds materials which seem to be truly congenial to him. "The Liar" has many awkward narrative passages, but it shows Faulkner dealing with characters who prefigure Ratliff, Uncle Will Varner, and the hill people of Frenchman's Bend. As Carvel Collins points out, there are other characters, motifs, incidents, and techniques in the New Orleans pieces which have definite analogues in the later fiction, and no truly comprehensive assessment of Faulkner's artistic development can fail to take account of them.[38]

Faulkner's short stories, Hassell A. Simpson has maintained, "dramatize the ultimate moments in otherwise quite ordinary lives."[39] This is, of course, true of a good many stories, but few of Faulkner's short stories deal with characters who are properly described as "ordinary," and the stories more often describe the consequences of the "ultimate moment" than the moment itself. We do not see Miss Emily kill Homer Barron, we do not see Mannie Hait shoot Snopes' mule, we do not see Ikkemotubbe's initial reaction to the news that Herman Basket's sister has married Log-in-the-Creek. W.M. Frohock has said that Faulkner's basic technique is to withhold the explanation of motive, rather than to withhold the final outcome of the action itself.[40] In his short stories and his novels, however, both the significant action and the motives for it are often apprehended indirectly. Though the reader can respond to the oblique presentation of action and motive, their nature and significance are rarely apparent to the characters themselves, at least in the earlier fiction. Miss Emily offers no explanation for what she has done, and there is indeed some question as to whether she knows precisely what she has done and why she did it. Sarty Snopes acts, but it is years before he can understand why.

The nature of the action in Faulkner's fiction also changes over the years. More and more in the later work, what happens is the result of good intentions, of coherent and admirable motives. The ironies of works like *The Sound and the Fury, Sanctuary,* "Dry September," and "That Evening Sun" are so pervasive that is is possible to misinterpret them, in the belief that Faulkner approves of villainy and torture because he describes a terrific world populated by villains and victims. Or, in the less charitable view, it was wrongly thought that he merely exploits his readers' fascination with violence and misery. In the later fiction he describes characters who are able and willing to act responsibly for the good, who are capable of articulating their understanding. The successes of the later characters provide a means by which the failures of the earlier characters may be understood, and the changes and development in Faulkner's fictional patterns reflect a substantial change in his attitude toward the world:

> ... every time any character gets into a book, no matter how minor, he's actually telling his biography — that's all anyone ever does, he tells his own biography, talking about himself, in a thousand different terms, but himself. (*FIU*, 275)

Faulkner, perhaps more than any other American writer of his time, was careful not to write disguised autobiography, or *romans à clef*. He went to considerable trouble to dissociate himself from his characters, just as he did to mislead friends and interviewers about the facts of his own background. But the testimony of his fiction reveals both the depth and complexity of the alteration in his personal mode of vision, and highly concentrated portions of that testimony may be read in his short stories.

4

The Matter of Snopes

Faulkner once surprised an interviewer by alluding to his writing of *The Hamlet* "in the late twenties." When reminded that the first novel of the Snopes trilogy was published in 1940, Faulkner explained, "It was mostly short stories. In 1940 I got it all pulled together" (*FIU* 14-15). Faulkner's practice of writing and rewriting short stories, of casting and recasting those stories into novels, and of revising this material to meet new fictional needs and new thematic purposes is nowhere more evident than in his numerous treatments of the Snopes family. The story of the remarkable rise of Flem Snopes from tenant farmer to bank president is at least implicit in *Father Abraham,* an unfinished work written in late 1926 or early 1927,[1] and is explicit in the published fiction from the time of *Sartoris* in 1929, but Faulkner did not complete his treatment of the Snopes phenomenon until 1959 when he published *The Mansion.* Members of the Snopes family are prominent in the three novels of the trilogy, and in *Sartoris* and *The Unvanquished,* and are alluded to in *As I Lay Dying, The Sound and the Fury, Sanctuary,* and *The Reivers.* They figure also, to a greater or lesser extent, in no fewer than fifteen of Faulkner's shorter prose works, not including at least three "non-Snopes" short stories which Faulkner adapted to his saga. Although it is best not to take literally Faulkner's assertion that *The Hamlet* was written in the 1920s, or that it was "mostly short stories," it is certainly true that each novel of the Snopes trilogy derives in significant part from material Faulkner had earlier developed in short stories. Taken all in all, the matter of Snopes is one of Faulkner's most important fictional achievements, and it reveals both his technical and thematic development over more than three decades of writing. The individual Snopes stories, as well as the non-Snopes stories eventually adapted for the trilogy, show that Faulkner was almost invariably willing to sacrifice his extrinsic design to meet the needs of a particular fictional text, and that his attitude toward the Snopes phenomenon, as well as his plotting of the saga, changed radically over the years.

Two contrasting statements Faulkner made late in his career demonstrate the paradox of autonomy and interdependence of the Snopes material. At the time of the publication of *The Town,* Faulkner told an audience at the

University of Virginia, "I thought of the whole story at once like a bolt of lightning lights up a landscape and you see everything at once but it takes time to write it, and this story [*The Town*] I had in my mind for about thirty years, and the one which I will do next — it happened at that same moment, thirty years ago when I thought of it, of getting at it" (*FIU*, 90). This statement implies that the main outlines of the entire trilogy were essentially constant from the beginning of Faulkner's Yoknapatawpha fiction to the end. When he came to publish *The Mansion,* however, Faulkner resisted attempts to reconcile details of the three volumes of the trilogy, and offered this comment in his headnote to the novel:

> This book is the final chapter of, and the summation of, a work conceived and begun in 1925. Since the author likes to believe, hopes that his entire life's work is a part of a living literature, and since "living" is motion, and "motion" is change and alteration and therefore the only alternative to motion is un-motion, stasis, death, there will be found discrepancies and contradictions in the thirty-four-year progress of this particular chronicle; the purpose of this note is simply to notify the reader that the author has already found more discrepancies and contradictions than he hopes the reader will — contradictions and discrepancies due to the fact that the author has learned, he believes, more about the human heart and its dilemma than he knew thirty-four years ago; and is sure that, having lived with them that long time, he knows the characters in this chronicle better than he did then.

In order to reconcile these two apparently contradictory statements, it is necessary to review the development of the Snopes material in both short story and novel forms. Though it is difficult to determine the precise chronology of the composition of many parts of the Snopes material, and though the chronology of publication of that material is sometimes seriously misleading in an attempt to discover the particulars of Faulkner's development, it is nevertheless possible to conclude that both the Virginia statement and the headnote to *The Mansion* are essentially accurate.

   The earliest treatments of the rise of Flem Snopes may be clearly placed. *Father Abraham,* written in late 1926 or early 1927, may be assumed to be the first Snopes story, and one on which Faulkner drew both generally and specifically in developing his later Snopes stories and novels. The bulk of the narrative is concerned with the story that would eventually be published as "Spotted Horses" in the June 1931 *Scribner's,* and was later adapted for Book Four of *The Hamlet.* But *Father Abraham* is far more than an early version of the story of the spotted ponies, a story which Faulkner was to write in a number of forms and under a number of titles before *Scribner's* finally accepted it;[2] it is Faulkner's introduction to the Snopeses, and as such is worthy of study as a single tale, independent of the material to follow. "Father Abraham," as Faulkner would make explicit in *Sartoris*, is not Ab Snopes (who does not make his appearance in the saga until "The Unvanquished" in 1936), but Flem himself.

The opening paragraphs of the story have a mock-epic tone:

> He is a living example of the astonishing byblows of man's utopian dreams actually func-
> tioning; in this case the dream is Democracy. He will become legendary in time, but he has
> always been symbolic. Legendary as Roland and as symbolic as a form of behavior; as sym-
> bolic of an age and a region as his predecessor, a portly man with a white imperial and a
> shoestring tie and a two gallon hat, was; as symbolic and as typical of a frame of mind as
> Buddha is today. With this difference: Buddha contemplates an abstraction and derives
> a secret amusement of it; while he behind the new plate glass window of his recently re-
> modelled bank, dwells with neither lust nor alarm on the plump yet still disturbing image
> of his silkclad wife passing the time of day with Colonel Winword in front of the post-
> office. (*FA*, 13)

Thus Faulkner's very first description of Flem posits his rise to the presidency of the Jefferson bank. It also anticipates his wife's adultery, which is discussed speculatively by the narrator of "Centaur in Brass" and confirmed in *The Town*. In addition, the phrase "neither lust nor alarm" may well prefigure both Flem's impotence (again confirmed in *The Town*) and his calculated tolerance of his wife's affair. But even more important than these narrative details is Faulkner's articulation of the symbolic implications of Flem's story. The mock-epic description continues:

> What boots it that for many years his corporeal illusion was not so smugly flourishing,
> that for many years he was too busy to sit down and, when he did, looked out not upon
> the world through plate glass? Buddha had his priests to invent a cult for him while he
> stirred not a finger; while he must be god cult priest and ritual simultaneously; Buddha
> drew followers by mouthsounds, he bought them with the very blood in his veins. This,
> behind its plate glass, its quiet unwinking eyes, its mouth like one of those patent tobacco
> pouches you open and close by ripping a metal ring along the seam, this is the man. It
> boots not that for thirty years the town itself saw him not four times a year, that for the
> next fifteen years the bank knew him only on the customer's side of the savings window,
> this was, is and will be, the man. The Lord said once to Moses; "I am that I am" and
> Moses argued with the good God; but when he spoke to one of his chosen, that one replied
> immediately: "Here am I, Uncle Flem." (*FA*, 13-14)

The comparisons of Flem with Roland, with the Southern Aristocrat, with Buddha, and with the God of the Old Testament evoke Flem as a figure of epic and cosmic proportions, embarked on the lonely and selfish quest for money, in provocative contrast to the selfless defenders of the community and the seek-ers of universal salvation. In this sense *Father Abraham* provides the beginning of Faulkner's description of the process by which the American Dream be-comes nightmare. Flem's inhuman greed and impersonal acquisitiveness are everywhere evident in the story, especially in his acquisition of Eula as wife and the "old Frechman's homesite" (*FA*, 18), and in his collaboration in the sale of the spotted ponies. Flem's bringing the spotted horses to Frenchman's Bend constitutes an interruption of the natural and communal orders of the small society. Throughout *Father Abraham* Faulkner presents a direct contrast between the land and the people who inhabit it, and implies a further contrast between Flem and the rest of the inhabitants of Frenchman's Bend. An omniscient and detached narrator presents his judgment of Flem and his victims against the background of the natural world:

> Then it was April. Peach and pear and apple were in bloom, and blackbirds swung and stooped with raucous cries like rusty shutters in the wind, and like random scraps of burned paper slanted across the fields; and new fledged willow-screens beyond which waters chuckled and murmured with the grave continuous irrelevance of children, and behind surging horses and mules men broke the land anew and the turned earth smelled like new calves in a clean barn, and sowed it, and nightly the new moon waxed in the windless west and soon stood by day though incomplete in the marbled zenith. Thus the world, and on a day Flem Snopes came up the road in a covered wagon, accompanied by a soiled swaggering man in a clay colored Stetson hat and a sweeping black moustache, and followed by a score of horses larger than rabbits and colored like patchwork quilts and shackled one to another with sections of barbed wire. (*FA*, 22)

The story of the sale of the spotted ponies, not radically different from the narrative contained in the *Scribner's* version of 1931 or *The Hamlet* in 1940, is framed by the general description of Flem's character: "... Flem had reduced all human conduct to a single workable belief: that some men are fools, but all men are no honester than the occasion requires" (*FA*, 19). Flem not only brings the spotted ponies into Frenchman's Bend, but by maintaining a shrewd distance from their auction he avoids taking responsibility for the havoc and destruction the ponies wreak there. If the mock-epic passages in *Father Abraham* serve to enhance Flem, both the meanness of his aims and the manner in which he achieves them contribute to a clear negative judgment of his behavior. The quality of his achievement, moreover, is strained by the pathetic foolishness of those he dupes; his trickster's triumph is commensurate with the stature of his opposition.

Father Abraham is remarkable in a number of ways: It introduces Flem Snopes and provides a rich perspective for observing and judging his actions; it forecasts his rise through the Frenchman's Bend and Jefferson economic hierarchies; it provides detailed allusions to the background of his marriage to Eula Varner; and it offers detailed or suggestive portraits of his Snopes kinsmen, Eck, Admiral Dewey, I.O., and Clarence, who would appear repeatedly in the later fiction. Most importantly, *Father Abraham* provides the *ur*-version of a story that continued to fascinate and challenge Faulkner, and it is practically unique among Faulkner's early fiction in that it holds his flights of lyricism and his passages of colloquial narrative in satisfactory tension.

Faulkner drew on the *Father Abraham* material, or at least on Flem's Jefferson phase of it, when he wrote *Flags in the Dust,* eventually published as *Sartoris.* Though Flem is, in this novel, rather less important than his cousin Byron, the embezzler and voyeur who writes obscene letters to Narcissa Benbow, he is given a rather detailed description for a minor character, and he is viewed as the most important manifestation of a disturbing phenomenon:

> Flem, the first Snopes, had appeared unheralded one day behind the counter of a small restaurant on a side street, patronized by country folk. With this foothold and like Abraham of old, he brought his blood and legal kin household by household, individual by individual, into town, and established them where they could gain money. Flem himself was presently manager of the city light and water plant, and for the following few years he was a sort of handyman to the municipal government; and three years ago, to old Bayard's profane astonishment and unconcealed annoyance, he became vice president of the Sartoris bank, where a relation of his was a bookkeeper. (*SAR,* 172. cf. *Flags,* 154)

The *Flags/Sartoris* account of Flem's rise looks back to *Father Abraham* in the cryptic allusion "like Abraham of old" and in its reference to his banking connection, though the discrepancy between the vice-presidency specified in *Sartoris* and the presidency implied in *Father Abraham* is worth noting. Flem's tenure in the city light and water plant looks forward to aspects of "Centaur in Brass" and the Byron Snopes-Narcissa Benbow episodes would lead eventually to the story "There Was a Queen." This, the first published allusion to Flem in the Faulkner canon, is significant not only because of the ways it recalls and extends the story of *Father Abraham,* but especially because in future accounts Faulkner would adhere to this outline, as far as it goes.

In the interval between *Sartoris* and "Spotted Horses," Faulkner made use of Snopes material in three different novels. In *The Sound and the Fury* there is a brief passage describing I.O. Snopes as a cotton speculator (*S&F,* 271). In *Sanctuary,* State Senator Clarence Snopes appears as an important character, along with his nephew Virgil, and in *As I Lay Dying,* Jewel Bundren attempts to tame one of the descendants of the spotted ponies that Flem had imported into the community.

In *Sanctuary,* the original version of which was written before *As I Lay Dying,*[3] Horace Benbow remembers Clarence Snopes as

> ... a hulking, dull youth, son of a restaurant-owner, member of a family which had been moving from the Frenchman's Bend neighborhood into Jefferson for the past twenty years; a family of enough ramifications to have elected him to the legislature without recourse to public polling. (*SAN,* 171)

Clarence Snopes is the caricature of the glad-handing, foul-smelling politician. He is convinced that Horace Benbow is "romantically" interested in Temple Drake. Clarence's function in *Sanctuary* is to show the extent of Temple's depravity. Because he is knowledgeable about the Memphis tenderloin, he is able, for a price, to tell Benbow where she is hiding. The incident also shows Benbow's inability to cope effectively with an unjust society, for the election of Clarence Snopes to the state Senate is symptomatic of the community with which Benbow must deal. Clarence's nephew, Virgil Snopes, and his companion Fonzo mistake Miss Reba's brothel for a boarding-house. They are crude instruments of comic relief, but their ignorance is of a kind which evokes only hollow laughter. Clarence enlightens them, and he quickly wins them over to his favorite vice. As with other early episodes of the Snopes saga, Faulkner drew on this material in *The Town* and *The Mansion*.

In *As I Lay Dying,* the spotted ponies episode is alluded to a number of times in a somewhat cryptic manner.

> "It's Bundren, from down beyond New Hope," Quick says. "There's one of them Snopes horses Jewel's riding."
> "I didn't know there was ere a one of them horses left," McCallum says. "I thought you folks down there finally contrived to give them all away."
> "Try and get that one," Quick says. The wagon went on. "I bet old man Lon never gave it to him," I says.
> "No," Quick says. "He bought it from pappy." (*AILD,* 106-7)

Jewel's purchase of the horse is recollected by Darl in a subsequent chapter:

> Then we saw him. He came up along the ditch and then turned straight across the field, riding the horse. Its mane and tail were going, as though in motion they were carrying out the splotchy pattern of its coat: he looked like he was riding on a big pinwheel, bare-backed, with a rope bridle, and no hat on his head. It was a descendant of those Texas ponies Flem Snopes brought here twenty-five years ago and auctioned off for two dollars a head and nobody but old Lon Quick ever caught his and still owned some of the blood because he could never give it away. (*AILD,* 127)

This descendant of the original spotted ponies figures importantly in the novel. Jewel's purchase of the pony from Lon Quick is a signal act of rebellious young manhood, a source of pride for Jewel and a cause of consternation and self-pity for Anse. Jewel's breaking of the horse is described in savage eloquence, and his determination to purchase it is evident in his exhausting work, such that the other Bundrens believe he has taken a woman.

The pony is prominent in the trade Anse eventually makes with another Snopes, apparently a nephew of Flem, who is a clerk in Varner's store. In order to secure the team of mules necessary to complete the journey to Jefferson with Addie Bundren's corpse, Anse trades Snopes a forty-dollar chattel mortgage on his cultivator and seeder, eight dollars appropriated from Cash (who had been planning to buy a phonograph with the money) and Jewel's horse. On learning that his horse has been included in the trade, Jewel deserts the family, apparently taking the horse with him, but the next day it is learned that he has delivered the horse himself to Snopes.

Before beginning to write *As I Lay Dying,* Faulkner had twice used the title on unpublished versions of the study of the spotted ponies.⁴ The explicit source of this phrase, as Carvel Collins has pointed out, is surely in Agamemnon's description of Clytemnestra in Book XI of *The Odyssey.*⁵ If we recall Clytemnestra as "the woman with the dog's eyes," we can see her Faulknerian counterpart not only in Addie Bundren, but also in Henry Armstid's wife, "with her desolate dog's eyes" (*FA*, 60). Mrs. Armstid offers her equivalent of Clytemnestra's curse to Buck: "Ef you takes that five dollars I earnt my chaps a'weaving', fer one of the hosses, hit'll be a curse onto you and your'n during all the time of man" (*FA*, 44). Of course it is Flem Snopes, rather than Buck, who finally takes and keeps the five dollars, refusing to return it to Mrs. Armstid. Thus the title "As I Lay Dying" is an appropriate, if obscure, description of the episode that damns Flem Snopes to eternal isolation within the human community.

The *Father Abraham* material provided Faulkner with the title for *As I Lay Dying* and with significant details for the Burden plot. The story of the pony highlights both Jewel's furious rebellion and Anse's abject self-pity and self-justification. In employing this material in a novel in which the Snopeses figure only peripherally, Faulkner was adhering to his unwritten law of fictional parsimony and demonstrating his own practice of self-reflexivity. Although *As I Lay Dying* was the first of Faulkner's *published* texts to include the spotted pony material, the form and substance of the allusions make it clear that he was availing himself of previously developed material. In novels and short stories, published and unpublished, Faulkner used the Snopes material reflexively almost from the beginning of his conception of the saga.

After completing *As I Lay Dying* in January 1930, Faulkner began, as Hans Skei demonstrates, his most intense and productive period of work in the short story form. During this period Faulkner returned to the *Father Abraham* material repeatedly, attempting to develop the story of the spotted ponies as an autonomous text for magazine publication. He finally succeeded with the text published by *Scribner's* under the title of "Spotted Horses" in June 1931. In the unpublished versions of the story which preceded the *Scribner's* text, Faulkner experimented with a variety of narrative strategies and a number of technical points-of-view before ascribing the narrative to a nameless countryman who is obviously one of the avatars of Suratt-Ratliff. In this text, the narrative is a genuine but grudging tribute to Flem's talents for sharp dealing. A version of Flem's marriage to Eula is given as background to the story of the spotted ponies:

> Well, one day about a year ago, one of them yellow-wheeled buggies and one of them curried saddle-horses quit this country. We heard they was heading for Texas. The next day Uncle Billy and Eula and Flem come into town in Uncle Bill's surrey, and when they come back, Flem and Eula was married. And on the next day we heard that two more of them yellow-wheeled buggies had left the country.

Anyway, about a month after the wedding, Flem and Eula went to Texas, too. They was gone pretty near a year. Then one day last month, Eula come back, with a baby. We figgered up, and we decided that it was as well-growed a three-month-old baby as we ever see. It can already pull up on a chair. I reckon Texas makes big men quick, being a big state. Anyway, if it keeps on like it started, it'll be chewing tobacco and voting time it's eight years old. (*USWF,* 166-67)

A significant alteration here from *Father Abraham* is that the sex of the child is not specified and a reader of "Spotted Horses" might infer that the child is a boy, though both *Father Abraham* and *The Hamlet* make clear that the child is female. Though the circumstances of Flem's marriage to Eula are ambiguous, they are generally consistent with the versions of *Father Abraham* and *The Hamlet.* Another detail omitted from "Spotted Horses" is the circumstance in which Flem receives the Old Frenchman place as Eula's dowry. These changes, alterations, and omissions show how Faulkner deliberately ignored or changed part of his mythology that would unnecessarily complicate a story. "Spotted Horses" is a frontier trickster tale, with heavy emphasis on the ironic humor of the unnamed narrator, who brags that Flem "skun me in two trades himself, and the fellow that can do that, I just hope he'll get rich before I do; that's all" (*USWF,* 166). Like Suratt in *Father Abraham* and Ratliff in *The Hamlet,* the unnamed narrator is ignominiously routed from his room by one of the spotted ponies, but where the first version is observed at a distance, the "Spotted Horses" version of this episode is described in broad colloquial humor, while Ratliff's version in *The Hamlet* combines both methods. With its broad humor and colloquial style, "Spotted Horses" invites comparison with stories such as "Fool About a Horse," "Shingles for the Lord," and "Race at Morning," and it stands as a story in its own right, even though it derives from and anticipates more sophisticated versions.

The next Snopes stories to be published, "Centaur in Brass" and "Lizards in Jamshyd's Courtyard," also center on Flem. Published in February 1932 in the *American Mercury* and the *Saturday Evening Post,* respectively, these two stories have very different subsequent histories. "Lizards" was substantially revised for incorporation in Book Four of *The Hamlet,* while "Centaur in Brass," set in Flem's Jefferson phase, was chosen for *Collected Stories* before being revised for incorporation in the opening chapter of *The Town.* "Lizards" does not mention Eula and explains that "Snopes had bought the Old Frenchman place from Varner" (*USWF,* 140), again indicating that Faulkner often chose to tell a commercial story economically rather than with a view to absolute consistency with other segments of his saga.

Like many other Faulkner stories, "Lizards" is framed in the present, describing Henry Armstid digging by himself at the Old Frechman place, "with a certain unflagging fury" (*USWF,* 136). The choric voices of the community comment on the situation:

"That Flem Snopes. I'll declare."

"He's a sight, sho. Yes, sir. Wouldn't no other man but him done it."

"Couldn't no other man done it. Anybody might a-fooled Henry Armstid. But couldn't nobody but Flem a-fooled Suratt."

"That's a fact, that's a fact. Sho." (*USWF,* 138)

The second section of the story casts back to establish both Suratt's grudging respect for Flem and his determination to get the better of him. This section continues the legend of the gold buried on the Old Frenchman place, describes Flem's having bested Suratt in a deal involving some goats (here also anticipating *The Hamlet*), and spells out Suratt's conviction that the gold must still be buried on the Old Frenchman place. Otherwise, Suratt reasons, Flem would not have bought it: "If Flem Snopes bought that place, he knows something about it that even Will Varner never knowed. Flem Snopes wouldn't buy a nickel mousetrap withouten he knowed beforehand it would make him back a dime" (*USWF,* 141). Section III of the story describes how Suratt, Vernon Tull, and Henry Armstid employ a local "dowser," Uncle Dick, who helps them find a few gold coins, which fixes their determination to acquire the property. The fourth and final section of the story describes how Suratt, Tull, and Armstid purchase the land at Flem's price, including Suratt's payment to Flem with a lien on his half-share of a Jefferson restaurant, a reference which looks back to *Father Abraham* and *Sartoris* and forward to *The Town*. After two nights of digging, Suratt and Tull discover they have been duped, for the "Civil War" treasure they have found parts of includes coins minted as recently as 1901. They attempt to share their discovery with Henry Armstid, who is, by now, oblivious to all reason and evidence and continues to dig insanely and jealously, a spectacle for the entire community:

> They had been watching him for a week, coming by wagon and on horse and mule back for ten miles, to gather, with lips full of snuff, along the fence with the decorum of a formal reception, the rapt and static interest of a crowd watching a magician at a fair. On the first day, when the first rider descended and came to the fence, Armstid turned and ran at him with the lifted shovel, cursing in a harsh, light whisper, and drove the man away. But he had quit that, and he appeared to be not even aware of them as on the successive days they gathered along the fence, talking a little among themselves in sparse syllables, watching Armstid spade the surface of the garden steadily down the slope toward the ditch, working steadily back and forth across the hillside. (*USWF,* 136-37)

While much of the emphasis in "Lizards" is on the contest between Suratt and Flem Snopes, it also more generally describes the cupidity of all those who buy and sell the Old Frenchman place. Suratt's ready humor is apparent here, but so is the fact that he, like Tull, Armstid, Snopes, and Varner, is looking out for the main chance. It is indeed an ironic world in which the grand house built by the Old Frenchman is torn down for firewood and its gardens ravaged by greedy men who are victims of the salted goldmine trick. The echo of Fitz-gerald's *Rubaiyat* — "They say the Lion and the Lizard keep/The Courts where Jamshyd gloried and drank deep" — in Faulkner's title sets the tone for the story, and Omar's Sixteenth Quatrain contains what might well be the more general motto of the story:

> The Worldly Hope men set their Hearts upon
> Turns Ashes — or it prospers; and anon,
>   Like Snow upon the Desert's dusty Face,
> Lighting a little hour or two — is gone.

The same theme is brought home by Uncle Dick, who, wanting no part of the gold himself, tells Suratt, Tull, and Armstid, "I feel four bloods lust-running.... Hit's four sets of blood here lusting for dross" (*USWF*, 146). The fourth blood is Flem's, but there is no indication in "Lizards" that his worldly hopes will turn to ashes. In "Lizards," as in *Father Abraham, Sartoris,* and "Spotted Horses," Flem is supremely successful.

This is not the case, however, with "Centaur in Brass," another story of the trickster tricked. In this story Flem Snopes is thwarted, at least temporarily, a victim of his own machinations. "Centaur" opens with the assertion that Flem Snopes has a "monument" in the town of the unnamed narrator, who tersely recapitulates the *Father Abraham* material:

> He came to Jefferson from the country, accompanied by his wife and infant daughter and preceded by a reputation for shrewd and secret dealing. There lives in our country a sewing-machine agent named Suratt, who used to own a half interest in a small back-street restaurant in town — himself no mean hand at that technically unassailable opportunism which passes with country folks — and town folks, too — for honest shrewdness.
>
> He travels about the country steadily and constantly, and it was through him that Snope's [sic] doings first came to our ears: how first, a clerk in a country store, Snopes one day and to everyone's astonishment was married to the store owner's daughter, a young girl who was the belle of the countryside. They were married suddenly on the same day upon which three of the girl's erstwhile suitors left the country and were seen no more.
>
> Soon after the wedding Snopes and his wife moved to Texas, from where the wife returned a year later with a well-grown baby. A month later Snopes himself returned, accompanied by a broad-hatted stranger and a herd of half-wild mustang ponies, which the stranger auctioned off, collected the money, and departed. Then the purchasers discovered that none of the ponies had ever had a bridle on. But they never learned if Snopes had had any part in the business, or had received any part of the money.
>
> The next we heard of him was when he appeared one day in a wagon laden with his family and household goods, and with a bill-of-sale for Suratt's half of the restaurant. How he got the bill-of-sale, Suratt never told, and we never learned more than that there was somehow involved in the affair a worthless piece of land which had been a portion of Mrs. Snopes's dowry. But what the business was even Suratt, a humorous, talkative man who was as ready to laugh at a joke on himself as at one on anyone else, never told. But when he mentioned Snopes's name after that, it was in a tone of savage and sardonic and ungrudging admiration. (*CS*, 149-50)

Thus, by the time he had written "Centaur in Brass" in August 1931,[6] Faulkner was confidently and explicitly drawing on his earlier Snopes stories in the process of making a new one. These paragraphs in "Centaur," of course, encapsulate the main action of *The Hamlet*, and the later description of the flirtation of Flem's wife (she is not named in this story) anticipates much of the central action of *The Town*. "Lizards in Jamshyd's Courtyard," according to Faulkner's short story sending schedule, was sent to the *Post* on May 27, 1930, while he continued to revise the *Father Abraham*/"Spotted Horses" material at least as late as February 13, 1931, and had completed a version of "Centaur in Brass" by March 11, 1931. Thus Faulkner had written "Lizards," which describes how Flem gained his toehold in Jefferson, before his story of the spotted ponies was revised in its magazine publication form, and he had also written "Centaur in Brass," in which Flem seems to be stymied, before either of the other two were published. This set of facts shows why it is dangerous to draw inferences about Faulkner's development by relying exclusively on the chronology of his stories' publication, and it further demonstrates not only his ability to use, reuse, and adapt his published and unpublished material to meet immediate narrative needs, but also demonstrates his amazing powers of withholding. If it is true that Faulkner had conceived of the main outlines of the Snopes saga as early as 1925, and, in any event, no later than early 1927, and if it is true that there is an essential consistency in his adherence to that outline in the early stories, it is also true that he chose not to reveal important elements of the Snopes outcome in every version of the saga.

"Centaur in Brass" implies that Flem manages to rise in the municipal government of Jefferson by acquiescing in and even manipulating his wife's presumed adultery with Major Hoxey, "the town's lone rich middle-aged bachelor, graduate of Yale and soon to be mayor of the town" (*CS*, 151). What outrages the town, according to the narrator, is not the adultery itself, if it has in fact occurred, but rather "the idea of their being on amicable terms" (*CS*, 151). "Centaur" thus expands the suggestion implied in the description of Eula and Colonel Winword in *Father Abraham,* and later developed at substantial length in the relations between Eula and Manfred de Spain in *The Town*. "Centaur" makes clear that Flem is not fooled by his wife, or, at least, that the town "believed that, whatever his wife was, she was not fooling him (*CS*, 152). Instead, the narrator observes, "It was another woman who did that..." (*CS*, 152).

The main plot, as revealed by the unnamed townsman who serves as narrator, concerns Flem's ultimately unsuccessful attempt at petty chicanery. Appointed superintendent of the municipal power plant, he seizes the opportunity to make a little money by removing both fixed and loose brass objects from the plant. His first theft nearly has disastrous consequences, for he replaces the brass safety valves, which he calls a "whistle" (*CS*, 152), with "one-inch steel screw plugs capable of a pressure of a thousand pounds" (*CS*,

153), threatening the safety of the power plant workers. Typically, neither Flem Snopes nor Turl, the night fireman who does Flem's bidding, is aware of the potential danger, and they are saved only by the knowledge and attention of Mr. Harker, the night engineer. But Flem persists in his avarice, using a horseshoe magnet to identify brass from among the "miscellaneous pile of metal junk, all covered with dirt: fittings, valves, rods, bolts and such" (*CS*, 155). He then asks Tom-Tom, the day fireman, to hide the pilfered brass for him. Flem's second thwarting occurs when the power plant equipment is audited and Flem is forced to pay, literally and immediately out of his own pocket, the sum of $304. 52 for the missing brass.

Twice warned that his behavior is both physically and legally dangerous, Flem nevertheless persists in his attempt to realize a financial gain from the stolen brass. Setting Tom-Tom and Turl against one another, he contrives to have Turl search Tom-Tom's corncrib for the hidden brass. Turl, however, focuses his attention on Tom-Tom's young wife, and the resulting triangle breaks under pressure, for Tom-Tom surprises Turl sneaking into his back porch and attempts to kill him:

> He leaped astride of Turl's neck and shoulders, his weight was the impetus which sent Turl off the porch, already running when his feet touched earth, carrying with him on the retina of his fear a single dreadful glint of moonlight on the blade of the lifted knife, as he crossed the back lot and, with Tom-Tom on his back, entered the trees — the two of them a strange and furious beast with two heads and a single pair of legs like an inverted centaur speeding phantomlike just ahead of the boardlike streaming of Tom-Tom's shirt-tail and just beneath the silver glint of the lifted knife, through the moony April woods. (*CS*, 164)

The wildly joined pair fall into a ditch and, recovering from their fall, discover their common enemy:

> He and Turl just sat there in the ditch and talked. Because there is a sanctuary beyond despair for any beast which has dared all, which even its mortal enemy respects. Or maybe it was just nigger nature. Anyway, it was perfectly plain to both of them as they sat there, perhaps panting a little while they talked, that Tom-Tom's home had been outraged, not by Turl, but by Flem Snopes; that Turl's life and limbs had been endangered, not by Tom-Tom, but by Flem Snopes. (*CS*, 165)

Tom-Tom and Turl complete the frustration of Flem's scheme by putting the brass in the town water tank, which becomes Flem's "monument":

> that shaft taller than anything in sight and filled with transient and symbolic liquid that was not even fit to drink, but which, for the very reason of its impermanence, was more enduring through its fluidity and blind renewal than the brass which poisoned it, than columns of basalt or of lead. (*CS*, 168)

In writing "Centaur in Brass" Faulkner accomplished a number of things, not the least of which was the making of a self-contained comic tale worthy of comparison with the best of Mark Twain's efforts in the same genre. Flem Snopes, like Jim Smiley in "The Notorious Jumping Frog of Calaveras County," is first established as a humorous character, in the sense that his nature marks him as radically different from that of the community in which he lives. His ignorance and miscalculation are shown in the episodes of the safety valves and the auditing, and these promises of reversal and frustration are exquisitely fulfilled in the final episode. For Flem, like Jim Smiley, assumes that his own trickery is sufficient to enable him to manipulate others to his own advantage, and Tom-Tom allows himself a subtle moment of retribution, when he explains to Flem that the brass "is where you said you wanted it" (*CS,* 167), just as Mark Twain's stranger more overtly taunts Jim Smiley by saying, "I don't see as how that ere frog is different from any other frog." In both stories, the trickster is tricked by those whom he had set out to deceive, as a result of his own arrogance and greed, and both stories are brilliant object lessons in the frustration of the comic overreacher.

"Centaur in Brass" also is the first Faulkner short story to center on Flem in Jefferson. No vestige of it appears in *The Hamlet,* and Faulkner did not use it again until he wrote *The Town* over twenty years later, where it is substantially reworked in the opening chapter. The story is even more significant, however, as the first text in which Flem is less than supremely successful. In *Father Abraham,* "Spotted Horses," and "Lizards in Jamshyd's Courtyard," Flem is completely triumphant, gaining admiration and respect for sharp dealing among the Suratts and Tulls and Varners at the same time that he evokes the reader's disgust. But "Centaur in Brass" shows him thwarted, stopped, sitting on the steps of his bungalow, "contemplating his monument" (*CS,* 168). Forced to pay out an additional sum as the result of a second audit, Snopes resigns from the power plant and makes an unsuccessful offer to buy the water tower after it is condemned by the town. There is poetic justice in his frustration by Tom-Tom and Turl, two men who in some sense have the same relation to one another that Flem has to Major Hoxey. Tom-Tom's direct and violent response to Turl's threat to his marriage stands in sharp contrast to Flem's devious tolerance of his own cuckolding. It is precisely his failure to anticipate the natural consequences of Turl's lust and Tom-Tom's jealousy that leads to Flem's downfall.

"Centaur in Brass" is also unusual among Faulkner's stories in that it was one of relatively few that he sold on its first submission, and unusual in that he did not first send it to the *Saturday Evening Post.* In accepting the story for *Scribner's,* which had made frequent pleas to Faulkner to send them more Snopes material following "Spotted Horses," editor Kyle Crichton complained that "Centaur in Brass" seemed to mark the end of Flem Snopes.[7] While

Crichton's objection was ill-founded in the sense that Faulkner, before and later, resurrected virtually any of his characters under any circumstances to meet the needs of a particular text, it is tempting to speculate that Crichton's observation that "Brass" marked a new and problematic phase for Flem Snopes was taken seriously by Faulkner, for Faulkner wrote no more stories centering on Flem until he came to write *The Hamlet*.

Although "Mule in the Yard," the next Snopes story, was not published until 1934, and though it was probably not written in its short story form until late in 1933, important elements of it are foreshadowed in *Sartoris*. In the first Yoknapatawpha novel Bayard Sartoris attempts to ride an untameable stallion, owned by a nameless horse-trader, who "was constantly engaged in litigation with the railroad company over the violent demise of his stock by its agency." MacCallum taunts him, saying that "the railroad company ought to furnish that stock of yourn with timetables." The trader attempts to defend himself, saying: "You talk like I might have druv them mules in front of that train. Lemme tell you how it come about—" (*SAR*, 131).

This relatively brief description, embedded in an important episode of *Sartoris*, apparently furnished Faulkner with the character of Lonzo Hait or I.O. Snopes of "Mule in the Yard," where it is reported that

> in the town they knew about him too — how he bought his stock at the Memphis market and brought it to Jefferson and sold it to farmers and widows and orphans black and white, for whatever he could contrive — down to a certain figure; and about how (usually in the dead season of winter) teams and even small droves of his stock would escape from the fenced pasture where he kept them and, tied one to another with sometimes quite new hemp rope (and which item Snopes included in the subsequent claim), would be annihilated by freight trains on the same blind curve which was to be the scene of Hait's exit from this world; once a town wag sent him through the mail a printed train schedule for the division. (*CS*, 252)

"Mule in the Yard" develops a single comic episode centering on I.O. Snopes and Miss Mannie Hait. Expanding and specifying the episode from *Sartoris,* the narrator explains how Snopes had once made a practice of hiring Mrs. Hait's husband to tie the mules on a blind curve on the railroad tracks, collecting damages from the railroad company when the mules were killed. Hait, however, was himself killed on one of these expeditions, and Mrs. Hait, much to the consternation of Snopes, received a large settlement from the railroad company. At the time present of the story one of I.O.'s mules runs loose in the widow's yard and Mrs. Hait, in her frantic efforts to drive the mule away, carelessly sets a scuttle of live coals on her cellar steps. When Snopes returns to the smoldering ruin to claim his mule, a complicated wrangle with Mrs. Hait ensues, and Snopes discovers, to his consternation, that Mrs. Hait has shot the mule. As Old Het summarizes it, "de mule burnt de house en you shot de mule. Dat's whut I calls justice" (*CS*, 264).

"Mule in the Yard" is one of Faulkner's finest comedies. The scene in which the mule circles the yard is a worthy successor to the epic chase in the *Nun's Priest's Tale*:

> With that unhasteful celerity Mrs. Hait turned and set the scuttle down on the brick coping of the cellar entrance and she and old Het turned the corner of the house in time to see the now wraithlike mule at the moment when its course converged with that of a choleric-looking rooster and eight Rhode Island Red hens emerging from beneath the house. Then for an instant its progress assumed the appearance and trappings of an apotheosis: hell-born and hell-returning, in the act of dissolving completely into the fog, it seemed to rise vanishing into a sunless and dimensionless medium borne upon and enclosed by small winged goblins. (*CS*, 251)

Like "Centaur in Brass," "Mule in the Yard" sounds a theme that would later be developed explicitly in *The Town* and *The Mansion*: the Snopeses, for all their cunning, can be overcome, both by their own petty overreaching and by the native wits of those who dare to oppose them. For all the criticism Faulkner received for "softening" the Snopes dilemma in the last two novels of the trilogy, he cannot be justly accused of inconsistency on this point, if the evidence of the stories is properly evaluated.

Having brought the Snopeses from Frenchman's Bend to Jefferson, Faulkner extended the saga backwards in time in developing Ab Snopes in the stories of *The Unvanquished*. This material, like that of *Father Abraham* and "Spotted Horses," was drawn on extensively in Faulkner's composition of *The Hamlet*. In that novel, Ratliff explains that the process of Ab's "souring" began during the Civil War:

> When he wasn't bothering nobody, not harming or helping either side, just tending to his own business, which was profit and horses — things which never even heard of such a thing as a political conviction — when here comes somebody that never even owned the horses even and shot him in the heel. And that soured him. And then that business of Colonel Sartoris's ma-in-law, Miss Rosa Millard, that Ab had done went and formed a horse-and-mule partnership with in good faith and honor, not aiming to harm nobody blue or gray but just keeping his mind fixed on profit and horses, until Miz Millard had to go and get herself shot by that fellow that called his-self Major Grumby, and then Colonel's boy Bayard and Uncle Buck McCaslin and a nigger caught Ab in the woods and something else happened, tied up to a tree or something and maybe even a heated ramrod in it too though that's just hearsay. (*HAM*, 29)

The episode referred to here is developed in the short stories "The Unvanquished" and "Vendée." In "The Unvanquished" it is clear that Granny Millard does not trust Ab, but the exigencies of the situation force her to rely on him in the procurement and sale of the mules. One indication of Ab's position in the Sartoris household is that Ringo refuses to call Ab "Mister," though Granny, punctilious as always, corrects him (*USWF*, 83). After the mule business is ruined, Granny still has forty-odd mules in a hidden pen. Ab tells the Yankees where the mules are concealed, and the last fruits of Granny's enterprise are taken from her. Ab has the temerity to pretend ignorance of his part in the Yankee "discovery." Even though she is aware of his treachery, Granny allows Ab to persuade her to ,make the fatal attempt to requisition horses from the dangerous Grumby. Ab, then, not only takes advantage of Granny and betrays her, he is also directly responsible for her death.

In "Vendée" it is discovered that Ab Snopes is travelling with Grumby. Momentarily Bayard thinks that Ab *is* Grumby, but Uncle Buck McCaslin sets him straight:

> "Him, Grumby?" he hollered. "Ab Snopes? Ab Snopes? By Godfrey if he was Grumby, if it was Ab Snopes that shot your grandmaw, I'd be ashamed to have it known. I'd be ashamed to be caught catching him." (*USWF*, 100)

Grumby turns Ab over to Bayard, Uncle Buck, and Ringo, hoping to protect himself. Grumby threatens to return and kill Ab, if Ab tells the others where he is headed. Thus the three pursuers have to pretend to be satisfied with Ab. He is bound and beaten, and Grumby is deceived. As in "The Unvanquished," Ab shows his determination to make the best of things, refusing to acknowledge that he is anything other than a loyal friend to the Sartorises:

> "Bayard ain't got no hard feelings against me. He knows hit was a pure accident; that we was doing hit for his sake and his paw and them niggers at home. Why, here hit's a whole year and it was me that holp and tended Miss Rosa when she never had ara living soul but them chil —" Now the voice began to tell the truth again; it was the eyes and the voice that I was walking toward. (*USWF*, 109)

After he is whipped, Ab again attempts to join his interests with those of the Sartorises. He is a contemptible figure, a man who inadvertently causes great harm through his own viciousness. He survives by shamelessly appealing to the good nature of his pursuers. There is no mention of Ab in the *Scribner's* text of "Skirmish at Sartoris," and the absence of Ab and Grumby from this story tends to support the assumption that it was written before "The Unvanquished" and "Vendée." "After Granny died," Bayard relates, "Ringo and Louvinia and I all slept in the cabin..." (*USWF*, 62). Since there is no allusion here to Granny's violent end, it is possible that Faulkner had not yet conceived of the incidents described in "The Unvanquished" and "Vendée." On the other hand, it may be that in preparing the story for publication he eliminated what would have been a complicating reference, as he eliminated Flem's marriage to Eula when he published "Lizards in Jamshyd's Courtyard." Neither is Ab mentioned in either the "Skirmish at Sartoris" or "An Odor of Verbena" sections of *The Unvanquished.* In the two magazine texts, as in the novel, Ab is rarely the center of interest. But Faulkner, in these stories, was extending and developing the Snopes saga, continuing the process of elaboration that would eventually culminate in *The Hamlet*.

Several other short stories of this period which Faulkner drew on for *The Hamlet* did not, in their original forms, feature Snopeses. "Fool About a Horse," "The Hound," and "Afternoon of a Cow" differ substantially from each other, and from the material in *The Hamlet* which assimilates them. "Fool About a Horse," like "Spotted Horses," is on the order of a tall tale. Its effects derive from the naive colloquial humor of the narrator, a twelve-year-old boy who tells how his father is bested in a horse-trade with Pat Stamper. The boy and his father set out for Jefferson to buy a cream separator for the boy's mother. In his desire to prove his superiority as a horse trader, the father trades his horse and mule for what Stamper claims is a matched span of mules. The new team barely gets the pair to Jefferson, where Pap purchases a pint of whisky and the cream separator before returning to trade for his original team. Stamper will not make the trade, and Pap ends up giving him the cream separator *and* Stamper's mules for his original mule and what appears to be a better horse. Returning home without the separator, they discover that the "new" horse is the old one, doctored by Stamper's black assistant who has blown it up with a bicycle pump and changed its color from bay to black. The mother is naturally incensed. She trades the horse and mule back to Stamper for the separator. Pap has as much as given Pat Stamper a horse and a mule, and in the process he has vindicated his wife's judgment that he is a fool about a horse.

As the boy tells it, "Fool About a Horse" emphasizes his affection for his father, with whom he is in complete sympathy. Pap is an overachiever whose downfall is comic, rather than tragic. "It was," the boy says, "pure fate" (*USWF*, 120). The boy describes Pap's minor faults, his willingness to trade property that is not his, his weakness for the demon rum, his excessive pride in his abilities as a horse-trader, and his inability to resist the temptation to trade with Pat Stamper. But the boy understands that his father is acting from the best of motives:

> It was Pat Stamper that rankled Pap. When a man swaps horse for horse, that's one thing. But when cash money starts changing hands, that's something else; and when a stranger comes into the county and starts actual cash money jumping from hand to hand, it's like when a burglar breaks into your house and flings your clothes and truck from place to place even though he don't take nothing: it makes you mad. So it was not jest to get Beasley's horse back onto Pat Stamper. It was to get Beasley's eight dollars back outen Pat some way. (*USWF*, 122-23)

There is little of the later Ab Snopes in Pap, but Faulkner uses the story in *The Hamlet* as Ratliff's explanation of how Ab becomes "soured." Ratliff takes the boy's place in the story, and Pap becomes Ab Snopes. Thus the horse-trade is put into the context of the other Snopes activity in *The Hamlet*. Ratliff's narrative humanizes Ab; it psychologizes him as Faulkner had earlier explained the behavior of Popeye in *Sanctuary*. Ratliff says that the incident was the final humiliation in Ab's life, the point at which "he just went plumb curdled" (*HAM,* 29). The novel text is complicated slightly by the necessity of explaining Ratliff's relation to Ab — the incident is said to have taken place in Ratliff's childhood when he and Ab were neighbors — but the novel text clarifies one ambiguity in the story. After she retrieves her cream separator from Stamper, the boy's mother runs the same gallon of milk through the separator over and over. In *The Hamlet* it is explained that Stamper refused to trade with her for Ab's original team, so Mrs. Snopes was forced to trade him the cow in order to recover her separator. This ironic recasting of O. Henry's "The Gift of the Magi" serves to demean Mrs. Snopes and shows that she is as stubborn and foolish as Ab. "Fool About a Horse," transposed into *The Hamlet,* loses something of its comic simplicity and directness. It follows Ratliff's narrative of the events described in "Barn Burning," and thus our knowledge of the kind of man Ab was in the trade with Pat Stamper is colored by our knowledge that he has become a barn-burner and the father of Flem. On the surface, the reworking of "Fool About a Horse" would seem to suggest that Faulkner was turning from comedy to irony as he did in revising stories for *Go Down, Moses,* but *Father Abraham* makes it clear that the Snopes chronicle was ironic from the beginning, and this is borne out by the Snopeses' appearances in other early stories and novels. The grafting of "Fool About a Horse" onto *The Hamlet* represents Faulkner's total reworking of a story which was originally very different in form and emphasis.[8]

There is a closer correspondence in tone between "The Hound" and the section of *The Hamlet* which deals with Mink Snopes' murder of Jack Houston. In *The Hamlet,* Houston's murder takes place during the long summer when Flem marries Eula and leaves for Texas. Mink is certain that Flem will come to rescue him, and Flem's failure to aid his kinsman is indicative of his lack of fellow-feeling. The incident may also anticipate the desire for respectability which Flem will manifest in *The Town*, and it provides the basis for his eventual undoing in *The Mansion*. But the central character in "The Hound" is Ernest Cotton, rather than Mink Snopes. Cotton murders Houston because of the latter's overbearing manner. There is a Snopes in "The Hound," a clerk in Varner's store who knows that Cotton has thrown his shotgun into a slough, but this Snopes does not appear elsewhere in the story. In *The Hamlet,* Mink is tormented by another Snopes, Lump, who has discovered that Mink murdered Houston. Lump badgers Mink for a share of the money Houston is supposed to have been carrying when he was killed. Another major difference is that in "The Hound" Cotton murders Houston in spite of the fact that he had won a judgment from him in a case involving a stray dog of Houston's. In *The Hamlet,* a heifer of Mink's "strays" onto Houston's land — the implication is that Mink has planned this — and the judgment is made in Houston's favor. Cotton's murder is thus even more horrible than Mink's, being less susceptible to rational explanation. Cotton resents Houston's overbearing manner, and his favored treatment of the hound which eventually betrays Cotton's guilt. "Swelling around like he was the biggest man in the county. Setting that ere dog on folks' stock," Cotton complains. "A dog that et better than me. I work, and eat worse than his dog" (*DM,* 60, *USWF,* 157).

In "The Hound" both Cotton and Houston are bachelors, while in *The Hamlet* Mink is a married man with children and Houston is a widower. These changes serve to connect Mink with the other Snopeses — his wife is bitterly resentful of Flem — while Houston's marriage and widowing go some way toward explaining his overbearing swagger:

> And they were married and six months later she died and he grieved for her for four years in black, savage, indomitable fidelity, and that was all. (*HAM,* 205)

The concentration and simplicity of "The Hound" are diffused and scattered in *The Hamlet,* but both Mink and Houston are more thoroughly explained and understood in *The Hamlet,* and their story is but one of many which help to define the character of Flem and the Snopes clan. Like "Wash" and "Barn Burning," "The Hound" is a powerful and self-contained story which bears only superficial resemblance to the episode developed in the novel.

Though not published until 1947, "Afternoon of a Cow" is related to *The Hamlet* in some ways. Some critics think it is the "germ" of the episode involving Ike Snopes and the cow in *The Hamlet.*[9] "Afternoon of a Cow" presents itself as a reminiscence of "Ernest V. Trueblood," a sententious character who announces that he has "been writing Mr. Faulkner's stories and novels for years" (*USWF,* 424). Trueblood is a prude, and he takes care to express his disdain for the manners and habits of his employer, "Mr. Faulkner." Trueblood's narrative tells how he, Faulkner, and the Negro hand, Oliver, undertake to aid a cow which has fallen into a ravine during a fire. Faulkner pushes and the other two pull, but the cow falls backward down the side of the ravine and onto Faulkner:

> I have been told by soldiers (I served in France, in the Y.M.C.A.) how, upon entering battle, there often sets up in them, prematurely, as it were, a certain impulse or desire which brings on a result quite logical and natural, the fulfillment of which is incontestible and of course irrevocable.— In a word, Mr. Faulkner underneath received the full discharge of the poor creature's afternoon of anguish and despair. (*USWF,* 430)

Having suffering this humiliation, Faulkner assumes the pose of Rodin's *Penseur,* and contrives to get the cow out of the ravine by the simple expedient of leading her along it to a point where there is easy access to the woods and pasture. Faulkner returns the cow to the barn, washes himself, dons a horse blanket, and orders a drink. Trueblood promises to describe the incident in the following day's writing, but he insists "upon my prerogative and right to tell this one in my own diction and style, and not yours." "By ——— !" Faulkner replies. "You better had" (*USWF,* 434).

The humor of "Afternoon of a Cow" derives from the disparity between style and subject, between "Trueblood's" grand manner and the earthy episode which he describes. It is primarily the presentation of the cow in high style which has led readers to conclude that the piece is related to *The Hamlet,* but in 1947 Faulkner recalled having drawn on the story in *The Hamlet.*[10] Faulkner is indeed parodying his own style here, and "Afternoon of a Cow" indicates Faulkner's awareness of the sometimes torturous involutions of his own prose. As Michael Millgate points out, there are no verbal parallels between this *jeu d'esprit* and *The Hamlet,*[11] and it is likely that Faulkner simply recalled the story rather than drawing on it directly in writing the Ike Snopes episode. In "Afternoon of a Cow" Faulkner wrote with feeling and sympathy, albeit feigned and to a comic purpose, of a cow which is, like the cows in *The Hamlet* and "Mule in the Yard," "misused."

Another Snopes story, which may have existed in Faulkner's mind and conversation, rather than on paper, is extant in a 1939 interview with Michael Mok for the *New York Post.* Describing the Snopeses as "a family who, by petty chicanery and unscrupulous politics, take possession of the county town of Jefferson, Miss." (*LIG,* 39), Faulkner claims to have been writing about them in his other fiction for fifteen years, and has put them into a book of their own. It would be, Faulkner said, "a big book, three or four volumes," of which the first book has been completed. The Snopes book, Faulkner said, presumably referring to the projected work in its entirety rather than only to *The Hamlet,* is "a humorous book — I mean it's a tribe of rascals who live by skullduggery and practice it twenty-four hours a day":

> Take Montgomery Ward Snopes. In the World War he was a Y.M.C.A. secretary. When he came back to the old home town he had a wad of money, earned, he said, by buying left-over stocks of cigarettes and candy and selling them cheap to the soldiers.
>
> Pretty soon the boys of the town discovered that Montgomery Ward had brought back a collection of French postcards, which he showed, for a fee, in a shack behind his house. His cousin, a State Senator in Jacksonville [*sic*], heard about the pictures and demanded to see them. As he was the most powerful member of the family, Montgomery Ward obliged.
>
> When the cousin had seen enough, he sent the cards back. A political enemy, who had long been planning the Senator's undoing, brought him up on charges of sending obscene matter through the mails. The Senator was arrested. Other influential members of the

tribe almost got him off on a technicality but the Senator insisted on making a long speech in court. Even the judge tried to stop him but his forensic impulse got the better of him and he talked himself right into jail. (*LIG*, 40)

This anecdote, of course, anticipates elements of the Atelier Monty episodes of *The Town,* but it also looks back to Montgomery Ward's previous appearance in *Sartoris/Flags,* as well as to the figure of State Senator Clarence Snopes in *Sanctuary.* In this anecdote, significantly, a Snopes receives his comeuppance, in part through his constitutional inability to resist violating the standards of Jefferson decency by exploiting human weakness, and it again foreshadows the developments through which the Snopeses destroy themselves. The Yoknapatawpha characters, Faulkner later said, had a continuous existence in his own mind quite apart from their avatars in particular stories and novels:

> I think that after about ten books, I had learned enough of judgment to where I could pick and choose the facet of the character which I needed at that particular time to move the story I was telling, so that I can take a facet of one character in one story and another facet of that character in another story. To me it's the same character, though sometimes to the reader it may seem as though the character had changed or developed more — to me he hasn't. (*FIU*, 24)

Thus, by the time he finally got *The Hamlet* "pulled together," Faulkner was able to draw on a wide range of short story and novel material, and on Snopes stories conceived but apparently not written. It is also evident that throughout the thirties Faulkner had in mind a Snopes trilogy, if not precisely what we now know as *the* Snopes trilogy. The trilogy was forecast at least as early as 1934, and was outlined by Faulkner in a 1938 letter to his Random House editor, Robert Haas:

> I am working at the Snopes book. It will be in three books, whether big enough to be three separate volumes I dont know yet, though I think it will. The first one I think will run about 80,000 words. I am half through with it. Three chapters have been printed in mags. as short stories, though not in my collections yet.
>
> The title is THE PEASANTS. Has to do with Flem Snopes' beginning in the country, as he gradually consumes a small village until there is nothing left in it for him to eat. His last coup gains him a foothold in Jefferson, to which he moves with his wife, leaving his successor kinsmen to carry on in the country.
>
> The second volume is RUS IN URBE. He begins to trade on his wife's infidelity, modest blackmail of her lover, rises from half owner of back street restaurant through various grades of city employment, filling each post he vacates with another Snopes from the country, until he is secure in the presidency of a bank, where he can even stop blackmailing his wife's lover.
>
> The third volume is ILIUM FALLING. This is the gradual eating-up of Jefferson by Snopes, who corrupt the local government with crooked politics, buy up all the colonial homes and tear them down and chop up the lots into subdivisions.

This is the plot, if any. Flem gets his wife because she is got with child by a sweetheart who clears out for Texas; for a price he protects her good name. No, before this, his youngest brother tries to keep his father from setting fire to his landlord's barn, believes he has caused the father to be shot, and runs away from home, goes west, has a son which the other Snopes know nothing about.

Flem moves to town with his wife whose child pretty soon sees what a sorry lot Snopes are. She goes to New York (has money from her actual father) and is overseas in the War with ambulance corps, where she meets the son of the boy who ran away from home, finds him a kinsman, finds how his father has tried to eradicate the Snopes from him. After the war she brings together this Snopes and the daughter of a collateral Snopes who also looks with horror on Snopeses. She and her remote cousin marry, have a son who is the scion of the family.

What this will tell is, that this flower and cream, this youth, whom his mother and father fondly believed would raise the family out of the muck, turns out to have all the vices of all Snopes and none of the virtues — the ruthlessness and firmness — of his banker uncle, the chief of the family. He has not enough courage and honesty to be a successful bootlegger nor enough industry to be the barber for which he is finally trained after Flem has robbed his mother of what money her father and husband left her. He is in bad shape with syphilis and all the little switch-tailed nigger whores call him by his first name in private and he likes it.

By this time Flem has eaten up Jefferson too. There is nothing else he can gain, and worse than this, nothing else he wants. He even has no respect for the people, the town, he has victimised, let alone the parasite kin who batten on him. He reaches the stage where there is just one more joke he can play on his environment, his parasite kin and all. So he leaves all his property to the worthless boy, knowing that no other Snopes has sense enough to hold onto it, and that at least this boy will get rid of it in the way that will make his kinfolks the maddest. (*SLWF,* 107-8)

It is difficult, as Noel Polk has observed, to know just how seriously to take this outline.[12] Faulkner's brief description of *The Peasants* is extremely close to the argument of *The Hamlet.* His description of *Rus in Urbe* and *Ilium Falling,* however, point only toward parts of *The Town* and *The Mansion.* The plot of "the youngest brother," of course, is diffused among "Barn Burning," *The Hamlet,* and the stories of Linda Snopes and Wallstreet Panic Snopes in *The Town* and *The Mansion.* The point is that at this stage of his career, Faulkner apparently viewed the Snopes saga in terms of bitter irony and biting satire from beginning to end.

Faulkner's description of the genesis and composition of *The Hamlet* to Malcolm Cowley in 1945 is more limited and more instructive. *The Hamlet,* Faulkner explained, was "incepted as a novel," with "Spotted Horses" as the beginning and, for a while, the end:

... two years later suddenly I had The HOUND, then JAMSHYD'S COURTYARD .... Meanwhile my book had created Snopes and his clan, who produced stories in their saga which are to fall in a later volume: MULE IN THE YARD, BRASS, etc. This over about ten years, until one day I decided I had better start on the first volume or I'd never get any of it down. So I wrote an induction toward the spotted horse story, which included

BARN BURNING and WASH, which I discovered had no place in that book at all. Spotted horses became a longer story, picked up the HOUND (rewritten and much longer and with the character's name changed from Cotton to Snopes) and went on with JAMSHYD'S COURTYARD. (*SLWF,* 197)

This letter, written twelve years before the appearance of *The Town* in 1957, suggests, again, that Faulkner's plan for a Snopes trilogy was in his mind for some time, but it also shows that his plan changed in several specific ways. We can only guess at the kind of connections Faulkner imagined between "Wash" and *The Hamlet.* Perhaps Wash Jones was to become Ab Snopes; perhaps Flem Snopes was to meet his end as Thomas Sutpen did; or perhaps Faulkner, remembering *Absalom, Absalom!,* simply confused two narratives featuring a young boy who is turned away from a big house. At any rate, the letter gives a fair idea of how Faulkner assimilated his stories into his novels, and it shows that the plans for the Snopes chronicle were altered during the period of composition.

Whatever his conception of the later volumes in 1940, Faulkner obviously felt no particular responsibility toward his previously published texts in writing *The Hamlet,* which, despite its occasional counterpoints of humor, is surely among his most despairing novels. Flem's triumph in Frenchman's Bend is total, and his success in Jefferson is foretold. *The Hamlet* begins with Flem's first appearance in the Frenchman's Bend community and it ends with his leaving it, bound for Jefferson, where he will become president of the bank. Flem's progress through the limited hierarchy of the Bend is marked in successive stages by episodes Faulkner had developed in the short stories. Though it is radically altered in *The Hamlet,* "Barn Burning" is the first of the stories employed in the structure of the novel. Flem uses his father's reputation as a barn-burner to secure a job as clerk in Varner's store. He then takes advantage of the opportunity to marry Eula and to get title to the Old Frenchman place from Ratliff, Tull, and Armstid. In the final scene of the novel, his wagon loaded for Jefferson, he joins the spectators who have come to watch the demented Henry Armstid digging for gold:

He did not pull out of the road into line. Instead, he drove on past the halted wagons while the heads of the women holding the nursing children turned to look at him and the heads of the men along the fence turned to watch him pass, the faces grave, veiled too, still looking at him when he stopped the wagon and sat, looking over their heads into the garden. (*HAM,* 365-66)

The pathetic Armstid, taunted by small boys, is unaware of Snopes' presence. He has no notion that Snopes is responsible for his plight. He is convinced, as he was in "Lizards," that everyone is after "his" treasure. He chases the boys until he falls exhausted.

> Then he got up, onto his hands and knees first as small children do, and picked up the shovel and returned to the trench. He did not glance up at the sun, as a man pausing in work does to gauge the time. He came straight back to the trench, hurrying back to it with that painful and laboring slowness, the gaunt unshaven face which was now completely that of a madman. He got back into the trench and began to dig.
>
> Snopes turned his head and spat over the wagon wheel. He jerked the reins slightly. "Come up," he said. (*HAM*, 366)

In *Father Abraham,* Flem is an absurd figure; in *The Hamlet* he is a menacing one. He not only endures, he prevails, and there is no hint that anyone in either Frenchman's Bend or Jefferson can do anything about him. There is no Wash Jones to rise up and destroy the man who has deceived him, no Miss Quentin to make off with his money, no Hightower or Byron Bunch to protect the Lena Groves of Frenchman's Bend. Only Ratliff understands the nature of the Snopes menace, and he, like Horace Benbow and Quentin Compson, is too weak to be effective in his opposition to Flem. *The Hamlet* lacks the detached comic attitude displayed toward the Snopeses in *Father Abraham,* and it has none of the good-humored admiration bestowed on Flem by the narrator of "Spotted Horses." Of the early Snopes stories, "Lizards in Jamshyd's Courtyard" is closest in tone to *The Hamlet,* but the story pays more attention to the weaknesses of Suratt and Armstid than to the viciousness of Flem Snopes.

Faulkner claimed that the story came to him all at once, and there were references to a forthcoming trilogy as early as 1934:

> I thought of the whole story at once like a bolt of lightning lights up a landscape and you see everything but it takes time to write it, and this story I had in my mind for about thirty years, and the one which I will do next [*The Mansion*] — it happened at that same moment, thirty years ago when I thought of it, of getting at it. (*FIU*, 30)

If Faulkner envisioned the destruction of Flem Snopes in his original moment of inspiration, he managed to withhold that element of his vision for thirty years. In the thirties stories of the Snopeses, published or unpublished, only in "Centaur in Brass" is there any indication that Flem is less than invincible. The impact of *The Hamlet* is the product of the meanness of Flem's ambitions, the baseness of his methods, and the totality of his triumph. There is no anticipation of his downfall in that novel, nor is there in any of the interviews Faulkner gave in the thirties and early forties. On the contrary, though Faulkner continued to announce his forthcoming chronicle, the implied content of the volumes subsequent to *The Hamlet* would appear to consist of the material expressed or hinted at in *Father Abraham.* In an interview at the time *The Hamlet* was published, Faulkner gave a brief definition of the clan:

The Snopeses are a family who, by petty chicanery and unscrupulous politics, take possession of the town of Jefferson, Miss. They creep over it like mold over cheese and destroy its traditions and whatever loveliness there was in the place.[13]

Faulkner's original conception of the Snopes saga, I believe, included Flem's triumph in Frenchman's Bend and in Jefferson, but did not include his destruction. Comments he made at Virginia indicate that Flem's desire for respectability was a late development in the conception:

... I say a scoundrel, to be a good one, must be an individualist, that only an individualist can be a first-rate scoundrel. Only an individualist can be a first-rate artist. He can't belong to a group or a school and be a first-rate writer.

Q. You could have some grudging admiration for Flem Snopes, who pretty well sticks to his character.

A. Well, until he was bitten by the bug to be respectable, and then he let me down....
(*FIU*, 33)

"The scoundrel in time is seduced away by the desire to be respectable," Faulkner continued, "so he's finished." Snopeses will always be opposed and conquered because "the impulse to eradicate Snopes is in my opinion so strong that it selects its champions when the crisis comes" (*FIU*, 34).

Thus, when he came to write *The Town*, Faulkner revised "Centaur in Brass" and "Mule in the Yard" in accordance with his altered conception of the Snopes dilemma.

In *The Town* the episode of the stolen brass is related by Charles Mallison, who has heard it from his cousin Gowan. The main factual revisions are that the middle-aged Hoxey is replaced by the dashing young de Spain, and that many more of the details of Flem's background are made explicit. A totally new feature in the novel emerges in Charles Mallison's description of his family's watchful attitude toward the Snopeses; Gavin Stevens and V.K. Ratliff are introduced as Snopes-watchers. The water tank with the brass in it, young Mallison asserts, is not a monument: "A monument only says *At least I got this far* while a footprint says *This is where I was when I moved again*" (*TWN*, 29). The whole "Centaur" episode in *The Town* is framed and decorated by Charles Mallison's references to the careful watching of Flem. Gavin Stevens cannot understand Flem's behavior, but Ratliff does. "Not catching his wife with Manfred de Spain yet," Ratliff tells Stevens, "is like that twenty-dollar gold piece pinned to your undershirt on your first maiden trip to what you hope is going to be a Memphis whorehouse. He dont need to unpin it yet" (*TWN*, 29).

Flem does not unpin the gold piece for years. He climbs in the social and commercial hierarchy of Jefferson on the strength of his wife's relationship to de Spain. But he is constantly embarrassed by the ignoble behavior of his relatives, and one by one he eliminates them from the community. Prime examples of this can be seen in Faulkner's reworking of "Mule in the Yard." In *The Town,* the main narrative of "Mule in the Yard" in unchanged, which substantiates Faulkner's admission that some of the writing in the novel is thirty years old (*FIU*, 108). The context of the novel, however, is entirely different from that of the story. We are aware throughout the episode in the novel of the watchful presence of Ratliff and Gavin Stevens, and in the end Flem Snopes steps forward to compensate Mrs. Hait for her loss and to bribe I.O. to leave Jefferson. Flem's action here, as Ratliff explains to Charles Mallison, is consistent with his desire for respectability, earlier demonstrated when he helps to close down Montgomery Ward's "photographic studio." The comic force of "Mule in the Yard" is undercut in *The Town* by the complexities of Charles Mallison's narration, and by the framing of the story within the context of Flem's activities in Jefferson.

Two new stories about the Snopeses, "By the People" and "Hog Pawn," were incorporated into *The Mansion,* the last novel of the trilogy. "By the People," published in 1955, shows Ratliff actually winning a battle against a Snopes. The Snopes in this case is Clarence Egglestone, the long-time State Senator who is now mounting a campaign for Congress. He is all that we would expect of a Snopes in politics, a turncoat racist demagogue who depends for his political life on Uncle Billy Varner's patronage. His career is recounted in ringing tones of mock-admiration by Charles Mallison, who observes the Snopeses with Ratliff and Gavin Stevens again in *The Mansion.* Gavin and Charles Mallison are horrified by Snopes' ambition, and Ratliff tells them they will have to adopt their opponent's methods. For Gavin, this is impossible, and he is completely dumbfounded when Snopes drops out of the race. This inexplicable fact is accounted for, reluctantly, by Ratliff, who admits that he humiliated Snopes. His method is to attract a series of dogs to the Senator, by drawing across the back of his trousers some recently used reeds from a favorite dogs' watering spot. Snopes does not notice that he has become a canine comfort station until it is too late, and Uncle Billy Varner withdraws his support from the man "that ere a dog passes can't tell from a fence post."[14]

This late Snopes story recalls *Father Abraham* in that it narrates low comedy in high rhetoric, but its result is precisely opposite to that of the first Snopes stories. Ratliff is in control and completely confident throughout, and in the story's first description of Snopes it is mentioned that he has withdrawn from the campaign. The prose of "By the People" is characteristic of Faulkner's later style, involuted and self-conscious. Ratliff is very much aware of his role as tutor to Gavin Stevens and Charles Mallison, and he makes the moral of the story explicit. As usual, when he has both the facts and the truth pointed out to him, Gavin can understand what has happened and what it means. In *The Mansion,* this episode, recounted in chapter 13, is simply one of many instances of the Snopeses' falling from prominence in Yoknapatawpha:

... Ratliff eliminated Clarence. Not that Ratliff shot him or anything like that; he just simply eliminated Clarence as a factor in what Charles's Uncle Gavin also called their constant Snopes-fear and -dread, or you might say, Snopes-dodging. (*MAN*, 295)

"Hog Pawn," which Faulkner sent to his agent in January 1955,[15] is another trickster tale. The story, narrated by Gavin Stevens' nephew Chick, intertwines the tale of a Jefferson feud between an old man named Meadowfill and a bachelor Snopes with the story of the romance of Essie Meadowfill and World War II veteran McKinley Smith. In its main outlines, "Hog Pawn" follows the classic argument of comedy, showing how the generating love of Essie and young Smith eventually triumphs over the opposition of *senex* Meadowfill. The Snopes-Meadowfill feud allows Gavin Stevens to perform again the feat he had achieved in "Knight's Gambit": anticipating and preventing an intended murder and setting the young lovers on the road to marriage. Both Snopes and Meadowfill are appropriately mean, cantankerous, and vicious. There is little, if anything, to choose between them, except that Snopes is willing to risk murder for the sake of victory in the feud.

As with the other stories revised for *The Town* and *The Mansion*, "Hog Pawn" is embedded in the larger contexts of the novel. In revising the story for Chapter 14 of *The Mansion*, Faulkner wrote a long induction establishing the feud between Meadowfill and Snopes (here named Orestes) as subsidiary to a lengthy contest between Flem Snopes and Jason Compson over the remainder of the original Compson property. Thus both Orestes Snopes and Meadowfill, like the hog over which they contend, are pawns in a larger game. Gavin's intercession in the feud constitutes one more manifestation of his desire to rid Jefferson of Snopeses, and at the end of the chapter he despairs in his knowledge that he has thwarted Orestes Snopes only to assist Flem. "It's hopeless," he tells Ratliff. "Even when you get rid of one Snopes, there's already another one behind you even before you can turn around." "That's right," Ratliff explains. "As soon as you look you see right away it aint nothing but jest another Snopes" (*MAN*, 349).

In *The Mansion*, the "Hog Pawn" story is placed just prior to the scenes describing Mink's completion of his revenge on Flem. As such, it stands in subtle and comic but clear juxtaposition to the story of how Mink came to murder Jack Houston, for Orestes Snopes, like Mink, allows his livestock to forage on another man's property. Postwar Jefferson, however, differs radically from 1908 Frenchman's Bend, and Mink's direct, primitive, and fatal obsession with Jack Houston is muted into Res Snopes' petty, inept, and ultimately harmless feud with Meadowfill. Faulkner's interpolation of the Flem Snopes-Jason Compson contest and the Ratliff-Stevens-Charles Mallison perspective reduces the comic force "Hog Pawn" displays in an isolated reading.

Other Snopes stories are similarly reworked or referred to in *The Mansion*.

Mink Snopes' murder of Houston is described again, and amplified. Eula's youthful affair with Hoke McCarron is recalled, and McCarron himself appears in the story. Many of the newer Snopeses, such as Wallstreet Panic, figure briefly, and Ab Snopes makes a final bow, but "for the moment Flem was the only true Snopes actively left in Jefferson" (*MAN*, 152). The novel includes brief reflexive vignettes of other characters from the Yoknapatawpha chronicle, almost all of them fond or neutral. Narcissa Benbow is mentioned as Bayard Sartoris' widow. Lucius Binford settles down with Miss Reba, who mourns his passing. Res Grier's work-unit dog is recalled. Captain McLendon appears as the defender of Tug Nightingale. The tragedies of the Compson family are alluded to briefly, and Jason is tricked by Flem. These allusions are clearly decorative, part of the reflexive lore of Yoknapatawpha. All the bits and pieces of previous stories and novels are arranged in the new design, which is essentially concerned with Mink's revenge on Flem.

One thing Faulkner apparently believed he had learned about the human heart and its dilemma in the thirty-four-year progress of the Snopes chronicle was that the Snopeses would destroy themselves. Those who read the Snopes trilogy as an entity ignore what seems to me to be the most pervasive evidence that there was a radical alteration in Faulkner's conception of the Snopes family. In his study Warren Beck contends that the trilogy "as now discovered whole is in its way the very crown of Faulkner's creativity." Beck's reading of the novels is a sensitive one, based on his agreement with those who feel that all of Faulkner's fiction is "basically and unequivocally humanistic."[16] Flem, he contends, is central to the trilogy as amoral aggressor, and although Flem is grotesque, those who oppose him are often provoked to extreme and grotesque actions of their own: |

> Irony, as concomitant of the grotesque, becomes medium of the tragicomic, comprehending the contradictory involvements of human affairs. Thus Faulkner's conceptual power, humanely based, expressed in empathy and irony, renders the vision of life as motion, the continuum of being in a transcendent human consciousness, immediately responsive, reverberant of past experience and projective of attitude and action, and thereby evocative of values, postulated relatively, but with ethical relevance."

A consideration of their specific grotesqueries shows why Faulkner's preoccupation with the Snopeses was as constant as Stevens' and Ratliff's. As individuals the Snopeses are comic figures, either laughable in themselves or the cause of the ludicrous posture in others. Collectively, however, the Snopeses originally appeared to be menacing, for they perverted the traditional institutions of marriage and the family and community solidarity and decency. The early Snopes stories and novels give no hint that they can be effectively combatted, or that they will ultimately destroy themselves, though in *The Hamlet* we are made to understand that the Snopeses are no more benevolent toward each other than they are toward others.

Flem's marriage to Eula is a perversion, an arrangement of financial convenience on which he would capitalize until her death. I.O. Snopes is a bigamist. Ike Snopes makes love to a cow. Byron Snopes is a voyeur and a writer of obscene letters. Of all the Snopeses, only Wallstreet Panic and Mink show anything like affective in their marriages, and these are distinctly later additions to the fiction.

In their perversion and exploitation of family loyalties the Snopeses are strikingly different from other Yoknapatawpha families. For the Compsons, for the Sartorises, for the McCaslins, for the Burdens, and in a slightly different way for individuals like Thomas Sutpen and Joe Christmas, family connections are of paramount importance. For Flem Snopes, they are nothing. He marries Eula to further his own advancement, and he allows her to cuckold him in order to achieve his ends. In the early descriptions of the Snopeses it appears that nepotism is one of Flem's primary concerns, but in Jefferson even this "human" attribute is denied him. He not only helps to put Montgomery Ward in jail, he determines which jail he will go to, and how long he will stay. As soon as another Snopes threatens Flem's position, he is dispatched from Jefferson. Flem is impotent, and he is concerned with neither patrimony nor progeny. He puts no stock in "background," and he is not willing to pretend that it is worth anything to him. "I had a grandfather," he says, in an uncharacteristically long speech, "because everybody had. I dont know who he was, but I know whoever he was he never had enough furniture for a room, let alone a house" (*TWN*, 222). It is instructive to compare a graphic representation of the Snopes genealogy with that of any of the other important Yoknapatawpha families. At the most there are four generations of Snopeses, beginning with Ab and ending with the four demented get of Byron Snopes and his Apache squaw. The Snopes genealogy is vertical rather than horizontal. They are all "cousins" of one kind or another, but there is no true kinship among them.

The Snopeses destroy, or seek to destroy, the community in which they live. Ab has no conception of loyalty, except to his own skin. His barn burning is symbolic of his fierce opposition to the established community. Flem bores from within, but he works outside the law as the occasion demands. Byron embezzles from the bank. Clarence moves from the legislature to Miss Reba's to teaching Sunday school without any apparent awareness of his hypocrisy. Lump sells tickets for his cousin's performances with the cow, as though he were a freak in a sideshow. The conduct of such characters provokes outrage and despair. In the early stories and novels no single member of the community can act effectively against them, for the individuals in the community are either weak and squeamish like Horace Benbow, or like Suratt-Ratliff they are not quite proficient enough to beat the Snopeses at their own game. Some, like Henry Armstid, are crippled and driven mad. Others, like the narrator of "Spotted Horses" and Ratliff in *The Hamlet*, can pause and admire their shrewdness.

But the Snopeses, Faulkner maintains, are finally self-destroying. Flem's apparent acquiescence in his own murder is the chief symbol. Ratliff and Stevens cannot prevent it, any more than they can stop any other Snopes activity. Mink's obsessive desire for revenge on Flem is sustained for thirty-eight years until it is fulfilled. There is a coherence to Mink's obsession which Flem, Ratliff, and Stevens all understand, but only Flem can control it to any significant extent. *The Mansion* has been scorned by those who feel that Faulkner's conclusion to the trilogy is contrived, an exercise in wishful thinking rather than the response to the fictional necessity of the characters he had created. Lawrance Thompson, for example, criticizes Faulkner's "erroneous decision to conclude the trilogy with the falsehood that Snopesism will always destroy itself."[18]

Erroneous or not, the conclusion to the trilogy is clearly a late conception of Faulkner's, and it is consistent with the plea for affirmation expressed at Stockholm and in the later fiction. Though much is made in *The Town* and *The Mansion* of "Snopesism," an examination of the Snopes phenomena throughout the short stories and novels shows that the Snopeses are multiple, particular, and eccentric, rather than homogeneous, universal, and typical. There is no one idea, attitude, motive, or action which is the dominant characteristic of all the different Snopeses. The imposition of a symbolic unity on this disparate family is an early ploy of Faulkner's, rejected in the later fiction. When Stevens talks about Snopesism he makes the mistake of assuming the family's unity and collective menace. Ratliff, on the contrary, is aware that Snopesism is simply another name for Flem. Faulkner finally admitted that his creation was, after all, a fictional device:

> There's probably no tribe of Snopeses in Mississippi or anywhere else outside my own apocrypha. They were simply an invention of mine to tell a story of man in his struggle. That I was not trying to say, This is the sort of folks we raise in my part of Mississippi, at all. That they were simply over-emphasized, burlesqued if you like, which is what Mr. Dickens spent a lot of his time doing, for a valid reason to him and to me ... which was to tell a story in an amusing, dramatic, tragic, or comical way. (*FIU*, 282)

Each short story involving the Snopeses is a separate work of art, and none of the Snopes texts, including the novels of the trilogy, is absolutely dependent on any of the others. If part of the pleasure in reading Faulkner's fiction is the discovery of old familiar characters and incidents, it is also a pleasure to discover the changes, to appreciate the fact that Faulkner's mythological characters are most palpable in their individual avatars. The Snopes stories, then, can and ought to be distinguished from their recasting in the Snopes novels, and all the Snopes material, viewed consecutively, reveals the dynamic nature of the design in the Faulkner canon.

5

Myriad Designs

Faulkner's short stories are at once autonomous works of art, structural units in his novels, and integral parts of his reflexive canon. By understanding their initial mode of existence as self-contained short stories, it is possible to determine their relations to the novels and to Faulkner's entire output. The relative neglect of the short stories to date is largely the result of the desire on the part of Faulkner's critics to seize on one or more "keys" to the author's art. Those who choose the mythological approach have assumed that the common denominator of Yoknapatawpha County and the reappearance of characters, incidents, and situations indicate that Faulkner followed a constant and discoverable design in populating his fictional universe. The short stories show that Faulkner's design was a dynamic one, and that Faulkner altered his characters, incidents, and situations to meet the artistic needs of the story or novel in question. Those who choose to emphasize Faulkner's role as a technical innovator have assumed that the primary interest of his fiction is in such matters as his manipulation of point-of-view, his articulation of a Bergsonian concept of fictional time, and his development of a contrapuntal fictional structure. The short stories embody each of these techniques, but they also show that no single technique is Faulkner's primary and constant concern. Those who emphasize Faulkner's relations with the Gothic tradition assume that he adapted a peculiarly Southern machinery to an old tradition of the romance in order to excite terror and loathing by distorting or ignoring reality. The short stories indicate that Faulkner often parodied the Gothic conventions as he employed them, and that he expressed an ironic disapproval of characters who acted always according to Gothic and romantic assumptions. Those who emphasize Faulkner's humanism assume that he was a fictional moralist whose lifelong concern was to celebrate in his fiction the eternal verities of human virtue he enumerated in the Nobel address. Read in the general order of their composition, the short stories show that Faulkner was a long time coming to his belief in the possibility of social justice, individual happiness, and responsible and benevolent individual and communal action. Those who emphasize the importance of Faulkner's style assume that there is a kind of writing that is peculiarly "Faulknerian,'' and that the discovery and description of this style is among the chief tasks of the Faulkner reader. The short stories show that Faulkner was capable of a wide variety of styles, and that his characteristic method of expression changed significantly over the years.

At the same time, the short stories provide substantial evidence in support of each major approach to Faulkner's fiction. The short stories are essential to an understanding of the Yoknapatawpha material. There are six distinct ways in which Faulkner drew on his "mythology" in writing his stories and novels. Some novels consist largely of material developed previously in short stories. In such novels, the original short stories were invariably modified in tone, fact, and emphasis to fit the larger structure of the novel. In writing other novels, Faulkner often incorporated single stories, either wholly or in part, again altering the original story to suit the needs of the novel. A third group of stories was apparently developed from characters or incidents originally treated in novels, and a fourth group consists of stories extracted and published from novels-in-progress, or from novels contemplated but not yet published. In such instances Faulkner was careful to distinguish between autonomous short stories and dependent excerpts. In each of these four relations, except for the clearly labelled excerpts, the short story and novel texts are significantly independent. A fifth relationship consists of general analogues between characters, situations, and techniques, and a sixth relationship is involved in the countless reflexive allusions which Faulkner made to specific characters and particular episodes developed in previous texts.

There are many differences between successive versions of the stories, and between similar or presumably identical characters and situations, and these differences point up the essential independence of Faulkner's separate texts. The differences between the short stories and novels dealing with the "same" characters and events in the Yoknapatawpha series are better explained by the exigencies of the newer work and by Faulkner's altered understanding of a character or situation rather than by his faulty memory of a previous text or by his attempt to supplement his declining imagination by availing himself of a character or situation or technique which had previously succeeded for him.

Faulkner's short stories are presently gathered in *Early Prose and Poetry, New Orleans Sketches, Knight's Gambit, Collected Stories, Big Woods,* and *Uncollected Stories,* and single texts are readily available in numerous anthologies. The careful organization of *Collected Stories* reflects Faulkner's concern with the integrated and contrapuntal arrangement of short story volumes which he first showed in *These 13* and continued in *Knight's Gambit* and *Big Woods.* Many of Faulkner's best stories were omitted from *Collected Stories,* and the plan of that volume represents his late assessment of the proper arrangement of the stories he did include, so the section headings of *Collected Stories* should not be taken as the definitive "key" to the stories therein. *The Unvanquished* and *Go Down, Moses,* often discussed as short story collections or "cycles," are best approached as novels, for the short stories revised for inclusion in these two books were originally simple, direct, and self-contained, while the seperable chapters of the Bayard Sartoris and Isaac McCaslin chronicles are complex, oblique, and dependent for their effects on material appearing in other sections of the text. The continued practice of including selections from these two texts in short story anthologies is a disservice to both Faulkner and his readers. At the very least, such excerpts should be prefaced with a clear explanation of the context from which they are taken.

The evidence of the short stories, then, suggests that the parts of Faulkner's mythology are more coherent than the whole, and that the individual text was more important to Faulkner than any extrinsic design, idea, or technique. The short stories show Faulkner's unrivalled versatility: his facility at the comedy of manners, at burlesque, at frontier and tall-tale humor, at detective stories, at hunting stories, at ironic narration, and at the depiction of horror, pathos, and tragedy. His short stories are remarkably various in their settings in place and time, in their points-of-view, and in their styles. Above all they are remarkable for the memorable characters who populate them. Because of their concentration, and their embodiment of Faulkner's aesthetic criteria of unity, coherence, and emphasis, the short stories often reveal Faulkner's mastery of the craft of fiction more strikingly than his longer and more diffuse novels.

The short stories are also vital in assessing Faulkner's development from an attitude of ironic determinism to a thoroughly comic artistic vision. "Life," Faulkner wrote Cowley in 1944, "is a phenomenon but not a novelty, the same frantic steeplechase toward nothing everywhere and man stinks the same stink no matter where in time."[1] It is apparent that Faulkner did not always hold this view, for his later fiction is considerably more positive and optimistic in its conclusions than that written in the twenties and thirties. The short stories are occasionally more useful than the novels in tracing the progress of this evolution, for most short story texts are the product of a relatively brief span of time, while several novels were years in the making. Through the work of Hans Skei, we now have more precise dates for the composition of the stories and novels than were previously available, this development can now be described with more precision than was formerly possible. At the moment we may begin by observing that the vast majority of the stories of the early thirties have tragic or ironic implications, and that nearly all the stories published after 1942 are essentially comic in nature.

The present consensus is that Faulkner's later fiction is distinctly inferior to his earlier works. The short stories do not give reason to modify this judgment substantially, because Faulkner wrote relatively few stories after 1942, and because his convoluted and discursive later style does not lend itself with grace to the medium of the short story. The grounds on which the later fiction is judged wanting, however, require examination. The earlier, more pessimistic fiction embodies the assumptions and world view of those who are opposed to evils, particularly social evils. *Light in August,* for example, treats Joe Christmas and Joanna Burden as victims of racial condescension and mob violence. On the one hand, the pessimistic works emphasize the dominance of vicious men such as Sutpen, Jason Compson, Popeye, and Flem Snopes. The reader is invited to exclaim, righteously, over the perfidy of these types. On the other hand when a Gavin Stevens is presented with approval in *Intruder in the Dust* in spite of his smugness and loquaciousness, his triumph seems too nearly a reward for vice. The later fiction presents an essentially sympathetic and affectionate view of the South, in contrast with the earlier fiction, which more nearly matched the stereotyped Northern expectations. The optimistic conclusions of the later fiction, particularly of *The Mansion,* have been dismissed as forced and mechanical, while the pessimistic endings of novels like *Absalom, Absalom!* or *The Hamlet* are thought to be the natural outcome of the tragic tendencies implicit in every human situation. Faulkner's later optimism seems to deny those tendencies, and is said to be a sentimental "soft" attempt to affirm the eternal verities described at Stockholm. The modern critical preference, in short, is for works which express a tragic, ironic, or apocalyptic view of the human condition, and those of Faulkner's works which do not express such a view are consequently thought inferior to those which do.

It is helpful to recognize these assumptions, for they play a large part in determining which of Faulkner's works are admitted to the larger canon. If we acknowledge that many of Faulkner's inferior stories and novels project the same philosophical attitudes as his superior works, we may come to understand, to learn again, that the merits of a work of art are not directly proportional to the extent that it embodies currently fashionable views. It is similarly assumed that Faulkner's short stories are "mere" magazine pieces, styled especially for the *Post, Collier's,* and the like. Faulkner's manuscripts, however, show that he was a deliberate artist and that he made few concessions to the proprieties of editorial taste. If he occasionally undertook a conscious piece of hackwork in fiction, as he claimed to have done in the first draft of *Sanctuary,* the trouble he took to rectify and explain that mistake ought to suggest that he seldom repeated it. His suppression of blatantly commercial stories such as "Two Dollar Wife" shows his consistent standards. Having written a story, however, he usually sought to publish it in the magazine that paid the most. The result is that some of Faulkner's *Post* stories, like "Red Leaves," leap out from their magazine contexts, like sapphires in the mud.

Two other assumptions have contributed to the neglect of Faulkner's stories, both having to do with the nature of the short story genre itself. The first assumption is implied by those critics who maintain that Faulkner's stories are of less importance than his novels because, as they put it, Faulkner contributed less to the development of the short story as a distinct literary form than he did to that of the novel. Though this assumption is highly debatable, it remains that Faulkner's short stories feature the same distinctions which earned him the title of innovator in the novel: the exploration of unusual points-of-view, the radical manipulation of narrative time, the sensitive and forceful evocation of an identifiable region, and the masterful delineation of the heroic, tragic, comic, or pathetic, but above all, *individual* characters of Yoknapatawpha County.

The final assumption is seldom stated, but it is nevertheless a pervasive one. It is that the novel is the quintessential form of fiction in our time, and that none of Faulkner's short stories is therefore worthy of the same serious consideration as his novels. Faulkner once told an interviewer, "I never wrote a short story I liked" (*LIG*, 59), and this comment might be thought to suggest his contempt for the form; his other comments on the short story indicate that he was less than satisfied with his stories because that genre demanded greater perfection than the novel. Faulkner's many excellent stories establish him as a master of the genre, and his short stories deserve the same close reading given his novels. In many instances they are deserving of even more, for the concentration of the short story on a single significant event in the life of a single significant character made the short story a form in which Faulkner often nearly realized his impossible dream of poetry.

Notes

Chapter 1

1. *The Faulkner-Cowley File* (New York: Viking Press, 1966), 14. Cowley dates the letter in which this statement appears from November 1944.

2. The most accurate and complete description of Faulkner's individual stories and story volumes is still James B. Meriwether's 1971 article, "The Short Fiction of William Faulkner: A Bibliography," *Proof* 1, pp. 293-329.

3. Hans H. Skei, *William Faulkner: The Short Story Career* (Oslo-Bergen-Tromsø: Universitetsforlaget, 1981).

4. For studies of Faulkner's "apprenticeship," see Richard P. Adams, *Faulkner: Myth and Motion* (Princeton: Princeton University Press, 1968), H. Edward Richardson, *William Faulkner: The Journey to Self-Discovery* (Columbia: University of Missouri Press, 1976). and Martin Kreiswirth, *William Faulkner: The Making of a Novelist* (Athens: University of Georgia Press, 1983). For the centrality of the 1929-1942 fiction, see Melvin Backman, *Faulkner: The Major Years* (Bloomington and London: Indiana University Press, 1966), and John Pilkington, *The Heart of Yoknapatawpha* (Jackson: University Press of Mississippi, 1981). Of Faulkner's "decline," Eric J. Sundquist's comment on *Go Down, Moses* is representative: "... this novel marks by its precariously extenuated form the end of Faulkner's major work, as though his creative powers, after a final draining surge, had broken under the pressures of the envisioned design." *Faulkner: The House Divided* (Baltimore and London: The Johns Hopkins University Press, 1983), 6.

5. On the revision of short stories for particular novels, see, among others, Joanne V. Creighton, *William Faulkner's Craft of Revision* (Detroit: Wayne State University Press, 1977) and James Early, *The Making of "Go Down, Moses"* (Dallas: Southern Methodist University Press, 1972). On the organization of short story volumes, see especially James G. Watson, "Faulkner: Short Story Structures and Reflexive Forms," *Mosaic* 11 (Summer 1978), pp. 127-37, and Arthur F. Kinney, "Faulkner's Narrative Poetics and *Collected Stories,*" *Faulkner Studies* 1 (1980), pp. 58-79.

6. James B. Meriwether and Michael Millgate, eds., *Lion in the Garden: Interviews with William Faulkner, 1926-1962* (New York: Random House, 1968). Hereafter cited parenthetically in the text as *LIG*.

7. Mark Spilka, "The Necessary Stylist: A New Critical Revision," *Modern Fiction Studies* 6 (Winter 1960-61), pp. 283-97. "Autonomy itself is relative: all works of art exist within surrounding contexts on which their quality depends." Critics who locate Faulkner's de-

sign "intertextually" include John T. Irwin, *Doubling and Incest/Repetition and Revenge: A Speculative Reading of Faulkner* (Baltimore: The Johns Hopkins University Press, 1975).

8. Faulkner wrote to a Mr. Thompson, circa 1931, "... I am availing myself of my prerogative of using these people when and where I see fit. So far, I have not bothered much about chronology, which, if I am ever collected, I shall have to do." Joseph Blotner, ed., *Selected Letters of William Faulkner* (New York: Random House, 1977), p. 50.

9. Quoted by Malcolm Cowley, *The Faulkner-Cowley File,* p. 90.

10. As is so often the case in Faulkner's career, individual story texts in these volumes overlap in ways that the chronology of their publication obscures. Some of the *Knight's Gambit* stories were written in the early thirties, and a version of the title story had been written before *Go Down, Moses* was published. Yet reviewers and critics persist in the unwarranted assignment of *Knight's Gambit* to the post-1942 or "declining phase" of Faulkner's career.

11. *Faulkner in the University: Class Conferences at the University of Virginia 1957-58,* Frederick L. Gwynn and Joseph L. Blotner, eds. (New York: Vintage, 1965). Hereafter cited in the text as *FIU. Faulkner at West Point,* Joseph L. Fant and Robert Ashley, eds. (New York. Random House, 1964).

12. Both *The Faulkner-Cowley File* and *Selected Letters* give numerous examples of Faulkner's private assessment of particular texts. More public commentary is in *Essays, Speeches & Public Letters,* ed. James B. Meriwether (New York: Random House, 1964).

13. For a comprehensive and reliable listing of Faulkner scholarship and criticism through 1973, see Thomas L. McHaney, *William Faulkner: A Reference Guide* (Boston: G.K. Hall, 1976). See also Skei, *The Short Story Career,* pp. 143-57.

14. See, for example, Faulkner's comments to Cowley on his preference of texts for "The Hound," "Barn Burning," and "Spotted Horses" (*The Faulkner-Cowley File,* p. 31).

15. See, among others, *FIU,* p. 145; *LIG,* p. 238; and *Faulkner at West Point,* pp. 78, 106.

16. Walter J. Slatoff, *Quest for Failure: A Study of William Faulkner* (Ithaca: Cornell University Press, 1960), p. 19.

17. Adams, *Faulkner: Myth and Motion,* p. vii.

18. Olga W. Vickery, *The Novels of William Faulkner* (Baton Rouge: Louisiana State University Press, 1964), p. 300. In her discussion of the relations of the short stories to the novels and to the entire matter of Yoknapatawpha, Prof. Vickery anticipates many of the issues of Faulkner's self-reflexivity.

19. Michael Millgate, *The Achievement of William Faulkner* (New York: Random House, 1966), pp. 259-76. Millgate's early observation that individual collections of Faulkner's stories "may conceivably possess a discernible internal organization of their own" has led to several useful studies.

20. Dorothy Y. Tuck, *Crowell's Handbook of Faulkner* (New York: Thomas Y. Crowell, 1964); Harry Runyan, *A Faulkner Glossary* (New York: Citadel, 1964); Walter K. Everett, *Faulkner's Art and Characters* (Woodbury, N.Y.: Barron's, 1969).

21. Lawrance Thompson, *William Faulkner: An Introduction and Interpretation* (New York: Barnes and Noble, 1963), p. 10.

22. Irving Howe, *William Faulkner: A Critical Appraisal* (New York: Vintage, 1962), p. 262.

23. Cleanth Brooks, *William Faulkner: The Yoknapatawpha Country* (New Haven and London: Yale University Press, 1963), *William Faulkner: Toward Yoknapatawpha and Beyond* (New Haven and London: Yale University Press, 1978), and *William Faulkner: First Encounters* (New Haven and London: Yale University Press, 1983).

24. See, for example, *Faulkner at West Point,* pp. 56-57, 81.

25. Meriwether, in "The Short Fiction of William Faulkner," makes careful distinctions.

26. *The Faulkner-Cowley File,* p. 80. Cf. *FIU,* p. 14.

27. Joseph Gold, *William Faulkner: A Study in Humanism from Metaphor to Discourse* (Norman: University of Oklahoma Press, 1966). Among the earliest developmental readings was provided by Russell Roth, "William Faulkner: The Pattern of Pilgrimage," *Perspective* 2 (1949), pp. 246-54. For an extended treatment of Faulkner's developing aesthetics, see Gary Lee Stonum, *Faulkner's Career: An Internal Literary History* (Ithaca and London: Cornell University Press, 1979). On thematic development, see Doreen Fowler, *Faulkner's Changing Vision: From Outrage to Affirmation* (Ann Arbor: UMI Research Press, 1983). A developmental reading of a particular issue is Karl F. Zender, "Faulkner and the Power of Sound," *PMLA* 99 (1984), 89-108.

28. Ray B. West, *The Short Story in America* (Chicago: H. Regnery, 1952).

29. Hugh Kenner, *Studies in Change: A Book of the Short Story* (Englewood Cliffs, N.J.: Prentice-Hall, 1965), p. 56.

30. *The Yoknapatawpha Country,* p. 337. In a subsequent discussion of the Compsons, Brooks notes: "It is curious that in 'That Evening Sun' Benjy is never mentioned." Such "curiosities" are the product of attempts to create interdependent texts. It is no more "curious" that Benjy is omitted from "That Evening Sun" than it is that the story, by Brooks' own chronology, is narrated by a character who has been dead for three or four years.

31. Tuck, *Crowell's Handbook of Faulkner,* pp. 177-78.

32. William Van O'Connor, *The Tangled Fire of William Faulkner* (Minneapolis: University of Minnesota Press, 1954), 68 n. The "Nancy" referred to in *The Sound and the Fury* is a mule.

33. Winthrop Tilley, "The Idiot Boy in Mississippi," *American Journal of Mental Deficiency* 59 (1955), pp. 374-77.

34. *SLWF,* 44. Another important difficulty of this kind concerns the racial identity of Joe Christmas in *Light in August.* Though many early readers and reviewers assumed that Christmas was a mulatto, Faulkner insisted that Christmas could never know for certain (*FIU,* 72, 97). But Faulkner permitted Cowley to add the tag "the mulatto" at the first mention of Christmas in *The Portable Faulkner.* (See *The Faulkner-Cowley File,* pp. 51, 55). Although Faulkner may have simply concluded that Cowley's excerpt, which concentrates on the proto-Nazi, Percy Grimm, would be improved by the elimination of the ambiguity, this episode is strikingly inconsistent with Faulkner's attitude toward other such changes.

35. See Elizabeth M. Kerr, *Yoknapatawpha. Faulkner's "Little Postage Stamp of Native Soil,"* (New York: Fordham University Press, 1976). See also Charles S. Aiken.

36.   Brooks, *The Yoknapatawpha Country,* pp. 5, 6.

37.   Robert Scholes and Robert Kellogg, *The Nature of Narrative* (Oxford: Oxford University Press, 1966), pp. 199, 200.

38.   John Cullen and Floyd C. Watkins, *Old Times in the Faulkner Country* (Chapel Hill: University of North Carolina Press, 1961), pp. 79-80. John Faulkner, *My Brother Bill: An Affectionate Reminiscence* (New York. Trident Press, 1963), pp. 271-73.

39.   On the origin of the rape scene in *Sanctuary,* see Carvel Collins, "A Note on *Sanctuary,*" *Harvard Advocate* 135 (November 1951), p. 16.

40.   Wayne C. Booth, *The Rhetoric of Fiction* (Chicago: University of Chicago Press, 1961). See also Joseph W. Reed, Jr., *Faulkner's Narrative* (New Haven and London: Yale University Press, 1973), esp. pp. 12-57.

41.   For an extended discussion of these matters, see Hugh M. Ruppersburg, *Voice and Eye in Faulkner's Fiction* (Athens: University of Georgia Press, 1983).

42.   "In no other writer in the world," Leslie Fiedler says, "do pejorative stereotypes of women appear with greater frequency and on more levels, from the most trivial to the most profound," *Love and Death in the American Novel* (New York: Meridian Books, 1962), p. 309. For more judicious studies of this subject, see Sally R. Page, *Faulkner's Women: Characterization and Meaning* (Deland, Fl.: Everett Edwards, 1972) and David Williams, *Faulkner's Women: The Myth and the Muse* (Montreal and London: McGill-Queen's University Press, 1977).

43.   See Elizabeth M. Kerr, *William Faulkner's Gothic Domain* (Port Washington, N.Y. and London: Kennikat Press, 1979) and Francois L. Pitay, "The Gothicism of *Absalom, Absalom!*: Rosa Coldfield Revisited," in *"A Cosmos of My Own": Faulkner and Yoknapatawpha 1980,* ed. Doreen Fowler and Ann J. Abadie (Jackson: University Press of Mississippi, 1981, pp. 199-226.

44.   Henry Seidel Canby, "School of Cruelty," *Saturday Review of Literature* 7 (March 21, 1931), pp. 673-74. Alan Reynolds Thompson, "The Cult of Cruelty," *The Bookman* 74 (1932), pp. 477-87.

45.   For recent treatments of Faulkner's language and rhetoric, see John T. Matthews, *The Play of Faulkner's Language* (Ithaca and London: Cornell University Press, 1982) and Gail L. Mortimer, *Faulkner's Rhetoric of Loss* (Austin: University of Texas Press, 1983).

46.   George Marion O'Donnell, "Faulkner's Mythology," *Kenyon Review* 1 (1939), p. 285.

47.   The legend persists that Faulkner, following the publication of *Sanctuary,* was able to place stories with the same editors who had previously rejected them. See John Faulkner, *My Brother Bill,* p. 156. For reason to doubt this legend, see Skei, *The Short Story Career,* p. 27.

Chapter 2

1.   *A Fable* was well underway when *Notes on a Horsethief* was published. Faulkner said that the germ of the novel came to him in 1942 (*FIU,* p. 27), and in a 1944 letter to Cowley he alludes to what is probably an early draft of the first part of *A Fable* (*The Faulkner-Cowley File,* pp. 16-17). By 1946 Faulkner referred to *A Fable* as "what seems now to be my magnum O" (*The Faulkner-Cowley File,* p. 91). See Chapter 5 of Keen Butterworth, *A Critical and Textual Study of Faulkner's "A Fable"* (Ann Arbor: UMI Research Press, 1983).

2. A sequel continues a story in time, while a "sibling" considers the same characters, events, and situation from another perspective, another location in fictional space. See Lawrence Durrell, headnote to *Balthazar* (New York: 1958).

3. See Michael Millgate, *The Achievement of William Faulkner,* pp. 11-12.

4. See James B. Meriwether, *The Place of* The Unvanquished *in William Faulkner's Yoknapatawpha Series,* Ph.D. Dissertation, Princeton, 1959,; Edwin M. Holmes, *Faulkner's Twice-Told Tales. His Re-Use of His Material* (The Hague : Mouton, 1966); and Joanne V. Creighton, *William Faulkner's Craft of Revision.*

5. See, for example, *LIG,* p. 132.

6. Irving Howe, *William Faulkner: A Critical Appraisal,* p. 238.

7. See Faulkner to Cowley, *SLWF,* p. 208, approving the publication of "Old Man" for *The Portable Faulkner.* But see also Faulkner to Saxe Commins in August 1953: "Dismembering THE WILD PALMS will in my opinion destroy the over-all impact which I intended. But apparently my vanity (if it is vanity) regarding my work has at last reached that pitch where I consider it does not need petty defending" (*SLWF,* p. 352). At Faulkner's suggestion, Chatto and Windus omitted "Old Man" from the British edition of *The Faulkner Reader* (*SLWF,* p. 359).

8. See W.T. Jewkes, "Counterpoint in Faulkner's *The Wild Palms,*" *Wisconsin Studies in Contemporary Literature* 2 (1961), pp. 39-54, and especially Thomas L. McHaney, *William Faulkner's* "The Wild Palms": *A Study* (Jackson: University Press of Mississippi, 1975).

9. Slatoff, *Quest for Failure, passim.* "Fool About a Horse," "Shingles for the Lord," and "A Courtship" apply this theme in a comic situation.

10. An often-cited reference to the Keats poem occurs at the end of the *Post* text of "The Bear" (*USWF,* pp. 293-95) and at the corresponding place in *Go Down, Moses* (*GDM,* 296-97).

11. Faulkner once said of Caddy Compson, "To me she was the beautiful one, she was my heart's darling" (*FIU,* p. 6). Those who persist in calling Faulkner a misogynist ignore his own negative characterization of misogynists such as Jason Compson, the Kansas police office in *Pylon,* and the tall convict.

12. See Meriwether, ed., *Essays, Speeches and Public Letters,* pp. 7-8.

13. *Essays, Speeches and Public Letters,* p. 7.

14. See Jack F. Stewart, "Apotheosis and Apocalypse in Faulkner's 'Wash,' " *Studies in Short Fiction* 6 (1969), pp. 586-600.

15. Volpe, *A Reader's Guide to William Faulkner,* p. 292.

16. Normal Podhoretz, in his famous blast at *A Fable,* observes. "The story which Faulkner worked into the allegory about the Cockney groom and the Negro preacher who steal a crippled race horse was written nine years ago, and though it is a good story, it certainly falls short of his best work on animals and men," *Doings and Undoings* (New York:. Farrar, Straus, 1964), p. 22.

17. In *Sartoris,* Elnora is described as "Simon's tall yellow daughter." This allusion, though it elliptically suggests a question regarding Elnora's paternity, is obscure and paradoxical compared to the explicit lineage described in "There Was a Queen."

18. See also Philip Castille, " 'There Was a Queen' and Faulkner's Narcissa Sartoris," *Mississippi Quarterly* 28 (1975), pp. 307-15.

19. "... silver so fine and soft that some of the spoons were worn now almost to paper thinness where fingers in their generations had held them; silver which Simon's grandfather Joby buried on a time beneath the ammoniac barn floor while Simon, aged three, in a single filthy garment, had looked on with a child's grave interest in the curious game." (*SAR*, p. 39)

20. "The Tall Men" features a McCallum (not MacCallum) family. An amputation similar to that described in "The Tall Men" also occurs in the novel (*SAR*, p. 140). The Snopes-Hait mule business of "Mule in the Yard" and *The Town* is also anticipated (*SAR*, p. 130). Late in the novel there is a drunken conversation involving Monaghan (who also figures in "Honor"), which includes references to the material of "Ad Astra," a version of which Faulkner had written by the end of 1927 (Skei, *The Short Story Career*, pp. 29, 36).

21. Faulkner's initial criticism of Hemingway was expressed in a 1947 classroom session at the University of Mississippi and was reported in blunt terms: "Hemingway — he has no courage, has never climbed out on a limb. He has never used a word where the reader might check his usage by a dictionary" (*LIG*, p. 58). Faulkner quickly regretted the publication of this statement and spent a good deal of time explaining and qualifying it. See, for example, *FIU*, pp. 143-44. For further discussion of this episode, see Joseph Blotner, *Faulkner: A Biography* (New York: Random House, 1984), pp. 482-85.

22. See Skei, *The Short Story Career*, pp. 59-60.

23. See *The Faulkner-Cowley File*, p. 26.

24. Millgate, *The Achievement of William Faulkner*, pp. 224-26. For more extended discussion of the structure of *Requiem*, see Noel Polk, *Faulkner's "Requiem for a Nun": A Study* (Bloomington and London: Indiana University Press, 1980).

25. Bertrand Russell, *A History of Western Philosophy* (New York: Simon and Schuster, 1945), p. 759.

26. Fiedler, *Love and Death in the American Novel*, p. 314.

27. For a more extended analysis of this scene, see James B. Carothers, "The Road to *The Reivers*" in *"A Cosmos of My Own": Faulkner and Yoknapatawpha,* 1980, Fowler and Abadie, eds. (Jackson: University of Mississippi Press, 1981).

Chapter 3

1. *The Faulkner-Cowley File*, pp. 15-16.

2. Booth, *The Rhetoric of Fiction*, p. 308.

3. Elmo Howell, "Faulkner's Country Church: A Note on 'Shingles for the Lord,' " *The Mississippi Quarterly* 21 (1968), pp. 205-10, criticizes Faulkner for making the church Methodist rather than Baptist, and objects to the differing characterizations of Whitfield in "Shingles" and *As I Lay Dying*. The Whitfield case is simply one of many in which a later Faulkner text treats with humor and sympathy a character who was unsympathetic or contemptible in an earlier text.

4. See Skei, *The Short Story Career*, pp. 40-41.

5.   *Requiem,* of course, was conceived as a novel, rather than as a play. As Noel Polk demonstrates in *Faulkner's "Requiem for a Nun,"* the dramatic passages must be read in juxtaposition to the long prose narratives.

6.   For further discussion of this story, see Tony J. Owens, "Faulkner, Anderson, and 'Artist at Home,' " *Mississippi Quarterly* 32 (1979), pp. 413-22, and Melvin E. Bradford, "An Aesthetic Parable: Faulkner's 'Artist at Home,' " *Georgia Review* 27 (1973), pp. 175-81.

7.   See Frank Cantrell, "Faulkner's 'A Courtship,' " *Mississippi Quarterly* 24 (1971), pp. 289-95.

8.   *Faulkner at West Point,* pp. 73-74, 100-102.

9.   For the genesis of "Turnabout," see Ben Wasson, *Count No 'Count. Flashbacks to Faulkner* (Jackson: University Press of Mississippi, 1983). For a discussion of "The Wasteland" stories see also Douglas Day, "The War Stories of William Faulkner," *Georgia Review* 15 (1961), 385-94.

10.   Millgate, *The Achievement of William Faulkner,* p. 261.

11.   O'Connor, *The Tangled Fire of William Faulkner,* p. 70.

12.   Tuck, *Crowell's Handbook of Faulkner,* p. 163. Runyan (*A Faulkner Glossary,* p. 103) and Holmes (*Faulkner's \Twice-Told Tales,* p. 102) also associate Midgleston with the protagonist of "Carcassonne."

13.   Slatoff, *Quest for Failure,* p. 23.

14.   Wright, *The American Short Story in the Twenties* (Chicago: University of Chicago Press, 1961), p. 185.

15.   Polk, "William Faulkner's 'Carcassonne'," *Studies in American Fiction* 12 (1984), pp. 29-43. See also M.E. Bradford, "The Knight and the Artist: Tasso and Faulkner's 'Carcassonne,' " *The South Central Bulletin* (Winter 1981), pp. 88-90, for an argument for a possible source of the severed horse image.

16.   John R. Thompson's translation of Nadaud's poem, *Poems of John R. Thompson,* ed. John S. Patton (New York: Scribner's, 1920), pp. 219-20.

17.   Most of the changes in "Shingles for the Lord" result from the change in the spelling of "frow" ("froe" in the *Post*) and from the more proper notation in *Collected Stories* of the different functions of the frow and the maul. Other alterations include "upended" (*CS*, p. 27) for "up-ended" in the *Post;* Quick's correct use of "modern" in *Collected Stories,* "modren" in the *Post* (Res Grier uses "modren" in both versions); and the addition of "at" in the line "And we went at it" (*CS*, p. 38). There are numerous differences between the *Story* version of "My Grandmother Millard" and the *Collected Stories* version, most being changes in punctuation. There seems to be a corruption of the text in the description of the Yankee soldiers "not so much peering as frantically gleeful" in their circuit of the outhouse where Cousin Melisandre is hiding (*CS*, p. 676). The *Story* version has "jeering," rather than "peering," and the earlier version, I think, fits the context better. It would be helpful in this and other instances to know precisely the extent to which Faulkner oversaw the setting of the text of *Collected Stories.*

18.   Cowley, *The Faulkner-Cowley File,* p. 5.

19.   Vickery, *The Novels of William Faulkner,* pp. 306, 308.

20. *LIG*, p. 54. Meriwether and Millgate note the dubious reliability of this interview. Another witness to the same interview, A. Wigfall Green, says Faulkner on this occasion called *Go Down, Moses* one of his favorite *novels*, "because it started as a collection of stories, but as he revised it he derived pleasure in creating of it seven different facets of one idea." *William Faulkner of Oxford*, James W. Webb and A. Wigfall Green, eds., (Baton Rouge: Louisiana State University Press, 1965), p. 132.

21. *The Faulkner-Cowley File*, p. 113.

22. *FIU*, p. 4. Faulkner was apparently here referring to the *Big Woods* text of "The Bear," which omits Part IV. But *The Faulkner Reader* includes the entire *Go Down, Moses* text.

23. Holmes, *Faulkner's Twice-Told Tales*, p. 16. The major tendencies in Faulkner's reuse of his material, Holmes argues, are "the habit of remolding short sections to integrate them into a longer work" and a simultaneous shift toward "complexity of diction, rhetoric, character, and theme."

24. Readers who have quickly and persistently identified Faulkner with such diverse "spokesmen" as Quentin Compson and Gavin Stevens also contrive to make Isaac McCaslin a spokesman-hero. Faulkner, however, has dissociated himself from all three. In Ike McCaslin's case he remarked, "I think a man should do more than just repudiate. He should have been more affirmative instead of shunning people" (*LIG*, p. 225). Of Quentin he noted, "There are too many Quentins in the South who are too sensitive to face its reality" (*FIU*, p. 17). Commenting on Stevens in *The Town*, Faulkner said that in trying to deal with people the lawyer "got out of his depth," displaying at times "a good deal less judgment than his nephew did." Stevens' pursuit of degrees and his failure to marry are related aspects of the character who fears that he would "get too involved with the human race if he married one of them" (*FIU*, pp. 140-41). On the general relationship between an author and his supposed spokesman, see *FIU*, pp. 25-26, 118.

25. For discussion of relations between "Gold is Not Always" and *Go Down, Moses* see Jane Millgate, "Short Story into Novel: Faulkner's Reworking of 'Gold is Not Always'," *English Studies* 45 (1964), pp. 310-17. On revisions of "Delta Autumn," see Carol C. Harter, "The Winter of Isaac McCaslin: Revisions and Irony in Faulkner's 'Delta Autumn'," *Journal of Modern Literature* 1 (1970), pp. 209-25.

26. Longley, *The Tragic Mask: A Study of Faulkner's Heroes* (Chapel Hill: University of North Carolina Press, 1963), p. 225.

27. Millgate contends that Faulkner's only substantial reason for including "Smoke" in *Knight's Gambit* would have been the "need to use every one of the Gavin Stevens stories in order to fill out what proved, even so, to be only a short book" (*The Achievement of William Faulkner*, p. 265). For a full discussion of Gavin Stevens in *Knight's Gambit*, see Mary Montgomery Dunlap, "William Faulkner's 'Knight's Gambit' and Gavin Stevens," *Mississippi Quarterly*, 23 (1970), pp. 223-39.

28. Auden, *The Dyer's Hand* (New York: Random House, 1968), p. 148. See also Mark Gidley, "Elements of the Detective Story in Faulkner's Fiction," *Journal of Popular Culture* 7 (1963), pp. 97-123.

29. Cowley, *The Faulkner-Cowley File*, p. 158.

30. Millgate, *The Achievement of William Faulkner*, p. 267.

31. The "Mississippi" piece illustrates Joseph Gold's thesis that Faulkner, in his later years, took for granted his readers' familiarity with his material. The essay fuses history and fic-

tion, as in the reflexive passage which incorporates the principal families of Yoknapatawpha into the pageant of the state:

> ... the Chicasaws and Choctaws and Natchez and Yazoos were as gone as the predeces-
> sors, and the people the boy crept with were the descendants of the Sartorises and De
> Spains and Compsons who had commanded the Manassas and Sharpsburg and Shiloh
> and Chickamauga regiments, and the McCaslins and Ewells and Holstons and Hoggan-
> becks, whose fathers and grandfathers manned them, and now and then a Snopes too
> because by the beginning of the twentieth century Snopeses were everywhere.... (*Essays,
> Speeches, and Public Letters,* p. 12)

32. See Hans H. Skei, "A Forgotten Faulkner Story: 'Thrift'," *Mississippi Quarterly* 32 (1979), pp. 453-60.

33. Meriwether, "The Short Fiction of William Faulkner."

34. See Skei, *The Short Story Career,* p. 53.

35. For a reading of the story, see Giliane Morrell, "Prisoners of the Inner World: Mother and Daughter in 'Miss Zilphia Gant'," *Mississippi Quarterly* 28 (1975), pp. 299-305.

36. For the history of "The Wishing Tree," see Meriwether, "The Short Fiction of William Faulkner," pp. 310-11; Skei, *The Short Story Career,* p. 27; and Blotner, *Faulkner: A Biography;* pp. 198, 207-8, 661-62; and especially Louis D. Brodsky, "A Textual History of William Faulkner's *The Wishing-Tree* and *The Wishing Tree,*" *Studies in Bibliography* 38 (1985), pp. 330-74.

37. See Michel Gresset, "Weekend, Lost and Revisited," *Mississippi Quarterly* 21 (1968), pp. 173-78.

38. Brooks, in *Toward Yoknapatawpha and Beyond,* gives a balanced view of the meaning and achievement of this phase of Faulkner's apprenticeship. Skei. *The Short Story Career,* pp. 17-25, helps to establish the chronology of composition for this period.

39. Simpson, *The Short Stories of William Faulkner:* Ph.D. Dissertation, Florida State University, 1962, p. 3.

40. Frohock, *The Novel of Violence in America* (Boston: Beacon Press, 1964), p. 158.

Chapter 4

1. See James B. Meriwether's Introduction to *Father Abraham* (New York: Red Ozier Press, 1984), for the background of this text.

2. See Skei, *The Short Story Career,* pp. 43-47, for the many points in this tangled history.

3. See Noel Polk's "Afterword" in his edition of *Sanctuary: The Original Text* (New York: Random House, 1981).

4. Skei, *The Short Story Career,* p. 47.

5. Collins, "The Pairing of *The Sound and the Fury* and *As I Lay Dying,*" *Princeton University Library Chronicle* 18 (1957), pp. 114-23.

6. Skei, *The Short Story Career,* p. 37.

7. For Crichton's remark, see James B. Meriwether, "Faulkner's Correspondence with *Scribner's Magazine,*" *Proof* 3 (1973), p. 266.

8. Meriwether points out that V.K. Suratt is named as a narrator in some manuscript and typescript versions of the story, and that Ab is substituted for Pap in one typescript. Since the change involving Ab is a later addition, it can still be maintained that Faulkner's first intention did not involve "Fool About a Horse" as a Snopes story.

9. Dwight Macdonald, however, mistakenly suggests that "Afternoon of a Cow" *derives* from *The Hamlet. Parodies: An Anthology from Chaucer to Beerbohm — and After* (New York: Modern Library, 1965), 473 n.

10. *SLWF,* p. 245.

11. Millgate, *The Achievement of William Faulkner,* p. 327.

12. Polk, "Idealism in *The Mansion,"* in *Faulkner and Idealism: Perspectives from Paris,* eds. Michel Gresset and Patrick Samway, S.J., eds., (Jackson: University Press of Mississippi, 1983), p. 113.

13. *LIG,* p. 39. I have taken the liberty of eliminating the interviewer's attempt to represent Faulkner's accent orthographically. Faulkner also used the mold-on-cheese metaphor in *Father Abraham* and at Virginia (*FIU,* p. 193).

14. "By the People," *40 Best Stories from 'Mademoiselle,' 1935-1960,* (New York: Harper, 1960), p. 280.

15. Skei, *The Short Story Career,* p. 108.

16. Beck, *Man in Motion. Faulkner's Trilogy* (Madison: University of Wisconsin Press, 1963), p. 5. See also James Gray Watson's conclusion that the trilogy is "unified in theme as in structure." *The Snopes Dilemma: Faulkner's Trilogy* (Coral Gables: University of Miami Press, 1970).

17. Beck, *Man in Motion,* p. 8.

18. Thompson, *William Faulkner: An Introduction and Interpretation,* p. 14.

Chapter 5

1. *The Faulkner-Cowley File,* p. 15.

Bibliography

Adams, Richard P. *Faulkner: Myth and Motion.* Princeton, N.J.: Princeton University Press, 1968.

Aiken, Charles S. "Faulkner's Yoknapatawpha County: A Place in the American South." *Geographical Review* 69 (1979). 331-48.

Auden, W.H. *The Dyer's Hand.* New York: Random House, 1962.

Backman, Melvin. *Faulkner: The Major Years.* Bloomington and London: Indiana University Press, 1966.

Beck, Warren. *Man in Motion: Faulkner's Trilogy.* Madison: University of Wisconsin Press, 1963.

Blotner, Joseph. *Faulkner: A Biography.* New York: Random House, 1984.

Booth, Wayne C. *The Rhetoric of Fiction.* Chicago and London: University of Chicago Press, 1961.

Bradford, Melvin E. "An Aesthetic Parable: Faulkner's 'Artist at Home'." *Georgia Review* 27 (1973). 175-81.

_____. "The Knight and the Artist: Tasso and Faulkner's 'Carcassonne'." *South Central Bulletin* 41 (Winter 1981). 88-90.

Brodsky, Louis D. "A Textual History of William Faulkner's *The Wishing-Tree* and *The Wishing Tree.* " *Studies in Bibliography* 38 (1985). 330-74.

Brooks, Cleanth. *William Faulkner: First Encounters.* New Haven and London: Yale University Press, 1983.

_____. *William Faulkner: The Yoknapatawpha Country.* New Haven and London: Yale University Press, 1963.

_____. *William Faulkner: Toward Yoknapatawpha and Beyond.* New Haven and London: Yale University Press, 1978.

Butterworth, Keen. *A Critical and Textual Study of Faulkner's "A Fable."* Ann Arbor: UMI Research Press, 1983.

Canby, Henry Seidel, "School of Cruelty." *Saturday Review of Literature* 7 (March 21, 1931). 673-74.

Cantrell, Frank. "Faulkner's 'A Courtship'." *Mississippi Quarterly* 24 (1971). 289-95.

Carothers, James B. "The Road to *The Reivers.*" In *"A Cosmos of My Own": Faulkner and Yoknapatawpha, 1980,* edited by Doreen Fowler and Ann J. Abadie. Jackson: University Press of Mississippi, 1981, pp. 95-124.

Castille, Philip. " 'There Was a Queen' and Faulkner's Narcissa Sartoris." *Mississippi Quarterly* 28 (1975). 307-15.

Collins, Carvel. "A Note on *Sanctuary.*" *Harvard Advocate* 135 (November 1951). 16.

_____. "The Pairing of *The Sound and the Fury* and *As I Lay Dying.*" *Princeton University Library Chronicle* 18 (1957). 114-23.

Cowley, Malcolm. *The Faulkner-Cowley File. Letters and Memories, 1944-1962.* New York: Viking Press, 1966.

Creighton, Joanne V. *William Faulkner's Craft of Revision.* Detroit: Wayne State University Press, 1977.

Cullen, John, and Floyd C. Watkins. *Old Times in the Faulkner Country.* Chapel Hill: University of North Carolina Press, 1961.

Day, Douglas. "The War Stories of William Faulkner." *Georgia Review* 15 (1961). 385-94.

Dunlap, Mary Montgomery. "William Faulkner's 'Knight's Gambit' and Gavin Stevens." *Mississippi Quarterly* 23 (1970). 223-39.

Durrell, Lawrence. *Balthazar.* New York: Dutton, 1958.

Early, James. *The Making of "Go Down, Moses."* Dallas: Southern Methodist University Press, 1972.

Everett, Walter K. *Faulkner's Art and Characters.* Woodbury, N.Y: Barron's, 1969.

Fant, Joseph L., and Robert Ashley, eds. *Faulkner at West Point.* New York: Random House, 1964.

Faulkner, John. *My Brother Bill. An Affectionate Reminiscence.* New York: Trident Press, 1963.

Faulkner, William. *Absalom, Absalom!* New York: Random House, 1936.

_____. *As I Lay Dying.* New York: Random House, 1964.

_____. *Big Woods.* New York: Random House, 1955.

_____. "By the People." *Mademoiselle,* 41 (October 1955). 86-89, 130-39. Rpt. *40 Best Stories from Mademoiselle, 1935-1960,* edited by Cyrilly Abels and Margarita G. Smith, pp. 263-82. New York: Harper, 1960.

_____. *Collected Stories of William Faulkner.* New York: Random House, 1950.

_____. *Doctor Martino and Other Stories.* New York: Random House, 1934.

_____. *Early Prose and Poetry,* edited by Carvel Collins. Boston: Little, Brown, 1962.

_____. *Essays, Speeches & Public Letters,* edited by James B. Meriwether. New York: Random House, 1966.

_____. *A Fable.* New York: Random House, 1954.

_____. *Father Abraham.* New York: Random House, 1984.

_____. *Faulkner in the University,* edited by Frederick L. Gwynn and Joseph L. Blotner. New York: Vintage, 1965.

_____. *Go Down, Moses and Other Stories.* New York: Random House, 1942.

_____. *The Hamlet,* 3rd ed. New York: Random House, 1964.

_____. *Knight's Gambit.* New York. Random House, 1949.

_____. *Light in August.* New York: Harrison Smith & Robert Haas, 1932.

_____. *Lion in the Garden: Interviews with William Faulkner, 1926-1962,* edited by James B. Meriwether and Michael Millgate. New York: Random House, 1968.

_____. *The Mansion.* New York: Random House, 1959.

_____. *Mayday.* South Bend, Ind.: University of Notre Dame Press, 1980.

_____. *New Orleans Sketches,* edited by Carvel Collins. New York: Random House, 1968.

_____. *Notes on a Horsethief.* Greenville, Miss.: Levee Press, 1951.

_____. *The Reivers.* New York: Random House, 1962.

_____. *Requiem for a Nun.* New York: Random House, 1951.

_____. *Sanctuary.* New York: Jonathan Cape and Harrison Smith, 1931.

_____. *Sartoris.* New York: Harcourt, Brace, 1929.

_____. *Selected Letters of William Faulkner,* edited by Joseph Blotner. New York: Random House, 1977.

_____. *Soldiers' Pay.* New York: Boni & Liveright, 1926.

_____. *The Sound and the Fury.* New York: Jonathan Cape and Harrison Smith, 1929.

_____. *The Town.* New York: Random House, 1957.

_____. *Uncollected Stories of William Faulkner,* edited by Joseph Blotner. New York: Random House, 1979.

———. *The Unvanquished.* New York : Random House, 1938.

———. *The Wild Palms.* New York: Random House, 1939.

Fiedler, Leslie. *Love and Death in the American Novel.* New York: Meridian Books, 1962.

Fowler, Doreen. *Faulkner's Changing Vision: From Outrage to Affirmation.* Ann Arbor: UMI Research Press, 1983.

Frohock, W.M. *The Novel of Violence in America.* Boston: Beacon Press, 1964.

Gidley, Mark. "Elements of the Detective Story in Faulkner's Fiction." *Journal of Popular Culture* 7 (1963). 97-123.

Gold, Joseph. *William Faulkner: A Study in Humanism from Metaphor to Discourse.* Norman: University of Oklahoma Press, 1966.

Gresset, Michel. "From Vignette to Vision. The 'Old, Fine Name of France' or Faulkner's 'Western Front' from 'Crevasse' to *A Fable.*" In *Faulkner: International Perspectives,* edited by Doreen Fowler and Ann J. Abadie, pp. 97-120. Jackson: University Press of Mississippi, 1984.

———. "Weekend, Lost and Revisited." *Mississippi Quarterly* 21 (1968). 173-78.

Harter, Carol C. "The Winter of Isaac McCaslin. Revisions and Irony in 'Delta Autumn'." *Journal of Modern Literature* 1 (1970). 209-25.

Holmes, Edwin M. *Faulkner's Twice-Told Tales: His Re-Use of His Material.* The Hague: Mouton, 1966.

Howe, Irving. *William Faulkner. A Critical Appraisal.* New York: Vintage, 1962.

Howell, Elmo. "Faulkner's Country Church. A Note on 'Shingles for the Lord'." *Mississippi Quarterly* 21 (1968). 205-10.

Irwin, John T. *Doubling and Incest/Repetition and Revenge: A Speculative Reading of Faulkner.* Baltimore and London: The Johns Hopkins University Press, 1975.

Jewkes, W.T. "Counterpoint in Faulkner's *The Wild Palms.*" *Wisconsin Studies in Contemporary Literature* 2 (1961). 39-54.

Kenner, Hugh. *Studies in Change: A Book of the Short Story.* Englewood Cliffs, NJ: Prentice-Hall, 1965.

Kerr, Elizabeth M. *William Faulkner's Gothic Domain.* Port Washington, N.Y. and London: Kennikat Press, 1979.

———. *Yoknapatawpha: Faulkner's "Little Postage Stamp of Native Soil."* New York: Fordham University Press, 1976.

Kinney, Arthur F. "Faulkner's Narrative Poetics and *Collected Stories.*" *Faulkner Studies* 1 (1980). 58-79.

Kreiswirth, Martin. *William Faulkner: The Making of a Novelist.* Athens: University of Georgia Press, 1963.

Longley, John L. *The Tragic Mask: A Study of Faulkner's Heroes.* Chapel Hill: North Carolina Press, 1963.

Macdonald, Dwight, ed. *Parodies: An Anthology from Chaucer to Beerbohm — and After.* New York: Modern Library, 1965.

Matthews, John T. *The Play of Faulkner's Language.* Ithaca and London: Cornell University Press, 1982.

McHaney, Thomas L. *William Faulkner: A Reference Guide.* Boston: G.K. Hall, 1976.

———. *William Faulkner's "The Wild Palms": A Study.* Jackson: University Press of Mississippi, 1975.

Meriwether, James B. "Faulkner's Correspondence with *Scribner's Magazine.*" *Proof* 3 (1973). 253-82.

———. "Introduction" to *Father Abraham.* New York: Random House, 1984.

———. *The Place of "The Unvanquished" in William Faulkner's Yoknapatawpha Series.* Ph.D. Dissertation, Princeton, 1959.

Millgate, Jane. "Short Story into Novel. Faulkner's Re-working of 'Gold is Not Always'." *English Studies* 45 (1964). 310-17.

Millgate, Michael. *The Achievement of William Faulkner.* New York: Random House, 1966.

Morrell, Giliane. "Prisoners of the Inner World. Mother and Daughter in 'Miss Zilphia Gant.' " *Mississippi Quarterly* 28 (1975). 299-305.

Mortimer, Gail L. *Faulkner's Rhetoric of Loss.* Austin: University of Texas Press, 1983.

O'Connor, William Van. *The Tangled Fire of William Faulkner.* Minneapolis: University of Minnesota Press, 1954.

O'Donnell, George Marion. "Faulkner's Mythology." *Kenyon Review* 1 (1939). 285-99.

Owens, Tony J. "Faulkner, Anderson, and 'Artist at Home'." *Mississippi Quarterly* 32 (1979). 413-22.

Page, Sally R. *Faulkner's Women: Characterization and Meaning.* Deland, FL: Everett Edwards, 1972.

Pilkington, John. *The Heart of Yoknapatawpha.* Jackson: University Press of Mississippi, 1981.

Pitavy, Francois. "The Gothicism of *Absalom, Absalom!:* Rosa Coldfield Revisited." In *"A Cosmos of My Own": Faulkner and Yoknapatawpha 1980,* edited by Doreen Fowler and Ann J. Abadie, pp. 199-226. Jackson: University Press of Mississippi, 1981.

Podhoretz, Norman. *Doings and Undoings: the Fifties and after in American Writing.* New York: Farrar, Straus, 1964.

Polk, Noel. *Faulkner's "Requiem for a Nun": A Study.* Bloomington and London: Indiana University Press, 1980.

_____. "Idealism in *The Mansion.*" In *Faulkner and Idealism: Perspectives from Paris,* edited by Michel Gresset and Patrick Samway, S.J., pp. 112-26. Jackson: University Press of Mississippi, 1983.

_____. *Sanctuary: The Original Text.* New York: Random House, 1981.

_____. "William Faulkner's 'Carcassonne'." *Studies in American Fiction* 12 (1984). 29-43.

Reed, Joseph W., Jr. *Faulkner's Narrative.* New Haven and London: Yale University Press, 1973.

Richardson, H. Edward. *William Faulkner: The Journey to Self-Discovery.* Columbia: University of Missouri Press, 1976.

Roth, Russell. "William Faulkner: The Pattern of Pilgrimage." *Perspective* 2 (1949). 246-54.

Runyan, Harry. *A Faulkner Glossary.* New York: The Citadel Press, 1964.

Ruppersburg, Hugh M. *Voice and Eye in Faulkner's Fiction.* Athens: University of Georgia Press, 1983.

Russell, Bertrand. *A History of Western Philosophy.* New York: Simon and Schuster, 1945.

Scholes, Robert, and Robert Kellogg. *The Nature of Narrative.* Oxford: Oxford University Press, 1966.

Simpson, Hassell A. *The Short Stories of William Faulkner.* Ph.D. Dissertation, Florida State, 1962.

Skei, Hans H. "A Forgotten Faulkner Story: 'Thrift'." *Mississippi Quarterly* 32 (1979). 453-60.

_____. *William Faulkner: The Short Story Career.* Oslo-Bergen-Tromsø: Universtetsforlaget, 1981.

Slatoff, Walter J. *Quest for Failure: A Study of William Faulkner.* Ithaca: Cornell University Press, 1960.

Spilka, Mark. "The Necessary Stylist: A New Critical Revision." *Modern Fiction Studies* 6 (Winter 1960-61). 283-97.

Stewart, Jack F. "Apotheosis and Apocalypse in Faulkner's 'Wash'." *Studies in Short Fiction* 6 (1969). 586-600.

Stonum, Gary Lee. *Faulkner's Career: An Internal Literary History.* Ithaca and London: Cornell University Press, 1979.

Sundquist, Eric J. *Faulkner. The House Divided.* Baltimore and London: The Johns Hopkins University Press, 1983.

Thompson, Alan Reynolds. "The Cult of Cruelty." *The Bookman* 74 (1932). 477-87.

Thompson, John R. *Poems of John R. Thompson.* Edited by John S. Patton, New York: Scribner's, 1920.

Thompson, Lawrance. *William Faulkner: An Introduction and Interpretation.* New York: Barnes and Noble, 1963.

Tilley, Winthrop. "The Idiot Boy in Mississippi." *American Journal of Mental Deficiency* 59 (1955). 374-77.

Tuck, Dorothy Y. *Crowell's Handbook of Faulkner.* New York: Thomas Y. Crowell, 1964.

Vickery, Olga W. *The Novels of William Faulkner.* Baton Rouge: Louisiana State University Press, 1964.

Volpe, Edmund. *A Reader's Guide to William Faulkner.* New York: Noonday Press, 1964.

Wasson, Ben. *Count No 'Count: Flashbacks to Faulkner.* Jackson: University Press of Mississippi, 1983.

Watson, James G. "Faulkner: Short Story Structures and Reflexive Forms." *Mosaic* 11 (Summer 1978). 127-37.

_____. *The Snopes Dilemma: Faulkner's Trilogy.* Coral Gables: University of Miami Press, 1970.

Webb, James W. and A. Wigfall Green, eds. *William Faulkner of Oxford.* Baton Rouge: Louisiana State University Press, 1965.

West, Ray B. *The Short Story in America.* New York: H. Regnery, 1952.

Williams, David. *Faulkner's Women: The Myth and the Muse.* Montreal and London: McGill-Queen's University Press, 1977.

Wright, Austin McGiffert. *The American Short Story in the Twenties.* Chicago: University of Chicago Press, 1961.

Zender, Karl F. "Faulkner and the Power of Sound." *PMLA* 99 (1984). 89-108.

Index